Is Anyone Really Good at Detecting Lies?

Professional Papers

Charles F. Bond Jr., Ph.D.

Bella DePaulo, Ph.D.

2011

CONTENTS

The development of deception detection skill: A longitudinal study of same-sex friends

On-the-job experience and skill at detecting deception

On lie detection "wizards"

Maintaining lies: The multiple audience problem

Accuracy of deception judgments

Individual differences in judging deception: Accuracy and bias

Preface

The two of us met in Toronto in August 1984. We had similar backgrounds and a common interest in the psychology of deception. We pursued our interests separately for many years, checking in with one another from time to time as one of us published a paper that excited the other. Then in 2002 we began a collaboration that has yielded two articles on deception and (with the current work) a book.

Here we present some of the professional papers we have authored over the years – two papers written by DePaulo (and associates), two written by Bond (and associates), and two papers that we wrote together as a team. All of the papers are about judgments of deception made from a liar's words, voice, or nonverbal behavior. These are research articles, written by psychologists for psychologists. Those who are unversed in the idiom of these articles may at first be put off by some of the technical language here. We advise these gentle readers not to worry about the results section of each article, where most of the technicalities lie. The psychological meat in these papers can be consumed with only a dash of statistics.

The first paper in the book "The development of deception detection skill: A longitudinal study of same-sex friends" concerns lying between friends. It examines lying in new friendships, and lying in friendships of longer duration. Is it easier to detect a friend's lie than a stranger's lie? Is it easier to detect a friend's lie the longer you have known the friend? These are some of the questions addressed.

The second paper is a study of "On-the-job experience and skill at detecting deception." It examines the ability of several groups of people to detect deception from a liar's words and voice. The lie detection abilities of college students, law enforcement recruits, and seasoned law enforcement professionals are compared. Results suggest that on-the-job experience has little to do with detecting lies, and that seasoned lie-detection professionals are overconfident in their ability to divine deceit.

The third paper in the book is titled "On lie detection 'wizards'." Maureen O'Sullivan and colleagues had identified a number of people whom they considered lie detection "wizards." This paper questions the rigor by which these individuals were identified and shows that a simple chance mechanism could have produced the lie detection performances that the earlier researchers considered wizard-like.

The fourth paper in this book "Maintaining lies: The multiple audience problem" concerns a challenge that liars may face if they tell different versions of a story to different parties. The challenge arises if later the topic of the story comes up and those various parties are present. Can liars maintain their credibility in these difficult circumstances? How will they deal with this "multiple audience" problem?

The fifth paper is a review article on "Accuracy of deception judgments." The article summarizes hundreds of studies on this topic. It provides evidence on the accuracy of lie detection and judges' general tendency to regard others as honest. It interprets this large body of evidence as evidence of a double-standard, in which people view others' lies more negatively than their own lies. For professionals with an interest in the details of the coding of the variables from each of the studies, the paper in this book includes an appendix that did not appear in the original published version of the article.

The final paper in the book is a review article on "Individual difference in detecting deception: Accuracy and bias." It considers individual differences on four different dimensions – the ability to detect lies, the tendency to perceive others as honest, the detectability of one's own lies, and one's tendency to be perceived as honest. People vary much more on certain of these dimensions than others, as a large-scale review of research reveals.

As a whole, these six papers cover many of the topics of current interest in the psychology of deception judgment. May readers dine well on the menu we are serving here.

Charles F. Bond, Jr.
Bella DePaulo

March 2011

Personality and Social Psychology Bulletin, 2002, Vol. 28, 536-545

The Development of Deception Detection Skill:
A Longitudinal Study of Same-Sex Friends

D. Eric Anderson
Bella M. DePaulo
University of Virginia

Matthew E. Ansfield
Lawrence University

One member of each of 52 pairs of friends told true and fabricated stories to a partner (the judge) who guessed whether each story was true. The procedure was followed when the friends had known each other for 1 month and again 5 months later. Across all of the pairs, accuracy at detecting deception did not improve over time. However, judges from the emotionally closer pairs did become more accurate at 6 months than they had been at 1 month. The judges from the less-close pairs instead became less inclined to regard the stories as truthful, especially when they actually were truthful. Results of a second study ruled out the alternative interpretation that the closer friends told stories that were more obviously truthful or deceptive at 6 months than they had at 1 month. On indirect measures of deception detection, all of the groups of judges could distinguish the truths from the lies.

People who do not know each other are not very successful at detecting each other's deceptions. Most often, in studies of deception detection skill, people are shown equal numbers of truths and lies and lie detection accuracy is defined as the percentage of both truths and lies that were accurately identified. There are now more than 100 estimates of the lie detection accuracy of people who do not know the person whose truths and lies they are trying to identify and who have no special training or experience at detecting deceit. In these studies, the mean accuracy achieved by the thousands of judges who participated in the studies was 54%. Two thirds of the group accuracy means were between 50% and 59%, and no groups scored higher than the mid-70th percentile. (DePaulo, Tornqvist, & Cooper, 2002).

One important reason for the low levels of accuracy at detecting deception may be that behavioral cues separate truths from lies only probabilistically and usually weakly (DePaulo, Lindsay, et al., 2002). Moreover, there may be important individual differences in cues to deception such that particular behaviors that separate truths from lies for many individuals may not do so for all, and conversely, particular individuals may behave in idiosyncratic ways when lying (cf. Zuckerman, Koestner, & Alton, 1984). If this is so, then a particular person's deception may be most successfully detected by people who have practice and experience at interpreting that person's behavior, such as the person's relationship partners. Over the course of a close personal relationship, people may come to learn the particular behaviors that betray each other's lies and underscore their truths. In addition, their understanding of each other may grow in ways that help them recognize the plausibility or implausibility of the stories they hear within the context of what they know about each other's lives.

In the early phases of a relationship, even relationship partners are unlikely to achieve high levels of accuracy at detecting each other's truths and lies. At first, partners, similar to strangers, have little more than general notions about cues to deception (often erroneous) on which to depend. It could take some time to learn the lie-telling code of another individual. Even over time, however, levels of accuracy will be constrained by inaccurate, delayed, and unsystematic feedback (cf. DePaulo & Pfeifer, 1986; Zuckerman et al., 1984). Subtle cues to deception will be difficult to learn when some lies are never recognized as such, and some unwarranted suspicions are never dispelled (DePaulo, Ansfield, Kirkendol, & Boden, 2002).

There are only a few studies of the deception detection success of groups differing in relationship status, but the results are in line with our dim prognosis. Whether the groups were friends or strangers (Fleming, Darley, Hilton, & Kojetin, 1990), romantic partners and strangers (Anderson, 1999), spouses and friends (Comadena, 1982), or mixed groups of friends and relatives who were compared to strangers (Fleming & Darley, 1991; Millar & Millar, 1995), there were never any unequivocal indications that people in closer relationships would be more successful than those in less-close relationships at detecting each other's deceptions and truths. A few other studies reported correlations between relationship closeness and success at detecting deception within groups of relationship partners, including dating couples (Levine & McCornack, 1992; McCornack & Parks, 1986) and friends (Stiff, Kim, & Ramesh, 1992). All of these correlations were near zero.

The development of a relationship brings not just opportunities to learn a partner's life stories and verbal and nonverbal styles but also emotional needs and investments. One of the most important of these may be people's desire to believe in the honesty of their partners. To sustain that belief, relationship partners may be more likely to show a preference for interpreting each other's communications as truthful than any special insight about deceptiveness. There is some evidence for this preference (typically called a "truth bias" in the deception literature). In the handful of studies comparing groups differing in relationship status, the relationship partners (relatives, friends, and romantic partners) showed an even greater inclination to judge messages as truthful than did strangers (Anderson, 1999; Buller, Strzyzewski, & Hunsaker, 1991; Millar & Millar, 1995). However, there were no indications that within groups of relationship partners (such as dating couples and friends), closeness and the tendency to judge communications as truthful are related (Levine & McCornack, 1992; McCornack & Parks, 1986; Stiff et al., 1992).

Relationship partners' faith in each other may be shaken during the first months of a relationship, as the initial glow of the early weeks gives way to tension and conflict later on (e.g., Hays, 1985). How will relationship partners then interpret each other's behavioral cues to deception and truth? We think that relationship partners who do not feel especially close to each other may no longer show the same generous interpretation of most communications as truthful that they may have shown at the outset. In fact, they may even become more grudging in their readings of each other and disbelieve some communications from their partner that are actually truthful. We predict that only those partners who remain close to each other in the face of the challenges that relationships face over time will show the even-handedness that skillful lie detection demands; that is, they will be secure enough to acknowledge that some of the stories their partner is telling them are lies and trusting enough to recognize the sincerity of the stories that really are truthful (cf. Holmes & Rempel, 1989). In sum, we are predicting that accuracy at detecting deceit will not improve over time for all relationship partners but only for those whose relationships are especially close. In relationships that are less close, we think that the tendency to perceive most communications as truthful will wane.

Our prediction that accuracy at detecting deception will improve over time for people in especially close relationships may seem at odds with the previous studies showing no link between relationship closeness and lie detection success. In some of those studies, the deception detection success of relationship partners was compared to that of strangers. But our prediction is not that relationships partners will outperform strangers, even at detecting the deceit of their own partners, nor is it that people in especially close relationships will do especially well at detecting deception. Instead, it is that especially close relationship partners will become more accurate over time at knowing when their partner is lying or telling the truth. That is a hypothesis that can only be tested longitudinally.

It is possible, however, that even our longitudinal study will uncover no evidence for the development of deception detection skill over the early months of a close personal relationship. But even if relationship partners showed no special detection ability when asked to categorize communications as either truths or lies, we thought we might find evidence for such ability by asking less direct questions. For example, we thought that if we asked participants how comfortable they felt during the interaction, they might report feeling more comfortable when the stories their partner was telling actually were truths than when they were lies. As DePaulo (1994) has suggested, this could occur even if the partners cannot successfully detect deception by their direct categorizations of the stories as truths or lies.

Although the first 100 or so studies in the deception detection literature focused on direct measures, there is now some evidence for indirect deception detection as well. One example comes from an incidental finding from a meta-analysis designed to assess the relationship between confidence and accuracy in the detection of deception (DePaulo, Charlton, Cooper, Lindsay, & Muhlenbruck, 1997). The primary analysis showed that the average correlation between confidence in one's judgments and the accuracy of those judgments was almost exactly zero. However, when the link between judges' self-reports of confidence and the actual truthfulness of the messages was examined, a different story emerged. Judges were more confident when the message they had just rated was a truth than when it was a lie. The judges' reports of differing levels of confidence in their ratings of the truths versus the lies showed that at some level, the judges could differentiate between truths and lies, even though their explicit deception detection accuracy in the same studies was sometimes poor (see also Anderson, DePaulo, Ansfield, Tickle, & Green, 1999).

In the present research, we examine indirect deception detection by relationship partners. We want to know whether friends might be able to detect each other's deception indirectly even when they appear not to have detected it directly (cf. Anderson, 1999). We also want to know whether indirect deception detection increases over time and at different rates than explicit deception detection.

We recruited pairs of men and pairs of women who had known each other for a month and who considered themselves friends. One member of each par, the sender, told four life stories to their friend, the judge, who tried to determine whether the stories were true or fabricated. The judge also completed a series of indirect measures, such as ratings of confidence, comfort, and suspiciousness. Five months later, all but one of the pairs of friends returned and completed the same procedure.

STUDY 1

Method

PARTICIPANTS

Experimenters contacted students from an introductory psychology class at the University of Virginia and asked them to sign up for a study on nonverbal behavior and friendship with a same-sex friend whom they had not known prior to the beginning of the semester. Those who turned in applications and met the criteria specified by the experimenters (including not knowing each other prior to the beginning of the semester and identifying each other as a friend) were contacted and scheduled for the first session of the study. They were then contacted again for a second session, approximately 5 months later. A total of 52 same-sex pairs (29 women, 23 men) completed both sessions.

At the beginning of each of the two sessions, senders and judges completed scales measuring their closeness to each other. The Subjective Closeness Index (see Aaron, Aaron, & Smollan, 1992) was the mean of participants' answers to two questions: "Relative to all your other relationships, how would you characterize your relationship with this person?" and "Relative to what you know about other people's close relationships, how would you characterize your relationship to this person?" Both were answered on scales ranging from 1 (*much less close than others*) to 9 (*much closer than others*). If the mean of the scores for both friends was greater than or equal to 6 at both sessions, the friends were considered especially close. We could have simply used the mean closeness ratings across both time periods; however, by that criterion, a pair of friends with a very high closeness rating at Time 1 but a much lower one at Time 2 (e.g., 7.75 and 5.00 for one of our pairs) would be classified as very close, even though their closeness to each other at Time 2 was only at the midpoint of the scale. We also could have used a simple change criterion to classify our groups, such that the pairs who showed the greatest increase in closeness from Time 1 to Time 2 would be considered the closer friends. However, by that criterion, friends showing a relatively big increase in closeness (e.g., 3.75 and 5.00 for one of our pairs) would be classified as close even thought their closeness was fairly low at both time periods.

According to the criterion we did choose, there were 24 especially close pairs of friends and 28 pairs of friends who were not especially close. The mean closeness ratings of the especially close friends were 6.84 and 7.02 at 1 month and 6 months; for the less-close friends, they were 5.46 and 4.50.

At both sessions, senders and judges also reported their levels of disclosure to each other by indicating whether they had discussed each of 18 topics (Ansfield, DePaulo, & Bell, 1995; Brauer & DePaulo, 1980). Mean scores (averaged across the sender and judge) could therefore range from 0 to 18. A Sex of Dyad X Closeness of Dyad X Time mixed-design ANOVA, with repeated measures on the Time factor, indicated that the closer friends disclosed more to each other than the less-close friends, $Ms = 10.81$ and 7.59, respectively; for the main effect of Closeness, $F(1, 48) = 22.70$, $p < .0001$. This difference did not change significantly over time; for the Closeness X Time interaction, $F(1, 48) = 2.29$, $p = 1.37$.[1]

PROCEDURE

Each pair of friends was tested individually. The friends completed a variety of communication tasks and self-report measures. Only the ones directly relevant to the present report will be described.

In the key task, the friends discussed in turn each of four life stories. One of the friends was randomly assigned to be the sender, who told the stories, and the other was assigned to be the judge, who asked questions about the stories and then tried to determine whether they were true stories. Before each conversation commenced, the judge was given typed instructions that indicated the topic of the story to be discussed (e.g., a story about a relationship; a family story; a story about something that someone once did for, or to, the sender). Story topics were randomly assigned. The judge was instructed to ask the sender to tell a story about that topic. The typed instructions also included hints the judge could use to help the sender think of a relevant story and suggestions for questions the judge could ask to keep the conversation going. The judge's task was to determine, over the course of the conversation, whether the sender was telling a true story. Judges were told that the sender might tell all true stories, all made-up stories, or any combination of true and made-up stories during each session.

Meanwhile, the sender was instructed to tell either a true story or to make up a story (randomly assigned) in response to the judge's questions. The sender could choose any life event that fit the assigned topic as long as it was a story that had never been discussed with the judge. The sender was instructed to make all stories convincing, such that anyone hearing the stories would believe that they were true. Within each session, each sender was instructed to tell two true stories and two fabricated stories. All senders were able to complete this task without difficulty.

After the judge had read the instructions and was ready to begin, the judge and sender sat face-to-face as they discussed the story. They could take up to 4 minutes for each conversation. After each conversation, the sender and judge faced away from each other while they answered a brief questionnaire about the conversation. The judges indicated whether they thought the story was a truth or a lie. They also reported, on 9-point scales, their confidence, comfort, and suspiciousness; the degree to which they tried to hide their suspiciousness; the degree to which they got enough information to make a veracity judgment; their perceptions of their friend's comfort; and their friend's perception of the judge's own suspiciousness. The friends who had told the stories reported whether the story that they had just told was a truth or a lie, as a manipulation check. All storytellers followed the instructions and told the appropriate true or made-up story according to the instructions given by the experimenter.

The same procedure was followed for each of the sessions. The senders and judges maintained their roles across the two sessions.

Table 1

Changes Over Time in Accuracy and Judgments of Truthfulness for the Less-Close Friends and Closer Friends

	Time 1	Time 2	Change
Percentage accuracy			
Less close	56.5	51.2	-5.3
Closer	46.8	61.4	14.6
Percentage judged as true			
Less close	73.9	56.9	-17.0
Closer	61.4	60.4	-1.0

Results

ACCURACY

Sex of dyad, closeness of dyad, and time (1 month, 6 months) were the factors in a mixed-design ANOVA. Time was a repeated-measures factor. Judges' perceptions of the stories as either truths or lies were the dependent measures. Judges were assigned a score of 0 if their perception was incorrect and 1 if it was correct (see Rosenthal & Rosnow, 1991; Snedecor & Cochran, 1967; Winer, 1971, for the use of ANOVA with dichotomous dependent variables). Means can therefore be interpreted straightforwardly as percentage accuracy scores.

The mean accuracy score across all factors in the design was 54.6%. This score, although greater than the chance value of 50%, was not significantly greater, $t(51) = 1.86$, $p = .068$. It is similar to the weighted mean score of 54% across more than 100 studies of lie detection among adults with no special relationship with each other (DePaulo, Tornqvist, & Cooper, 2002). We found no evidence that the judges were better at detecting deception in the closer friendship pairs ($M = 54.1\%$) than in the less-close pairs ($M = 53.8\%$), $F(1, 48) < 1$. Also, across all of the pairs of friends, accuracy did not improve significantly from 1 month (51.6%) to 6 months (56.3%); for the main effect of Time, $F(1, 48) = 1.04$, $p = .313$.

As predicted, closer friends did become more accurate at detecting deception over the course of their relationship (see Table 1); for the Closeness X Time interaction, $F(1, 48) = 4.77$, $p = .034$. From Time 1 to Time 2, closer friends improved from 46.8% correct to 61.4%, $F(1, 48) = 5.94$, $p = .019$. For less-close friends, there was a nonsignificant decrease in accuracy from 56.5% to

51.2%, $F = .78$, $p = .381$. The difference in accuracy between the closer and the less-close friends was not significant at either point in time. For Time 1, $F(1, 48) = 2.66$, $p = .109$; for Time 2, $F(1, 48) = 2.41$, $p = .127$.[2]

Table 2

Changes Over Time in Percentage of Truths and lies Judged as Truths by the Closer and the Less-Close Friends

| | Less-Close Friends | | | Closer Friends | | |
	Time 1	Time 2	Change	Time 1	Time 2	Change
Truths	80.4	58.1	-22.3	58.2	71.8	13.6
Lies	67.4	55.8	-11.6	64.6	48.9	-15.7

PERCENTAGE OF STORIES JUDGED AS TRUE

Sex and closeness were again between-dyad factors, and time and truthfulness of the story (truth, lie) were repeated-measures factors in an ANOVA with truth judgments as the dependent variable. Judges were assigned a score of 0 if they judged the story to be a lie and 1 if they judged it to be a truth. Means therefore indicate the percentage of messages judged to be truths.

Even though only half of the stories they heard really were truths, judges believed that 63.7% of them were truths. Therefore, as in many previous studies (DePaulo, Tornqvist, & Cooper, 2002; Levine, McCornack, & Park, 1999), judges showed a tendency to judge significantly more than half of the messages as truths, $t(51) = 5.58$, $p < .0001$. This tendency decreased from 1 month (67.7%) to 6 months (58.6%); for the main effect of Time, $F(1, 48) = 5.43$, $p = .024$.

There was no difference between the closer friends (60.9%) and the less-close friends (65.4%) in their overall tendency to judge the stories as truthful; for the main effect of Closeness, $F(1, 48) = .82$, $p = .371$. However, the decrease over time in the tendency to judge stories as truthful was specific to the less-close friends; for the Closeness X Time interaction, $F(1, 48) = 4.22$, $p = .046$. As shown in Table 1, the less-close friends believed that 73.9% of the stories were true at Time 1 but only 56.9% at Time 2. In contrast, the closer friends consistently judged about 60% of the stories to be true.

The three-way interaction of Closeness, Time, and Truthfulness of the story (statistically identical to the significant two-way interaction of Closeness X Time in the accuracy ANOVA) addresses the question of whether the closer friends' improvement in accuracy resulted from an improvement in identifying truths as truths or in identifying lies as lies, or both. It also indicates whether the less-close friends made any particular error (misidentifying truths as lies or lies as truths) more often at one time than another. As shown in Table 2, the closer friends improved over time both in seeing the truths as truths, $F(1, 48) = 2.31$, $p = .135$, and the lies as lies, $F(1, 48) = 3.08$, $p = .086$, although neither individual comparison was significant. The less-close friends tended to see all of the messages as less truthful at Time 2 than at Time 1, and this drop in truthfulness judgments was significant for the messages that actually were truthful, $F(1, 48) = 6.22$, $p = .016$. (For the lies, $F[1, 48] = 1.68$, $p = .201$.)

INDIRECT MEASURES

To assess indirect deception detection, we asked the judges how confident they were in their guesses, how comfortable they were, how comfortable they thought the senders were, how suspicious they were, how much they tried to hide their suspicion, how suspicious the senders thought they were, and the extent to which they had gotten enough information to make their judgments of truthfulness. The answers to these questions were analyzed in a MANOVA using the same factors as in the ANOVA conducted on the explicit guesses.

As predicted, there was a main multivariate effect for the actual truthfulness of the story, $F(7, 41) = 4.16$, $p = .002$. All seven of the univariate tests were significant or nearly so. The univariate analyses revealed that judges were more confident in their guesses when the story was true ($M = 6.38$) than when it was made up ($M = 5.75$), $F(1, 48) = 10.78$, $p = .0019$, were more comfortable when the story was true ($M = 7.56$) than when it was false ($M = 7.13$), $F(1, 47) = 14.27$, $p = .0004$, were less suspicious during the true stories ($M = 4.88$) than during the made-up ones ($M = 5.51$), $F(1, 48) = 9.13$, $p = .004$, tried to hide suspicion slightly less during the true stories ($M = 3.62$) than during made-up stories ($M = 3.97$), $F(1, 48) = 3.78$, $p = .058$, and felt that they got more information during the true stories ($M = 6.52$) than during the made-up stories ($M = 5.82$), $F(1, 48) = 19.48$, $p = .0001$.

Judges also thought that the senders were more comfortable during the true stories ($M = 6.83$) than during the made-up ones ($M = 6.36$), $F(1, 48) = 7.73$, $p = .008$, and believed the senders perceived them as less suspicious during the true stories ($M = 4.60$) than during the made-up stories ($M = 5.01$), $F(1, 48) = 4.14$, $p = .048$.

There was also a main, multivariate effect for time of measurement, $F(7, 41) = 2.52$, $p = .030$. The significant univariate effects indicated that judges saw the senders as more comfortable at Time 1 ($M = 6.88$) than at Time 2 ($M = 6.31$), $F(1, 48) = 6.67$, $p = .013$, and that the judges tried to hide their suspicion more at Time 1 ($M = 4.21$) than they did at Time 2 ($M = 3.38$), $F(1, 48) = 6.88$, $p = .012$.

If the closer friends were more accurate than the less-close friends on the indirect measures, the Truthfulness of the Story X Closeness interaction would be significant. If the closer friends, relative to the less-close friends, became more accurate on the indirect measures only over time, then the Truthfulness of Story X Closeness X Time interaction would be significant. However, neither of these effects was significant. (For the two-way interaction, $F[7, 35] = 1.96$, $p = .089$; for the three-way interaction, $F[7, 41] = 1.64$, $p = .152$.)[3]

Discussion

It was only the judges from the closer friendship pairs in Study 1 who improved significantly in deception detection accuracy from about 1 month into their friendship until 5 months later. These closer friends did not seem to have selected each other on the basis of their initial ability to detect each other's truths and les because, at Time 1, the closer friends were slightly less accurate than the less-close friends. The closer friends were not even better than the less-close friends in the degree to which they could distinguish the truths from the lies on dimensions other than truthfulness, because indirect accuracy was the same for both groups at both points in time. Instead, our preferred explanation is that only the closer judges learned to interpret cues more accurately over time.

However, there are other possible explanations. For example, the senders from the closer pairs may have told truths and lies that were more clearly recognizable as such at Time 2 than they had at Time 1. If this did in fact occur, then anyone watching the Time 2 tapes of their stories should be able to show the same accuracy at detecting the truths and lies that their friends did. To test this, we recruited raters who were strangers to the original participants to view the videotapes of the friends' interactions and record their impressions.

Study 1 also left unanswered several questions about the interpretation of the indirect deception detection effects. Both the less-close and the closer friends could detect deception on these measures. Does that suggest that even the less-close friends, who were inept at detecting deception directly, did have some special ability to discriminate truths from lies or would even strangers be able to make these distinctions when watching the interactions on videotape? Again, the recruitment of strangers as raters allows us to answer this.

Finally, the indirect deception detection measures were continuous measures, whereas the direct deception detection index was dichotomous. Perhaps it is this measurement difference that accounts for the greater accuracy on indirect than direct measures. To address this, we added a continuous measure of truthfulness.

STUDY 2

Method

PARTICIPANTS

Raters for this study were undergraduate research assistants who received course credit for their work. Eight raters (4 men, 4 women) each rated all 104 of the tapes (52 pairs x 2 sessions).

PROCEDURE

Raters watched the conversations from Study 1 in a counterbalanced order. Half of the raters watched tapes from Time 1 first, whereas the other half watched tapes from Time 2 first. Furthermore, half of the raters in each of those two conditions watched the tapes of the male dyads first, whereas the other half watched the tapes of the female dyads first. Finally, half of the raters in each condition watched the tapes of the particular friendship pairs in the order in which they were originally run and the other half watched the tapes in the reverse order.

The raters filled out many of the same measures as the friends in Study 1, including the question about whether they thought each story was the truth or a lie, and a measure that the friends did not complete, a 9-point rating of the truthfulness of the communication (1 = *not at all truthful*, 9 = *completely truthful*). They also indicated their perceptions of the sender's comfort and the judge's comfort and the judge's suspiciousness. In addition, they rated their own comfort, suspiciousness, and confidence in their judgments and indicated the degree to which they felt that they had gotten enough information to make their judgments.

Results

ANALYSES

Accuracy and truth bias were computed for the Study 2 raters as they were for the Study 1 friends. Friendship pairs were again the units of analysis. Within-pair factors were time (1 month, 6 months); order of judgment (Time 1 tapes first, Time 2 tapes first); sex of rater; and for the ANOVA on judgments that the story was true, truthfulness of the story (truth, lie). Sex of dyad and closeness of the pair were the between-pairs factors. All of those factors were also included in an ANOVA in which the 9-point ratings of truthfulness were the dependent measures. Finally, a MANOVA with the same factors was computed on all of the indirect deception detection measures.

COULD STRANGERS DISTINGUISH TRUTHS FROM LIES?

There were three assessments of whether the raters in Study 2, who were strangers to the people they were judging on the videotapes, could distinguish the truths from the lies: the dichotomous, explicit measure of detection accuracy that was used in Study 1; a set of indirect measures; and a continuous scale of truthfulness. As in Study 1, explicit accuracy based on judgments of the stories as truths or lies was not significantly greater than chance, $M = 50.6\%$, $t(51) = 1.43$, $p = .159$.

To determine whether the raters detected deception indirectly, their answers to questions about their confidence in their guesses, their level of suspicion, their perceptions of the judge's level of suspicion, the extent to which they got enough information to make their veracity judgments, and their perceptions of both the sender's and judge's levels of comfort were entered into a MANOVA. As in Study 1, the indirect measures separated the truths from the lies. There was a significant multivariate main effect for the truthfulness of the story, $F(6, 43) = 42.70$, $p < .0001$. Raters were more confident of their guesses when the story was true ($M = 5.30$) than when it was made up ($M = 5.21$), $F(1, 48) = 12.71$, $p = .0008$, thought that the senders were more comfortable during true stories ($M = 5.90$) than during fabricated stories ($M = 5.78$), $F(1, 48) = 21.17$, $p < .0001$, and thought that the judges were more suspicious during the fabricated stories ($M = 5.05$) than during the true stories ($M = 4.48$), $F(1, 48) = 307.0$, $p < .0001$. Raters were also more suspicious when viewing clips of the lies ($M = 4.81$) than when they saw clips of the truths ($M = 4.26$), $F(1, 48) = 96.1$, $p < .0001$. Raters also reported that they got more information on which to base their judgment of truthfulness when they heard a true story ($M = 5.10$) than when they heard a fabricated one ($M = 5.03$), $F(1, 48) = 7.37$, $p = .009$.

The third index of detection ability, the continuous measure of truthfulness, was new to this study. The main effect of the truthfulness of the story was significant for this measure, $F(1, 48) = 8.92$, $p = .004$, and showed that accuracy on this measure was greater than chance: Raters judged the stories that were actually true to be more truthful ($M = 5.10$) than the stories that were actually made up ($M = 4.98$).

DID THE DECEPTION OF THE CLOSER FRIENDS BECOME MORE OBVIOUS OVER TIME?

In Study 1, the judges from the closer pairs showed significant improvement over time at detecting their friend's deception. If this result occurred because the senders in the closer dyads told lies that were more easily distinguished from truths at 6 months than at 1 month, then the lies should be especially distinguishable from the truths even to strangers. This would be evident in a Closeness X Time of Measurement effect for raters' accuracy. This effect was not significant, $F(1, 48) = 2.49$, $p = .121$. (The direction of the effect indicated that the raters were less accurate at judging both the closer and the less-close friends from the Time 2 tapes, $Ms = 50.4$ and 47.5, respectively, than from the Time 1 tapes, $M = 52.5$ for both groups.)

Were there any indications that the lies told by the closer friends became more detectable over time on the indirect measures of detection or on the continuous truthfulness scale? Such effects would result in a three-way interaction of Closeness, Time of Measurement, and Truthfulness of the Story. This interaction was not significant in the multivariate analysis, $F(6, 43) = .75$, $p = .614$, or in the truthfulness ANOVA, $F(1, 48) = .59$, $p = .445$.

GENERAL DISCUSSION

The Development of Deception Detection Skill: Relationship Closeness

The present study is the first to trace deception detection accuracy over the development of a friendship, from the first month to 6 months into the relationship. Overall, the friends in our first study were as successful at detecting deception as strangers. Their accuracy was slightly, but not significantly, above chance, and they guessed that more of the stories were true than made up, despite hearing equal numbers of each. As a group, the judges showed only an insignificant degree of improvement at detecting the deception of their friends from the time when they had known them only for about a month until 5 months later. In fact, the overall accuracy of the friends across both time periods, 54.6%, was very similar to the 54% accuracy for strangers, documented across more than 100 estimates (DePaulo, Tornqvist, & Cooper, 2002). If we had examined only our group of friends as a whole, we would have come to the same conclusion as previous cross-sectional studies, namely, that there is no unqualified evidence that relationship partners are better than strangers at detecting deception (Anderson, Ansfield, & DePaulo, 1999).

In previous research, the link between closeness and accuracy at detecting deception also had been assessed by correlating closeness with accuracy within groups of relationship partners. We computed analogous correlations from our data separately for Time 1 and Time 2. As in the earlier studies, we too found unimpressive results when we treated our data as if they were cross-sectional. The correlation of closeness with accuracy was $r(50) = -.112$ at Time 1 and .102 at Time 2.

We thought that friends who remained especially close after knowing each other for 6 months would show greater accuracy than they had at 1 month. Close friends' ability to maintain and sometimes even deepen their intimacy, we thought, could have been gained by their success at dealing with annoyances, inconveniences, and threats (Holmes & Rempel, 1989). They would thereby have less need than other relationship partners either to believe that their friend would never tell lies or to be overly suspicious of their friend.

As we predicted, the closer friends showed a significant improvement in deception detection accuracy from 1 month to 6 months, whereas the less-close friends showed a trivial decrease in accuracy. We considered the alternative that accuracy improved in the closer friendship pairs not because the judges were becoming more insightful but because their friends who were telling the stories were becoming more obvious. However, our Study 2 data were inconsistent with that alternative. The strangers rating the videotapes were no more successful at detecting the closer friends' truths and deceptions told at Time 2 than those told at Time 1.

The failure of the judges in the less-close pairs to show any improvement over time was accounted for by a consistent mistake they made: At 6 months, they often disbelieved their friends, even when their friends deserved to be believed. Whereas at 1 month they believed in the truthfulness of 80.4% of the stories that actually were true, by 6 months, they believed that only 58.1% of the truthful stories were true. The emotionally closer friends instead became increasingly well calibrated in the appropriateness of their faithfulness and skepticism. From 1 month to 6 months, they believed more of their friends' truths and disbelieved more of their lies (although neither of these comparisons, tested individually, was significant).

We have been focusing on the differential interpretation of cues by the closer and less-close friends once those cues have been noticed. It is also possible that the closer friends were more attentive to each other and thereby recognized more of the potentially relevant cues in the first place. We were able to assess the degree to which the judges noticed some differences between truths and lies by our measures of indirect deception detection. Of interest, both the closer and the less-close judges, at both points in time, successfully separated the truths from the lies on these indirect measures; so did the raters from Study 2, who were strangers to the senders. The levels of indirect deception detection were very consistent. They were comparable for the closer and the less-close judges, and they were stable from Time 1 to Time 2. From what we can discern from the results of our indirect measures, then, differential recognition of potentially relevant cues did not account for the development of skill at detecting a partner's deception that was unique to the closer friends.

Given that all of the groups and subgroups showed significant indirect deception detection at both time periods, why is it that only the closer friends at Time 2 performed significantly better than chance on the direct, dichotomous measure of deception detection? The distinctions that perceivers made on the indirect measures, although quite reliable statistically, were not large when considered in terms of points on the rating scales. For example, on the 9-point scale of suspiciousness, judges recorded a mean rating of 5.51 when their friends were telling lies, compared to a mean rating of 4.88 when their friends were telling the truth. To the friends making these judgments, their impressions probably seemed more like hints than compelling evidence. That left lots of room for the judges to interpret their intuitions in the context of their wishes and fears about their relationship partners. For the close friends at Time 2, who had maintained their closeness over the course of the 6 months, despite any conflicts and disappointments that may have arisen, it was possible to take the glimmer of sincerity they heard in the honest stories and believe in their friends' truthfulness. At the same time, the close friends were also willing to accept rather than deny the whiff of insincerity they discerned in the dishonest stories and call those stories lies. For the less-close friends, however, faith in their partners had apparently eroded over time. A mere glimmer of sincerity was not reason enough to give their friends credit for being truthful, whereas a whiff of insincerity was considered more than sufficient justification for calling their friends liars (see also Holmes & Rempel, 1989; Rempel, Holmes, & Zanna, 1985). This explanation is, however, admittedly speculative.

Because our direct measure of deception detection in Study 1 was dichotomous, whereas our indirect measures were continuous, it is possible that judges only seemed to be more accurate on the indirect measures because those were more sensitive measures. To clarify this point, we added a continuous measure of truthfulness, which is a direct assessment of perceptions of truthfulness on a more sensitive scale. The Study 2 raters did show significant deception detection accuracy on the continuous measure, even though they did not perform significantly better than chance on the direct dichotomous measure. This suggests that the dichotomous and indirect measures may differ more importantly on measurement sensitivity than on directness.

However, we are cautious about this conclusion for a number of reasons. First, ratings on several of the indirect measures separated the truths from the lies even more strongly than did the ratings on the truthfulness scale. Second, in several previous studies (e.g., DePaulo, Jordan, Irvine, & Laser, 1992; DePaulo, Rosenthal, Green, & Rosenkrantz, 1982), both the direct and the indirect perceptions were assessed on the same type of rating scale but accuracy was greater on the indirect measures. The only study other than the present ones designed specifically to address direct and indirect deception detection was Anderson's (1999) investigation of the detection of deception by romantic partners and strangers. In that study, judges were given the potentially threatening task of assessing the truthfulness of people (sometimes their romantic partners) who were answering the question of whether they found a specific other person attractive. On the direct dichotomous measure, perceivers were significantly less accurate when the person they were judging was a romantic partner than when that person was a stranger (cf. Simpson, Ickes, & Blackstone, 1995). On the indirect, continuous measures, however, judgments of the romantic partners were significantly more accurate. The results for the rating scale measures of truthfulness, which was a direct but sensitive measure, were the same as for the direct dichotomous measure: When judges had to make direct ratings of deceptiveness, they were less insightful about their own romantic partners than they were about total strangers. The Anderson (1999) findings, together with our own, point to the importance of continuing the study of direct and indirect deception detection in different relationship types and with deception tasks varying in the potential threat they pose to the relationship.

Other Alternatives and Qualifications

We have argued that close friends' improved success at detecting deception followed from their increasingly accurate interpretation of specific behavioral cues. Alternatively, the judges from the closer pairs may have become more accurate because they had come to know their friends more deeply and therefore could interpret the plausibility of their stories more knowledgeably (cf. Stinson & Ickes, 1992). Within the context of an especially intimate relationship, the same stories that might seem convincing to a stranger could be more transparently false to a friend. We know that in the present research, the friends in the closer pairs, relative to those from the less-close pairs, did disclose more to each other. However, when we included the mean disclosure scores from the friendship pairs at each point in time as covariates, the previously significant Sex X Time effect, $F(1, 48) = 4.77$, $p = .034$, dropped only slightly to $F(1, 47) = 3.27$, $p = .077$. Therefore, we think it is unlikely that this explanation fully accounts for the closer friends' improvement in accuracy.

Another alternative explanation is that at Time 2, the senders from the closer pairs deliberately told truths and lies that would be distinguishable only to their friend and not to strangers (cf. Fleming & Darley, 1991; Fleming et al., 1990). Because the participants followed the experimental procedure in every other way, we think it is unlikely that they chose to subvert it in this one way, but we cannot rule it out.

One limitation of our study is that we tracked our friends for only 6 months. Although there is a deepening and stabilizing of friendships within that time frame (Hays, 1985), it is possible that 6 months marks just the beginning of the development of skills as difficult as detecting deceit. If we followed our friends for a much longer period of time, they may have shown much more impressive gains. Although this possibility may be worth pursuing, we are not very optimistic. The 61.4% accuracy achieved by the closer friends at 6 months is a score bested by fewer than 10% of the groups of strangers recently reviewed meta-analytically (DePaulo, Tornqvist, & Cooper, 2002). Even among professionals whose jobs involve daily attempts to detect lies, accuracy scores greater than the mid-60th percentile are uncommon (e.g., DePaulo & Pfeifer, 1986; Ekman & O'Sullivan, 1991; Ekman, O'Sullivan, & Frank, 1999). Relationship partners, similar to experienced professionals, have many opportunities to learn about cues to deception, but under many circumstances, the behavioral indicators of deception are likely to remain subtle and ambiguous. Whether relationship partners draw the correct inferences from those cues may depend importantly on whether they are willing to own up to the implications of those inferences – for example, that their partner is not so saintly as they had wished or so demonic as they had alleged.

NOTES

1. There was also a main effect for Sex of Dyad, $F(1, 48) = 7.75$, $p = .008$, indicating that the female friends disclosed more to each other ($M = 10.14$) than did the male friends ($M = 8.26$).

2. About ½ hour after judges indicated their guesses as to whether their friends had told the truth or lied about each story, they were asked to record their guesses once again about the same stories. When the two different guesses were added to the analysis as levels of a repeated-measures factor, the Sex of Dyad X Time interaction became significant, $F(1, 50) = 4.49$, $p < .05$. This interaction showed that, averaging across the two guesses, the women's accuracy improved from 48% at Time 1 to 59% at Time 2, whereas the men's accuracy decreased slightly from 52% to 48%. The interaction of Sex and Time with the particular guess was not significant, suggesting that the pattern of means was essentially the same for the two guesses. However, the Sex X Time interaction was not significant in the analysis reported in this article, $F(1, 48) = 1.62$, $p = .210$, which was conducted on just the first guesses.

3. Because this effect was important to our interpretation, we checked the results of the univariate analyses. The effect was not significant in any of those analyses either.

Authors' Note: The studies were supported in part by grants from the National Science Foundation and the National Institute of Mental Health to the second author. We thank Reginald B. Adams for his help with this research.

REFERENCES

Anderson, D. E. (1999). *Cognitive and motivational processes underlying the truth bias.* Unpublished doctoral dissertation, University of Virginia.

Anderson, D. E., Ansfield, M. E., & DePaulo, B. M. (1999). Love's best habit: Deception in the context of relationships. In P. Philippot, R. S. Feldman, & E. J. Coats (Eds.), *The social context of nonverbal behavior* (pp. 372-409). Cambridge, UK: Cambridge University Press.

Anderson, D. E., DePaulo, B. M., Ansfield, M. E., Tickle, J. J., & Green, E. (1999). Beliefs about cues to deception: Mindless stereotypes or untapped wisdom? *Journal of Nonverbal Behavior, 23,* 67-88.

Ansfield, M. E., DePaulo, B. M., & Bell, K. L. (1995). Familiarity effects in nonverbal understanding: Recognizing our own facial expressions and our friends'. *Journal of Nonverbal Behavior, 19,* 135-149.

Aron, A., Aron, E. A., & Smollan, D. (1992). Inclusion of the Other in the Self Scale and the structure of interpersonal closeness. *Journal of Personality and Social Psychology, 63,* 592-612.

Brauer, D. V., & DePaulo, B. M. (1980). Similarities between friends in their understanding of nonverbal cues. *Journal of Nonverbal Behavior*, *5*, 64-68.

Buller, D. B., Strzyzewski, K. D., & Hunsaker, F. G. (1991). Interpersonal deception: II. The inferiority of conversational participants as deception detectors. *Communication Monographs*, *58*, 25-40.

Comadena, M. E. (1982). Accuracy in detecting deception: Intimate and friendship relationships. In M. Burgoon & N. E. Doran (Eds.), *Communication yearbook 6* (pp. 446-472). Beverly Hills, CA: Sage.

DePaulo, B. M. (1994). Spotting lies: Can humans learn to do better? *Current Directions in Psychological Science*, *3*, 83-86.

DePaulo, B. M., Ansfield, M. E., Kirkendol, S. E., & Boden, J. M. (2002). *Serious lies*. Manuscript submitted for review.

DePaulo, B. M., Charlton, K., Cooper, H., Lindsay, J. J., & Muhlenbruck, L. (1997). The accuracy-confidence correlation in the detection of deception. *Personality and Social Psychology Review*, *1*, 346-357.

DePaulo, B. M., Jordan, A., Irvine, A., & Laser, P. S. (1982). Age changes in the detection of deception. *Child Development*, *53*, 701-709.

DePaulo, B. M., Lindsay, J. J., Malone, B. E., Muhlenbruck, L., Charlton, K., & Cooper, H. (2002). *Cues to deception*. Manuscript submitted for review.

DePaulo, B. M., & Pfeifer, R. L. (1986). On-the-job experience and skill at detecting deception. *Journal of Applied Social Psychology*, *16*, 249-267.

DePaulo, B. M., Rosenthal, R., Green, C. R., & Rosenkrantz, J. (1982). Diagnosing deceptive and mixed messages from verbal and nonverbal cues. *Journal of Experimental Social Psychology*, *18*, 433-446.

DePaulo, B. M., Tornqvist, J. S., & Cooper, H. (2002). *Accuracy at detecting deception: A meta-analysis of modality effects*. Manuscript in preparation.

Ekman, P., & O'Sullivan, M. (1991). Who can catch a liar? *American Psychologist*, *46*, 913-920.

Ekman, P., O'Sullivan, M., & Frank, M. G. (1999). A few can catch a liar. *Psychological Science*, *10*, 263-266.

Fleming, J. H., & Darley, J. M. (1991). Mixed messages: The multiple audience problem and strategic communication. *Social Cognition*, *9*, 29-46.

Fleming, J. H., Darley, J. M., Hilton, J. L., & Kojetin, B. A. (1990). Multiple audience problem: A strategic communication perspective on social perception. *Journal of Personality and Social Psychology*, *58*, 593-609.

Hays, R. B. (1985). A longitudinal study of friendship development. *Journal of Personality and Social Psychology*, *48*, 909-924.

Holmes, J. G., & Rempel, J. K. (1989). Trust in close relationships. In C. Hendrick (Ed.), *Review of personality and social psychology: Close relationships* (Vol. 10, pp. 187-220). Newbury Park, CA: Sage.

Levine, T. R., & McCornack, S. A. (1992). Linking love and lies: A formal test of the McCornack and Parks model of deception detection. *Journal of Social and Personal Relationships*, *9*, 143-154.

Levine, T. R., McCornack, S. A., & Park, H. S. (1999). Accuracy in detecting truth and lies: Documenting the "veracity effect." *Communication Monographs*.

McCornack, S. A., & Parks, M. R. (1986). Deception detection and relationship development: The other side of trust. In M. L. McLaughlin (Ed.), *Communication yearbook 9*. Beverly Hills, CA: Sage.

Millar, M., & Millar, K. (1995). Detection of deception in familiar and unfamiliar persons: The effects of information restriction. *Journal of Nonverbal Behavior*, *19*, 69-84.

Rempel, J. K., Holmes, J. G., & Zanna, M. P. (1985). Trust in close relationships. *Journal of Personality and Social Psychology*, *49*, 95-112.

Rosenthal, R., & Rosnow, R. L. (1991). *Essentials of behavioral research* (2nd ed.). New York: McGraw Hill.

Simpson, J. A., Ickes, W., & Blackstone, T. (1995). When the head protects the heart: Empathic accuracy in dating relationships. *Journal of Personality and Social Psychology*, *69*, 629-641.

Snedecor, J. C., & Cochran, W. G. (1967). *Statistical methods* (6th ed.). Ames: Iowa State University Press.

Stiff, J. B., Kim, H. J., & Ramesh, C. N. (1992). Truth biases and aroused suspicion in relational deception. *Communication Research*, *19*, 326-345.

Stinson, L., & Ickes, W. (1992). Empathic accuracy in the interactions of male friends versus male strangers. *Journal of Personality and Social Psychology*, *62*, 787-797.

Winer, B. J. (1971). *Statistical principles in experimental design* (3rd ed.). New York: McGraw-Hill.

Zuckerman, M., Koestner, R., & Alton, A. O. (1984). Learning to detect deception. *Journal of Personality and Social Psychology*, *46*, 519-528.

Received March 1, 2000
Revision accepted August 2, 2001

Journal of Applied Social Psychology, Vol. *16,* No. *3,* 249-267.

On-the-Job Experience and Skill at Detecting Deception[1]

Bella M. DePaulo
University of Virginia

Roger L. Pfeifer
Federal Law Enforcement Training Center
Glynco, Georgia

The role of on-the-job experience in fostering skill at detecting deception was examined. A deception-detection test was administered to three samples of more than 100 students each: a group of undergraduates with no special experiences at detecting deceit; a group of new recruits to a federal law enforcement training program, who had some limited on-the job experience at detecting deceit; and a group of advanced federal law enforcement officers, with years of experience working at jobs in which the detection of deception is very important. Although the officer samples were more confident about their judgments of deceptiveness than were the students, they were no more accurate than the students. None of the three groups showed a significant improvement in deception-detection success from the first half to the second half of the test; however, the advanced officers felt increasingly confident about their performance as they progressed through the test. Correlational analyses of the relationship between accuracy and confidence provided further evidence that experience does not improve people's awareness of the accuracy or inaccuracy of their judgments. The findings from this research are compared to the results of research on other kinds of professional decision-makers (e.g., clinical psychologists), and several theoretical perspectives on the role of experience in decision making are discussed.

The detection of deception from verbal and nonverbal cues is a very difficult task. Although most groups of subjects whose skills have been assessed have performed at a level that exceeds chance, very few groups have ever achieved an accuracy level greater than 60% (in tasks for which 50% accuracy would represent a chance level), and some have even performed worse than chance (for reviews, see DePaulo, Stone, & Lassiter, 1985; Kraut, 1980; Zuckerman, DePaulo, & Rosenthal, 1981). The skill profile of the human lie-detector, then, is not a very impressive one. But perhaps this pessimistic picture can be blamed on the nearly-exclusive study of inexperience deception-detectors. Perhaps if researchers were to turn their attention to groups of people who have had years of experience at detecting lies – for example, people who have long been employed in jobs in which the detection of deception is particularly important – a more flattering portrait would emerge. This is the optimistic perspective on the role of experience in fostering skill at detecting deceit.

A variety of intuitively compelling hypotheses can be derived from the optimistic perspective. The most obvious of these is that experience at detecting deception should facilitate lie-detection success. More experienced deception-detectors, if indeed they are more successful, might also be expected to report appropriately high degrees of confidence in their judgments of deceptiveness. There may be other benefits of experience, too. Although even the most experienced lie-detectors are unlikely to be correct all the time, perhaps experience improves people's discernment of which their judgments are and are not likely to be valid. That is, experience at detecting deceit might increase the correlation between accuracy and confidence. Finally, in new deception-detection contexts, experienced detectors may also be especially skilled at learning how to learn. For example, when they are observing strangers telling lies and truths in situations which are not entirely akin to the situations they encounter on the job, their success at identifying these messages might increase especially quickly.

Recently, in their review of the literature on deceiving and detecting deceit, DePaulo et al (1985) proposed a very different hypothesis about the effects of experience on deception-detection success. They suggested that in many occupations in which the detection of deception is important, detectors receive inadequate and unsystematic feedback on the accuracy of their judgments of deceptiveness. To illustrate their point, they describe the feedback received by customs inspectors:

> Consider, for example, customs inspectors, who as part of their job have perhaps hundreds of experiences daily at trying to detect deceit. What kind of feedback do they get? From the many travelers whom they decide not to search, they get virtually no feedback at all. Some of those persons may in fact be smugglers, but once the inspectors let them pass unsearched, they will almost never find out that they made a mistake. Even when inspectors do decide to search travelers who are in fact smuggling illegal goods, they may not always find those goods. In those instances, the inspectors would classify the travelers as nonsmugglers, when in fact they are smugglers.

Einhorn (1982) has suggested that it is in just these types of situations, in which feedback is unsystematic and people have an inadequate understanding of the structure of the decision-making task, that people are especially unlikely to learn from their experiences. He further suggests that positive feedback can actually impair the learning of more valid decision-making rules, by undermining people's motivation to determine exactly how their successes were achieved. In the case of customs inspectors who learn immediately and definitively that the traveler they searched was indeed smuggling illegal goods, they may regard this success experience as support for their theory about which verbal and nonverbal behaviors are indicative of deception. In fact, however, it is possible that their success occurred in spite of their beliefs about cues to deceptions – beliefs which may have actually been erroneous.

The first prediction, then, from this more pessimistic perspective, is that experienced lie-detectors will not be any more successful than inexperienced lie-detectors at detecting deceit. Such a result would be consistent with a large literature on decision making in other work-related settings (e.g., clinicians making diagnostic judgments); in those settings, the more experienced decision-makers are often no more accurate than the less experienced ones (Goldberg, 1968). Also supportive of t his predictions is a study in which a group of customs inspectors and a group of laypersons watching videotapes of travelers were both unsuccessful in deciding which travelers should be searched (Kraut & Poe, 1980). Similarly, in a study in which undergraduates and police detectives observed interrogations of suspects in a mock crime, the detectives were no more accurate than the undergraduates in their judgments of guilt and innocence (Hendershot & Hess, 1982).

Even if experienced detectors are not especially successful, will they perhaps be more aware of their own knowledge and its limitations? Research by Lichtenstein and Fischhoff (1977) suggests that they will not. In their studies of factors influencing the appropriateness of confidence judgments, they found that when subjects were answering questions relevant to their particular area of expertise, they reported confidence levels that were no better calibrated to their actual decision-making success than when they were answering questions about topics for which they had no particular expertise.

Will experienced detectors learn more quickly than less experienced detectors when confronted with a new lie-detection task? Once again, research suggests that they will not. In a study of clinical decision making which included three groups of subjects with very different amounts of task-relevant experience, Oskamp (1965) found that as subjects received more and more information about a clinical case, the accuracy of the judgments made about the case showed no significant improvement for any of the three groups. Interestingly, however, even though subjects' accuracy did not improve as they received more information, their level of confidence did increase markedly.

To study the relationship between experience at detecting deception and (a) success at detecting deception, (b) confidence in judgments of deceptiveness, (c) the appropriateness of these confidence judgments, and (d) the ability to learn more about deception, we recruited several different groups of subjects. The "experienced" sample was comprised of federal law enforcement officers who worked at a variety of jobs in which the importance of detecting deception varied, but was generally quite high. Within this officer sample were two subsamples with very different amounts of on-the-job experiences: new recruits, who had been officers for an average of only 5 months, and more advanced officers, who had been officers for an average of more than 7 years. Our least experienced sample was a group of undergraduates who were not selected for their experience at detecting deceit.

All subjects listed to an audiotape of 16 senders who varied in their motivation to lie successfully. Each sender told two lies and two truths; one of the lies and one of the truths was planned in advance, and the others were told spontaneously. Subjects recorded their judgment of deceptiveness and their confidence in that judgment after each message. This particular stimulus tape was selected for several reasons. First, it has been used in previous research (DePaulo,

Lanier, & Davis, 1983), in which untrained judges were able to detect deception at a level that was significantly better than chance. Hence, we knew that the messages on this tape did include valid and discernible clues to deception and truth. Second, the inclusion on the tape of a variety of different types of communications (planned and unplanned, motivated and unmotivated) allowed us to put together a more comprehensive profile of the skills of experienced and inexperienced detectors.

Method

SUBJECTS

One group of students and two groups of federal law enforcement officers served as subjects. The student sample consisted of 161 undergraduates (77 males and 84 females) from the University of Virginia who volunteered to participate in a study of deception-detection for course credit. The mean age was 19.21 years (SD=1.05).

The officer sample consisted of 258 subjects (215 males and 43 females) who volunteered to participate in a study of deception-detection while attending classes at the Federal Law Enforcement Training Center in Glynco, Georgia. Of these officers, 144 (112 males and 32 females) were *new recruits* who had been federal officers for an average of only 5.25 months (range = less than 1 month to 36 months). Their mean age was 28.79 years (SD=7.88). The other 114 officers (103 males and 11 females) were *advanced officers* who were at the training center for refresher courses, advanced training, or retraining in a different area of law enforcement. The advanced officers had been officers for an average of 7.52 years (range = 1 year to 32 years). Their mean age was 33.04 years (SD=7.53).

The officers were recruited by notices that were posted at the training center, and by announcements made during classes. The study was described as a project designed to measure the ability to detect deception. It was specified on the notices and in the announcements that all responses would be confidential. And in fact, subjects in all samples (including the undergraduate sample) completed all testing materials anonymously.

The officers were employed in a wide variety of agencies, including, for example, divisions of the Secret Service, the U.S. Customs Service, and the Army, Navy, Air Force, Coast Guard, and Marine Corps. Most officers employed by a branch of the military worked for either the Military Police or the Criminal Investigative Division. The job duties of the latter officers included the investigation of cases involving theft, fraud, and narcotics.

In order to obtain an estimate of the importance of detecting deception in each of the employing agencies, four officers who conducted and supervised training sessions at the training center answered two questions about each category: (1) To what extent is the detection of deception involved in the day-to-day activities of a person who works in this agency? And (2) How important would it be to a person in this agency to be able to detect deception successfully? Both questions were answered on 9-point scales, with the high endpoint labelled "very much" for the first question and "very important" for the second. The interjudge reliabilities (coefficient alpha) for these questions were .67 and .57, respectively. For each question, the ratings of the four judges were averaged. Across the 43 different agencies, the correlation of the mean rating of question one with the mean rating of question two was .82. Therefore, the two ratings were combined into one composite mean score. For the sample of new recruits, this mean detection score was 6.96; for the advanced officers, it was 7.52. These two means differed significantly, $F(1,253)=9.85$, p =.002; d = .39,[2] indicating that the more advanced officers, compared to the new recruits, worked in agencies in which the detection of deception was especially important.

Of the many formal training sessions which the officers attend while at the training center, the one most relevant to the detection of deception is a 3-hour session on interviewing techniques. In the session, the officers practice interviewing hired role-players. The role-players are people who have studied scripts depicting real suspects in actual cases, and who attempt to simulate the behaviors of those suspects. The interview involving the officers and the role-players are videotaped, and replayed for the officers. As the tape is replayed, the officers are periodically asked whether they believe that the role-player is lying or telling the truth, and they are also asked to provide reasons for their responses. For some – though not all – of the role-players' responses, objective evidence relevant to the veracity of the responses is available from the case materials. In those instances, officers are provided with feedback about the accuracy of their truth/lie judgment.

STIMULUS MATERIALS

Stimulus materials used to assess subjects' ability to detect deception were the 64 audiotaped communications conveyed by 16 of the 32 "senders" who participated in the DePaulo et al. (1983) study. The senders were eight male and eight female undergraduates who had answered four questions about their attitudes and opinions in front of a panel of six of their peers. Senders lied in response to two of the questions and told the truth in response to the other two. They were allowed to plan in advance one of their truthful responses and one of the deceptive responses. All senders answered the same four questions in the same order. The particular questions that senders were to answer truthfully versus deceptively, and those that were planned versus unplanned, were counterbalanced. One half of the male senders and one half of the female senders were given instructions designed to motivate them to lie successfully (for example, they were told that research findings had demonstrated that the ability to lie successfully was linked to professional success). To the other senders -- those in the low motivation condition – the study was described as a guessing game. (For further details, see DePaulo et al., 1983.)

PROCEDURE

The procedure and the task instructions were the same for all three groups. All subjects were tested in small groups. Subjects were first given a general introduction to the purpose of the study (to test their ability to detect deception); next they completed (anonymously) a brief questionnaire which included questions primarily about demographic characteristics such as age and education.

Subjects were then told that they would hear four answers conveyed by each of 16 senders, and the senders might be lying or telling the truth on any number of their answers. Subjects were given a list of the four questions that the senders were asked, in the order in which they were asked. Subjects were not told about the motivational manipulation.

During the rating pause following each response, subjects indicated whether they believed the response was a truth or a lie, and they also indicated their confidence in that judgment by circling a number on a 9-point scale with endpoints labeled "not very sure at all" (1) and "very sure" (9). After completing their ratings, subjects were debriefed and thanked for their participation.

Results

PRELIMINARY ANALYSES

Accuracy scores. Subjects' accuracy at detecting deception and truth was defined as the percentage of correct truth/lie judgments. The mean accuracy score across all subjects and all types of items was 53.6 (SD=6.0, range = 35.9 to 73.4). This level of accuracy is significantly greater than chance, $t(418) = 12.00$, $p < .001$; $d = 1.17$, and is representative of the most common finding in this area of research – that is, that accuracy is significantly better than chance but less than 60%. Preliminary analyses of subjects' raw truth-lie judgments showed that the groups did not differ significantly in their tendency to label messages as lies.

Covariates. Subjects' age was significantly correlated both with the "group" variable (i.e., the officers were older than the students) and with accuracy (older subjects were less accurate). Therefore, age was used as a covariate in all analyses using accuracy scores as dependent variables. Subjects' level of education (number of years past seventh grade) was also related to both measures; however, the addition of this factor as a covariate to the accuracy analyses did not appreciably change any of the results. Therefore, only age was included as a covariate in the accuracy analyses. (Preliminary analyses showed that age did not interact with the group factor.) All of the means that are reported are unadjusted means.

The inclusion of background variables as covariates in the analyses of confidence ratings had no significant effects on the results; therefore, no covariates were included in those analyses.

Contrasts. For every significant effect involved the group factor (students/new recruits/advanced officers), two nonorthogonal contrasts were computed. The first, which will be called the *linear* contrast, assigned weights of -1, 0, and +1 to the students, new recruits, and advanced officers, respectively. This contrast summarizes the effects on the dependent measure of increasing amounts of experience. The second contrast, which will be referred to as the *students/officers* contrast, compared the officer sample as a whole to the student sample (the weights were -2, +1, and +1, respectively, for the students, new recruits, and advanced officers).

Accuracy. Subjects' accuracy scores (percentage correct) were the dependent measures in a 3 (Group: students / new recruits / advanced officers) × 2 (Sex of Subject) × 2 (Motivation of Sender: low / high) × 2 (Sex of Sender) × 2 (Planning: unplanned/ planned) × 2 (Message Type: truth / lie) analysis of variance, with age as a covariate. The first two factors were between-subjects; the others were within-subjects factors.

The effects relevant to the present report are those involving the Group factor, either as a main effect or in an interaction.[3] Most importantly, the main effect for Group was not significant, $F(2,410) < 1$. Thus, the officers were no more accurate than the students at detecting deception and truth; in fact, they did slightly – though not significantly – worse (see Table 1). [4]

Table 1

Accuracy and Confidence of Deceptiveness Judgments

Group	Accuracy [a]	Confidence [b]	Appropriateness of confidence [c]
Students	54.3	6.20	.03
New recruits	52.9	6.51	.02
Advanced officers	52.3	6.54	.01

Notes: [a] Percentage of correct identifications of truths and lies. [b] Confidence ratings recorded on a 9-point scale; higher numbers indicate greater confidence. [c] Within-subject correlations between accuracy and confidence

---

Two significant interactions indicate that although the overall level of skill did not vary significantly from group to group, the patterning of skills did vary. The more interpretable of these is the Group × Motivation interaction, $F(2,411) = 3.04$, $p = .05$. As shown in Table 2, the officers, compared to the students, did *relatively* better at identifying the lies and truths told by the senders who were highly motivated to succeed, compared to those who were less highly motivated. (In an absolute sense, however, the officers were less successful than the student at identifying the messages of the low-motivation senders, and equally successful at judging the highly-motivated senders.) The linear contrast for this effect was not quite significant, $F(1,411) = 3.40$, $p = .07$; $d = .18$; however, the students / officers contrast was significant, $F(1,411) = 5.84$, $p = .02$; $d = .24$.

The other higher-order interaction is of no apparent theoretical import. The Group × Sex of Sender × Planning interaction, $F(2,411) = 3.19$, $p = .04$, showed that as experience increased (from students to new recruits to advanced officers) , subjects did relatively better at identifying the planned messages conveyed by the female senders than the unplanned messages conveyed by the males. For the linear contrast, the $F(1,411)$ was 6.14, $p = .01$; $d = .24$; for the students / officers contrast, it was 5.72, $p = .02$; $d = .24$.

Table 2

Accuracy at Identifying Low and High Motivation Messages

Group	Motivation of sender		
	Low	High	High minus low
Students	54.8	53.8	-1.0
New recruits	51.8	54.0	2.2
Advanced officers	51.0	53.6	2.6

32

Confidence. The same analysis – Group × Sex of Subject × Motivation of Sender × Sex of Sender × Planning × Message Type, without the covariate, was computed with confidence scores as the dependent measure. Again, the effects of primary interest are those involving the Group factor. [5] Most importantly, the significant overall main effect for Group, $F(2,413) = 3.07, p = .05$, suggested that the groups did differ in their levels of confidence. The students / officers contrast, $F(1,413) = 5.64, p = .02; d = .23$, indicated that the officers were significantly more confident about their truth / lie judgments than were the students (see Table 1). (The linear contrast did not reach significance, $F(1,413) = 2.91, p = .09; d = .17$).

Only one other interaction with Group was significant. The Group × Message Type interaction, $F(2,413) = 6.76, p = .001$, showed that the more experienced subjects were relatively more confident of their judgments of the lies than of the truths (see Table 3). Both the linear contrast, $F(1,413) = 9.29, p = .002; d = .30$, and the students / officers contrast, $F(1,413) = 13.46, p < .001; d = .36$, were significant.

In summary, although the officers were not any more accurate than the students at detecting deception and truth, they were more confident.

Table 3

Confidence in Judgments of Truths and Lies

Group	Message Type		
	Truth	Lie	Lie minus truth
Students	6.25	6.14	-.11
New recruits	6.50	6.52	.02
Advanced officers	6.49	6.58	.09

The relationship between confidence and accuracy was computed on both a between-subjects and a within-subjects basis. For the between-subjects analysis, each subject was assigned an overall accuracy score (percentage correct across all items) and an overall confidence score (mean confidence rating across all items). Across all three groups, the correlation was .02. This is very similar to the median correlation of .06, across six studies, reported in the Zuckerman et al. (1981) review. The correlations for the students, new recruits, and advanced officers were .14, .10, and -.12, respectively. None of these correlations differed significantly from zero. However, the student correlation was significantly higher than the advanced officer correlation, $Z = 2.13$, $p = .03$, and the new recruit correlation was slightly higher than the advanced officer correlation, $Z = 1.75$, $p = .08$. Thus, as experience increases, the relationship between accuracy and confidence (on a between-subjects basis) becomes increasingly negative, such that people who generally are more confident than others tend also to be less accurate than others.

For the within-subjects analysis, a separate Pearson correlation was computed for each subject. This correlation summarized the relationship between the accuracy of each truth/lie judgment and the reported confidence in that judgment across the 64 messages. These correlations were transformed (Fisher's Z), then entered as the dependent variable in a 3 (Group) × 2 (Sex of Subject) between-subjects ANOVA. None of the Fs from these analyses approached significance. For the students, new recruits, and advanced officers, respectively, the mean correlations were .03, .02, and .01. These low correlations are consistent with the literature showing poor calibration for difficult tasks (e.g., Lichtenstein & Fischhoff, 1977; Lichtenstein, Fischhoff, & Phillips, 1982). Thus, there is no evidence from the present study to suggest that experience at detecting deception improves people's awareness of when their deceptiveness judgments are right and when they are wrong.

LEARNING ABOUT DECEIT: WITHIN-TEST CHANGES IN ACCURACY AND CONFIDENCE

Changes in accuracy. To determine whether the more experienced subjects learned more about how to detect deception over the course of the test, we computed separate accuracy scores for performance during the first half (first 32 items) versus the second half of the test. These accuracy scores were the dependent variables in a 3 (Group) × 2 (Sex of Subject) × 2 (Motivation of Sender) × 2 (Planning) × 2 (Message Type) × 2 (Part of Test: first half/second half) analysis of variance, with age as a covariate. The effects of primary theoretical interest are those involving both the Group and Part of Test factors. None of these effects were significant. The very small F-value (<1) for the Group × Part of Test interaction indicates that the more experienced groups showed no greater changes in accuracy than the less experienced groups over the course of the test (see Table 4).

Table 4

Within-Test Changes in Accuracy and Confidence

Group	Accuracy			Confidence		
	First half	Second half	Learning [a]	First	Second half	Increase [b] half
Students	56.0	52.6	-3.4		6.21	6.18	-.03
New recruits	54.1	51.7	-2.4		6.51	6.52	.01
Advanced officers	52.7	52.9	-0.8		6.44	6.64	.20

Notes: [a] Second half accuracy minus first half accuracy.
[b] Second half confidence minus first half confidence.

Overall, performance decreased from the first half (M=54.3) to the second half (M=52.0) of the test, $F(1,411)$=9.94, p = .002; d = .31. However, the level of accuracy achieved during the second half was still greater than chance, $t(418) = 6.75, p < .001; d$=.66.[6] Because the sequence of items on the test was not systematically manipulated, it is impossible to know whether this overall decrement in performance was due to differences in item difficulty, decreases in subjects' motivation or attentiveness, the learning of erroneous rules, or some other factor. For the purposes of the present investigation, however, the important point is that this decrement did not occur differentially across the three groups.

Changes in confidence. Confidence scores were also computed separately for the first half versus the second half of the test, and entered as dependent variables into a Group × Sex of Subject ×

Motivation of Sender × Planning × Message Type × Part of Test analysis of variance. Again the effects of central interest are those involving both the Group and the Part of Test factors. The linear contrast on the Group × Part of Test interaction was significant, $F(1,413) = 4.62$, $p = .03$, $d = .21$. (The students/officers contrast on this interaction was nearly significant, $F(1,413) = 3.33$, $p = .07$, $d = .18$.) As experience increases, subjects became more confident from the first to the second half of the test. As Table 4 shows, this increment in confidence was most pronounced for the advanced officers; it was negligible for the new recruits; and for the students, the change in confidence was also tiny and in the opposite direction.

The main effect for Part of Test was not significant, $F(1,413) = 2.08$, $p = .15$, $d = .14$, indicating that across all groups, there was no overall change in confidence over the course of the test.

In summary, the officer samples did not learn any more or less about detecting deception from the first to the second half of the test than the student sample; however, over the course of the test, the advanced officers did become more confident of the accuracy of their judgments.

Appropriateness of changes in confidence. To determine whether the subjects who became more (or less) accurate over the course of the test were those who also became more (or less) confident, the change in accuracy score (second half minus first half) was correlated with the change in confidence score. This correlation was .08 across all groups, and .16, .12, and -.12, respectively, for the students, new recruits, and advanced officers. Only the student correlation differed significantly from zero ($p = .04$). The student correlation was significantly bigger than the advanced officer correlation, $Z = 2.30$, $p = .02$, and the new recruit correlation was slightly bigger than the advanced officer correlation, $Z = 1.90$, $p = .06$. With experience, then, changes in confidence correspond less and less closely to changes in accuracy.

CORRELATIONS WITH OTHER EXPERIENTIAL VARIABLES

To further examine the role of experience in skill at detecting deception, we correlated all of the major dependent variables – overall accuracy, overall confidence, the correlation between accuracy and confidence (transformed by Fisher's Z), change in accuracy from the first to the second half of the test (i.e., second-half accuracy minus first-half accuracy), and change in confidence from the first to the second half of the test – with the amount of time that the officers had been employed as officers (in months) and with the rating of the importance of detecting deception in the agencies in which each officer worked. These correlations were computed for the officer sample as a whole, and separately for the new recruits and advanced officers. For the accuracy variables, both zero-order correlations and partial correlations (with age) were computed. More than 40 correlations were computed, and only one reached statistical significance – a result which was probably due to chance.

DISCUSSION

Overall, our results supported the pessimistic view of the role of on-the-job experience in fostering skill at detecting deception. We tested three samples of more than 100 subjects each – a group of undergraduates with no special experiences at detecting deceit; a group of new recruits to a federal law enforcement training program, with some limited on-the-job experience at deception-detection; and a group of advanced federal law enforcement officers, with years of experience working at jobs in which the detection of deception is very important. The more experienced samples did no better than the undergraduates at detecting deception; they were no better attuned to the accuracies and inaccuracies of their deceptiveness judgments than were the undergraduates; and they showed no special ability to learn quickly how to detect deception while working through the 64 items of the deception-detection test. Other measures of experience also failed to supply evidence of any special skill. Although the general level of importance of skill at detecting deception in the various federal agencies was quite high, it did vary from agency to agency. However, working in an agency in which deception-detection was particularly important did not seem to facilitate officers' skill development; the "importance" variable did not correlate significantly with overall accuracy, improvements in accuracy over the course of the test, nor with the appropriateness of the officers' confidence ratings. Similarly, total years of experience as an officer failed to predict any of these skills.

To the extent that these federal officers really did fail to learn from experience, they are not unlike many other professional decision-makers, such as clinical psychologists, whose judgmental skills have, for at least some tasks, not outstripped those of untrained undergraduates. Why is it that so many years of job-relevant experiences can apparently have so little salutary effect on the development of judgmental skills? Following Einhorn (1982), we believe that the nature of the feedback that these deception-detectors receive, together with their inadequate understanding of the limitations of that feedback, deserve much of the blame. In most, if not all, of these law-enforcement jobs, the officers do not receive feedback after every deception-detection attempt. Even when they do receive feedback, it may be delayed in time; suggestive rather than definitive; or even inaccurate (as in the case of false confessions).

Outcome feedback in the form of successes and failures may be problematic for still another reason: It does not provide subjects with information about the specific rules or processes that led them to the right or wrong answer. It simply tells them that – for some unspecified reason – their truth / lie judgment was either right or wrong. Human deception-detectors – even inexperienced ones – seem to develop theories about cues to deception. When this global feedback does occur – particularly if it is positive – they may interpret it as further support for their theories. In this way, erroneous theories can be maintained, and sometimes even strengthened (see also Lord, Ross, & Lepper, 1979).

From a more optimistic perspective, the foregoing analysis can be used to formulate a set of conditions under which human lie-detectors might successfully learn from their experiences. Such learning might occur when feedback is unambiguous, and when it is provided consistently over many trials, systematically, and in close temporal proximity to the judgmental process. Learning might also be facilitated by a training procedure in which many elements of the communicative interaction are held constant, so that trainees can focus their attention on a small number of critical features. (For a more extended discussion of these points and other suggestions for improving judgmental accuracy, see DePaulo & Jordan 1982; DePaulo et al., 1985; Goldberg, 1968; and Lichtenstein et al., 1982). Training procedures which have incorporated several of these features have already been reported (Zuckerman, Koestner, & Alton, 1984; Zuckerman, Koestner, & Colella, 1984), and some limited improvement in lie-detection success has in fact occurred. [7]

Even with intensive training, however, officers' biases and errors are unlikely to be totally eliminated, for reasons similar to those suggested by Fischhoff (1982). For example, the feedback that officers receive during their actual on-the-job experiences will remain ambiguous and unsystematic. Also, when ground truth cannot be definitively established, officers may be rewarded according to criteria other than the accuracy of their judgments (e.g., consistency of those judgments with the currently-favored hypothesis). Further, in law enforcement occupations (and many others), convincing expressions of confidence may be advantageous, even when high levels of confidence are not entirely warranted.

An alternative interpretation of our results is that the deception-detection task that we used simply was not a fair measure of the officers' talents. The test included only verbal and vocal cues – perhaps officers' special skills in here in the ability to interpret visual nonverbal behaviors. Or perhaps officers are especially adept at discerning the communicative intents of people who are even more highly motivated to succeed than were the highly motivated senders on the tape used in the present study. Or perhaps the officers were disadvantaged by the fact that the senders were undergraduates, who were more similar to the "nonexpert" undergraduate judges than to the officers. We cannot definitively rule out these interpretations nor a variety of others that are similar to these. Yet, for a number of reasons, we find them unconvincing. First, the results of this study are consistent with the results of studies of other kinds of experienced decision-makers (e.g., Goldberg, 1968), and with studies that used tasks of a similar level of difficulty (e.g., Fischhoff, 1982). They are also the results that were predicted by a theoretical analysis of the nature of naturally-occurring learning experiences (e.g., Einhorn, 1982). Finally, in the specific domain of decision making about deception and truth, other types of tasks have been used (e.g., stimulus materials that included visual cues; deceptive interactions that may have been much more similar to the ones that experienced detectors encounter on the job; and senders who were more similar, demographically, to the experienced judges than were the senders involved in the present research); even on these tasks, though, the experienced judges failed to outperform the inexperienced ones (Hendershot & Hess, 1982; Kraut & Poe, 1980).

Another interpretation may be that the officers perceived the task as a measure of their professional skill, and therefore were more highly motivated to succeed at the task than were the undergraduates. The fact that all responses made by the subjects in all three groups were made anonymously should have contributed to an equalization of the level of motivation across groups. It is possible, though, that difference in motivation still remained. Since we know of no research pertaining to the effects of motivation on deception-detection success, we cannot know what the effects of such motivational differences might have been.

As in all research in which the groups are not equivalent at the outset, it is impossible to rule out the interpretation that the groups performed differently not because of their differential experience at detecting deceit, but because of some other unmeasured factor that was correlated with group status. It is also possible that the analyses of covariance did not optimally correct for

38

even the one factor (age) which was included as a covariate in the design (see Cochran, 1957). Short of randomly assigning persons to occupations, we can never respond definitively to these interpretations. However, once again, we believe that the congruence of our findings with relevant theoretical formulations and bodies of research adds to the credibility of the interpretations we have forwarded.

Still, we do not want to claim on the basis of this evidence that federal officers are no better than college students would be at detecting the deceptions and truths that they really do encounter in their day-to-day work experiences. Using a variety of clues – including, perhaps, demographic information about the senders, factual evidence about the case, and other kinds of data that were not part of the deception-detection task used in the present research – federal officers may indeed succeed quite often at detecting job-related deceptions and truths. What we *are* suggesting, though, is that these officers do not seem to have learned from their experiences how to interpret verbal and nonverbal behaviors apart from other kinds of evidence. In fact, any successes that they do achieve at detecting deceptions and truths may occur in spite of their theories about verbal and nonverbal indicants of deception, which may actually be quite flawed.

Although the more experienced groups of subjects that we tested showed no special skill on any of our measures, they did report greater feelings of confidence. First, across all of the communications that they heard, the two officer samples reported higher confidence in their truth / lie judgments than did the group of undergraduates. We are reluctant to suggest that this is an experiential effect of several reasons: The advanced officers were not significantly more confident than the new recruits, and within each officer sample (and for the two samples considered together), subjects who had been officers longer were not more confident than those who had less time on the job. Most likely, then, this overall difference in confidence is linked to selection into this particular type of work, or even selection into this particular study, which was advertised as a test of deception-detection skill.

The more theoretically interesting confidence result was the differential increase in confidence over the course of the test shown by the more experienced samples – particularly the advanced officers. Although these very experienced lie-detectors (like other two less experienced samples) did not show any improvement at all in the level of accuracy that they attained over the course of the test, they became increasingly confident that they were doing well. Many explanations have been proffered to account for the overconfidence that so often occurs on judgmental tasks of moderate to extreme difficulty (see, for example, Fischhoff, Slovic, & Lichtenstein, 1977; Koriat, Lichtenstein, & Fischhoff, 1980). Our task, however, is not to explain overconfidence per se, but to account for its differential display by the most experienced of our deception-detectors.

Previous research suggests that experienced lie-detectors may have theories about cues to deception that are very similar in content to the theories of inexperienced detectors (DePaulo et al, 1985; Kraut & Poe, 1980). Experience may affect theories not by changing their content, but by changing the tenacity with which their proponents adhere to them, and the facility with which these proponents glean from new samples of behavior evidence which seems to them to be theory-consistent. Also, because the theories of experienced detectors are used so often, they may be more tightly-structured, and more readily accessed and implemented, than the theories of inexperienced detectors. Applied to the present investigation, this suggests that the advanced officers, while listening to the messages, may have discovered theory-consistent cues more quickly than did the other subjects; they may also have noticed more such cues; and they may have felt more certain that these cues were indeed valid ones. All of these factors would bolster their feelings of confidence over the course of the test. However since the theories they were applying were in fact no more valid than those of the less experienced subjects, their rate of learning would not eclipse that of the other groups. Further testing and refinement of this highly speculative explanation may be warranted. The hypothesized process may not be limited to the domain of deception-detection, but may also occur in other judgmental contexts in which intuitive theories are readily formulated and applied, but rarely rigorously tested.

REFERENCES

Cochran, W.G. (1957). Analysis of covariance: Its nature and uses. *Biometrics, 13*, 261-281.

Cohen, J. (1977). *Statistical power analysis for the behavioral sciences* (rev. ed.). New York: Academic Press.

DePaulo, B.M., & Jordan, A. (1982). Age changes in deceiving and detecting deceit. In R.S. Feldman (Ed.), *Development of nonverbal behavior in children* (pp. 151-180). New York: Springer-Verlag.

DePaulo, B. M., Lanier, K., & Davis, T. (1983). Detecting the deceit of the motivated liar. *Journal of Personality and Social Psychology, 45*, 1096-1103.

DePaulo, B. M., & Rosenthal, R. (1978). Age changes in nonverbal decoding as a function of increasing amounts of information . *Journal of Experimental Child Psychology, 26*, 280-287.

DePaulo, B.M., Stone, J.L., & Lassiter, G.D. (1985). Deceiving and detecting deceit. In B.R. Schenkler (Ed.), *The self and social life* (pp. 323-370). New York: McGraw-Hill.

Druckman, D., Rozelle, R.M., & Baxter, J.C. (1982). *Nonverbal communication.* Beverly Hills, CA: Sage.

Einhorn, H.J. (1982). Learning from experience and suboptimal rules in decision making. In D. Kahneman, P. Slovic, & A. Tversky (Eds.), *Judgment under uncertainty: Heuristics and biases* (pp. 268-283). Cambridge: Cambridge University Press.

Fischhoff, B. (1982). Debiasing. In D. Kahneman, P. Slovic, & A. Tversky (Eds.), *Judgment under uncertainty: Heuristics and biases* (pp. 422-444). Cambridge: Cambridge University Press.

Fischhoff, B., Slovic, P., & Lichtenstein, S. (1977). Knowing with certainty: the appropriateness of extreme confidence. *Journal of Experimental Psychology: Human Perception and Performance, 3*, 552-564.

Goldberg, L. (1968). Simple models or simple processes? Some research on clinical judgments. *American Psychologist, 23*, 483-496.

Hendershot, J., & Hess, A.K. (1982). *Detecting deception: The effects of training and socialization levels on verbal and nonverbal cue utilization and detection accuracy.* Unpublished manuscript, Auburn University, Auburn, AL.

Koriat, A., Lichtenstein, S., & Fischhoff, B. (1980). Reasons for confidence. *Journal of Experimental Psychology: Human Learning and Memory, 6*, 107-118.

Kraut, R.E. (1980). Humans as lie detectors: Some second thoughts. *Journal of Communication, 30,* 209-216.

Kraut, R.E., & Poe, D. (1980). Behavioral roots of person perception: The deception judgments of customs inspectors and laymen. *Journal of Personality and Social Psychology, 39,* 784-798.

Lichtenstein, S., & Fischhoff, B. (1977). Do those who know more also know more about how much they know? *Organizational Behavior and Human Performance, 20,* 159-183.

Lichtenstein, S., & Fischhoff, B. (1980). Training for calibration. *Organizational Behavior and Human Performance, 26,* 149-171.

Lichtenstein, S., Fischhoff, B., & Phillips, L.D. (1982). Calibration of probabilities: The state of the art to 1980. In D. Kahneman, P. Slovic, & A. Tversky (Eds.), *Judgment under uncertainty: Heuristics and biases* (pp. 306-344). Cambridge: Cambridge University Press.

Lord, C.G., Ross, L., & Lepper, M.R. (1979). Biased assimilation and attitude polarization: The effects of prior theories on subsequently considered evidence. *Journal of Personality and Social Psychology, 37,* 2098-2109.

Oskamp, S. (1965). Overconfidence in case-study judgments. *Journal of Consulting Psychology, 29,* 261-265.

Rosenthal, R., Hall, J.A., DiMatteo, M.R., Rogers, P.L., & Archer, D. (1979) *Sensitivity to nonverbal communication: The PONS test.* Baltimore, MD: The Johns Hopkins University Press.

Zuckerman, M., DePaulo, B.M., & Rosenthal, R. (1981). Verbal and nonverbal communication of deception. In L. Berkowitz (Ed.) *Advances in experimental social psychology* (Volume 14, pp. 1-59). New York: Academic Press.

Zuckerman, M., Koestner, R., & Alton, A.O. (1984). Learning to detect deception. *Journal of Personality and Social Psychology, 46,* 519-528.

Zuckerman, M., Koestner, R., & Colella, M.J. (1985). Learning to detect deception from three communication channels. *Journal of Nonverbal Behavior, 9,* 188-194.

Footnotes

[1] This research was supported in part by grants from the National Academy of Education and the National Institute of Mental Health. We thank the students and officers for their participation in this study, and the staff of the Federal Law Enforcement Training Center for their cooperation. We also thank Tim Wilson for his comments on an earlier draft of this paper, Pam Holley-Wilcox for statistical consultation, and Jeff Gates, Susan Kirkendol, Jose Macaranas, Carissa Smith, and Charles Valadez for their help in conducting their research..

[2] The statistic d is an estimate of the size of the effect, expressed in standard deviation units (Cohen, 1977).

[3] Other effects were also significant, but are not of central importance to the topic of the present report. For example, consistent with 11 of 15 previous studies on this issue (Zuckerman et al., 1981), subjects were much more successful at identifying truths ($M = 64.2$) than lies ($M = 42.1$), $F(1,411)=169.07, p < .001; d = 1.28$. Also, consistent with the findings reported by DePaulo et al. (1983), (a) subjects were especially accurate at identifying the likes and truths told by the highly motivated male senders and the less-highly motivated female senders, $F(1,411)$ for the Motivation × Sex of Sender interaction = 35.70, $p < .001; d = .59$; and (b) when listening to female senders, subjects were more accurate at identifying the unplanned responses of the highly motivated senders and the planned responses of the less-highly motivated senders; when listening to male senders, subjects were relatively less accurate at identifying those messages, $F(1,411)$ for the Motivation × Sex of Sender × Planning interaction = 61.27, $p < .001; d =.77$.

[4] In the same analysis conducted without the covariate, the main effect for Group came closer to reaching statistical significance, $F(2,409) = 2.61, p < .07$.

[5] Other effects were also significant. For example, males ($M = 6.59$) were more confident than females ($M = 6.24$), $F(1,413)$ for Sex of Subject = 5.20, $p = .02; d = .22$. Subjects were more confident when judging female senders ($M = 6.45$) than when judging male senders ($M = 6.38$), $F(1,413)$ for Sex of Sender = 5.28, $p = .02; d = .23$. Subjects were more confident when judging the communications of highly motivated senders ($M=6.46$) than when judging those of less highly motivated messages ($M=6.37$), $F(1,413)$ for Motivation = 8.36, $p = .004; d = .28$; this pattern was particularly characteristic of the messages conveyed by females senders, $F(1,413)$ for Motivation × Sex of Sender = 8.19, $p = .004; d = .28$. Subjects were relatively more confident of their judgments of the lies told by males and the truths told by females, $F(1,413)$ for Sex of Subject × Message Type = 4.09, $p = .04; d = .20$. Also, subjects were more confident of their judgments of the planned truths and unplanned lies than the unplanned truths and planned lies, $F(1,413)$ for Planning × Message Type = 8.37, $p = .004; d = .28$.

[6] Since subjects received no feedback on the accuracy of their responses, perhaps it should not be surprising that no improvement in accuracy was demonstrated (cf. Lichtenstein & Fischhoff, 1980). However, in studies of skill at understanding nondeceptive messages on the basis of nonverbal cues alone, subjects often do show significant increments in accuracy over the

course of the test (e.g., DePaulo & Rosenthal, 1978; Rosenthal, Hall, DiMatteo, Rogers, & Archer, 1979).

[7] Druckman, Rozelle, and Baxter (1982) have also described training procedures that have facilitated deception-detection success. However, the senders in their testing tapes were people who had been instructed to behave in particular ways. Hence, their deceptive and truthful communications may have been a stylized version of those that occur more spontaneously.

Law and Human Behavior, 2007, *31*, 109-115.

On Lie Detection "Wizards"

Charles F. Bond Jr. and **Ahmet Uysal**

M. O'Sullivan and P. Ekman (2004) claim to have discovered 29 wizards of deception detection. The present commentary offers a statistical critique of the evidence for this claim. Analyses reveal that chance can explain results that the authors attribute to wizardry. Thus, by the usual statistical logic of psychological research, O'Sullivan and Ekman's claims about wizardry are gratuitous. Even so, there may be individuals whose wizardry remains to be uncovered. Thus, the commentary outlines forms of evidence that are (and are not) capable of diagnosing lie detection wizardry.

Legal professionals have an interest in deception. Many of them believe that deception is common. Many of them have views about their own ability to detect deceit.

Psychologists have been writing about deception for decades. They base their writings on psychological research. Hundreds of relevant research studies have been conducted over the years, and these have been summarized in a recent review (*Bond & DePaulo, in press*). The accumulated research literature suggests that people are not good at detecting deception. In judging whether or not others are lying, the average person is accurate roughly 54% of the time when 50% would be expected by chance.

Deception researchers have studied topics of forensic interest. Some have documented the lie detection abilities of relevant occupational groups (Meissner & Kassin, *2002*). Others have attempted to develop lie detection training procedures that would be of use in forensic settings (Kassin & Fong, *1999*). Many have focused their research efforts on the sorts of high-stakes lies that would be of interest in the legal arena (Garrido, Masip, & Herrero, *2002*). For book-long treatments of these and other forensic aspects of deception, see Vrij (*2001*) as well as Granhag and Stromwall (*2004*).

O'Sullivan and Ekman (*2004*) have recently reported a curious result. They found 29 "wizards" of deception detection. Interviews reveal that these "geniuses" of lie detection have "an intense focus and investment in their performance" (O'Sullivan, *2005*, p. 246).

Lie detection wizards should be of interest to forensic researchers. It would be smart for researchers to scrutinize wizards' occupational backgrounds, to see if legal professionals are overrepresented. Those who are attempting to develop lie detection training procedures should wish to uncover wizards' detection strategies. All forensic researchers should be interested in wizards who have demonstrated an ability to detect high-stakes lies, and this is precisely the ability claimed for these 29 wizards (O'Sullivan & Ekman, *2004*). Some of the lies they detected were told under threats of punishment. On the more practical side, law enforcement agencies would be wise to hire lie detection wizards. The US government should also want to hire them. Recognizing this latter point, O'Sullivan and Ekman (*2004*) have already "suggested to government officials that wizards … might be consulted on cases of extraordinary importance" (p. 284).

Before concluding that these 29 individuals have extraordinary abilities, let us scrutinize the statistical evidence for wizardry at lie detection. In this commentary, we show that a simple chance mechanism could produce the wizard-like performances O'Sullivan and Ekman observed. We also describe the forms of evidence that would be needed to determine whether or not people are lie detection wizards.

"WIZARDS" OF LIE DETECTION

O'Sullivan and Ekman (*2004*) found 29 individuals who performed well on three high-stakes lie detection tests. Test 1 involves lies about opinions; test 2 involves lies about a mock crime; and test 3 involves lies about emotion. These tests are in a videotaped format. Ten people appear on each tape—five who are lying and five who are telling the truth. Test-takers see each person on each tape. In response to each videotape segment, test-takers indicate whether or not the person on the tape is lying.

Results on the opinion, crime, and emotion tests have appeared in seven journal articles (Ekman & O'Sullivan, *1991*; Ekman, O'Sullivan, & Frank, *1999*; Etcoff, Ekman, Magee, & Frank, *2000*; Frank & Ekman, *1997*; Frank, Paolantonio, Feeley, & Servoss, *2004*; O'Sullivan, *2003*; O'Sullivan, Ekman, & Friesen, *1988*). Let us summarize the findings presented in those professional outlets while confining our attention to test results for college students. Accuracy rates on the opinion, crime, and the emotion test are available for 353, 113, and 464 undergraduates who judged those tapes. On the average, these students correctly judged 56.06, 60.19, and 50.00% of the opinion, crime, and emotion segments.

O'Sullivan and Ekman have screened over 12,000 professionals for their expertise at lie catching. Twenty-nine of the 12,000 met the researchers' criteria for wizardry. To convince readers of the genius displayed by these individuals, O'Sullivan and Ekman report a statistical computation. It shows that there is an extremely low probability that any given person would achieve a "wizard" performance by chance. For purposes of the computation, the researchers define a "chance" performance as one in which a test-taker responds to video segments as though s/he were flipping coins—thus having a 50/50 chance of being correct on each of 30 lie-or-truth segments.

We have several statistical concerns about this work. Let us begin by noting that people do not respond to the crime and opinion video segments as though they were flipping coins. They judge more than 50% of these lies and truths correctly, as journal articles report. Also, O'Sullivan and Ekman (*2004*) report the probability of *one* individual achieving a wizard-qualifying test score, even though more than 12,000 individuals have been tested. Although the probability of any one person excelling at these tests is low, it may nonetheless be quite likely that one (or more) *of 12,000* test-takers would achieve a high score (cf., Nickerson & Hammond, *1993*). An appropriate model for these data would need to acknowledge the large number of people who have taken the tests.

Here we consider the possibility that none of the 12,000 test-takers were wizards. Under this null hypothesis, we compute the probability that 29 (or more) of the test-takers would meet the criteria O'Sullivan and Ekman have used to identify wizards. We determine this probability under two statistical models: a coin-flipping model and a research-based model. We regard the first model as inappropriate and are presenting it only because it formalizes an assumption made by O'Sullivan and Ekman. We regard the second model as more realistic.

Let us explain these two models. The coin-flipping model begins with an assumption that is false, according to earlier research—that people have a 50/50 chance of being accurate on each video segment of each test O'Sullivan and Ekman use to identify wizards. It assumes that 50% of nonwizards would judge the average lie accurately, when more than 50% have judged it accurately in prior research. Because the model assumes that fewer nonwizards would make correct judgments than the number who would actually make them, it should lead to an underestimate of the number of "wizards" on these tests. Anyone who gets substantially more than 50% right will be labeled a "wizard." But the average judge gets more than 50% right, as previous research shows.

The research-based model uses results from earlier student judges to estimate a chance level of accuracy on each segment. If (despite Meissner & Kassin, *2002*), we entertain the possibility that students are less accurate on these lie detection tests than professionals, this model may also be conservative. Even so, the research-based model for predicting professionals' lie detection accuracy is more realistic than the coin-flipping model. Hence, it will be interesting to compare the number of "wizards" O'Sullivan and Ekman found with a research-based prediction for the number of wizards.

Let us now offer a few statistical details. By the O'Sullivan and Ekman (*2004*) definition, a person is a "wizard at deception detection" if the person

(a) reports correct judgments to at least nine opinion video segments, and gives correct judgments to *either*

(b) at least eight crime video segments *or*

(c) at least eight emotion video segments.

We begin with the simplifying assumption that all of the video segments on a given lie detection test are equally difficult. Given our simplifying assumption, we use the binomial distribution to determine the probability of a performance on each test that satisfies the cutoff score prescribed by the authors.

Let us symbolize the probability of such a performance as x for the opinion test, y for the crime test, and z for the emotion test. Then for reasons that are explained by Howell (_2002_), the overall probability of a person meeting the O'Sullivan and Ekman criterion for wizardry can be determined from the equation $x(y + z - yz)$. Let us symbolize this overall probability as p. If 12,000 randomly selected nonwizards took these tests, we would expect $12,000 \times p$ of those individuals to be classified as wizards.

Let us now present some of the numerical results from two statistical models: the coin-flipping model and the research-based model. Under the coin-flipping model, $x = .0114$, $y = .0553$, and $z = .0553$. These figures imply that $p = .00122$. Thus, we would expect 14.71 of the 12,000 test-takers to meet the O'Sullivan and Ekman criterion for being a wizard. Under the research-based model, $x = .0270$, $y = .1701$, and $z = .0553$. This model implies that $p = .00583$. Thus if we use results from earlier student judges, we would expect 69.98 of the 12,000 individuals to meet the criterion for being a wizard.

O'Sullivan and Ekman tested 12,000 individuals for wizardry. They classified 29 of those 12,000 as wizards (95% confidence interval = 18.46–39.54 wizards). O'Sullivan and Ekman found more wizards than would be expected under the coin-flipping model. In our way of thinking, this discrepancy verifies what was already known—that people do not respond to these video segments as though they were flipping coins. The coin-flipping model classifies anyone who achieves substantially more than 50% accuracy on these deception tests as a wizard. But the average student achieves more than 50% accuracy. That is why more people are classified as "wizards" than the coin-flipping model predicted.

O'Sullivan and Ekman classified only 29 professionals as wizards. This is fewer than the 70 wizards our research-based model would seem to predict. This discrepancy is not easy to explain. One possible explanation relates to a detail of our research-based model—its use of only student judges to predict lie detection accuracy. In addition to the 930 students who judged the three relevant videotapes, 508 other people had judged these tapes before the wizards made any judgments. Suppose we constructed a research-based model from the accuracy of _all_ 1438 judges of these videotapes. Although one might expect this more inclusive research-based model to yield more accurate predictions, it in fact predicts that 155 of the 12,000 professionals should be classified as wizards. Thus, it does nothing to explain why only 29 "wizards" were found.

Although we cannot be sure why the observed number of wizards is so much lower than our research-based prediction, let us venture two possible explanations: one is methodological, the other statistical. The methodological explanation is that these 12,000 professionals took lie detection tests under different conditions than earlier judges. For example, the professionals took two of the tests in their private residences; whereas, the earlier judges took those tests in an academic group setting. Perhaps the professionals were tested under conditions less conductive to lie detection.

The second, statistical explanation begins by noting that only a subset of the 12,000 professionals studied by O'Sullivan and Ekman took all three lie/truth discrimination tests. Let us elaborate on the researchers' testing protocol. The 12,000 professionals in this study attended group workshops on detecting deception. At the outset of each workshop, participants judged 10 opinion lie-or-truth segments. After completing this opinion test, participants were given the correct answers "and asked to report to the group (by a show of hands) how many items they got right" (O'Sullivan & Ekman, _2004_). Workshop participants who reported scoring 90% or better were invited to take additional tests. Some accepted the invitation and subsequently completed the crime and emotion tests.

We do not know how many professionals completed the three-test lie detection battery, but if we are allowed a post hoc assumption about that number, we can fit the research-based model to these data perfectly. To do so, we note that under the research-based model there is a .00583 probability of a nonwizard being classified as a wizard. Thus, the assumption that we must make is that N people took all three lie detection tests, where N can be found from the equation $29 = .00583 N$. Algebra then reveals that to "predict" 29 wizards, we must assume that 5,390 of the 12,000 professionals completed all three lie detection tests. Perhaps it is implausible to assume that 5,390 of 12,000 professionals completed all three of the researchers' lie detection tests. Readers need to make this judgment for themselves, after studying the article by O'Sullivan and Ekman (_2004_).[1]

DIAGNOSTIC EVIDENCE

As statisticians, we are in no position to conclude that the 29 individuals whom O'Sullivan regards as lie detection wizards are _not_, in fact, wizards. Following standard null hypothesis logic, failures to find significant evidence may represent Type II errors. Thus, the current evidence may simply be insufficient to uncover these 29 individuals' wizardry. Indeed, it is conceivable that many more of the 12,000 professionals in question are wizards, and the authors' procedures lack sufficient power to detect this fact. In light of this logical possibility, it is important to consider the forms of evidence that could (and could not) diagnose lie detection wizardry.

To be diagnostic, tests for wizardry must meet certain psychometric and statistical criteria. The tests must be internally consistent. Because the tests must show high composite reliability, they may need to be long (Nunnally, _1978_). An a priori statistical definition of wizardry needs to be specified. Computations must demonstrate that the cutoff score to be used for identifying wizards has sufficient statistical power to detect this statistically defined "wizard." This cutoff score should take into account probabilistic arguments of the sort we have outlined above. Evidence of an extra-chance detection performance should be required before any wizardry is inferred. A second, lower cutoff score should also be developed for the identification of nonwizards.

Of course, there are other considerations in testing. If a lie detection test is to be diagnostic of a general forensic ability, it should expose test-takers to a variety of forensically relevant lies. There would be advantages if the person who developed this test was not the person who interpreted the test. If the test developer and interpreter had different theoretical orientations, it would be hard to contend that the content of the test and the interpretation of the test were related to one another in a way that reflected "bias" (Rosenthal, *1994*).

Standardized testing procedures should be used. No one should be allowed to score their own test of lie detection ability, nor should anyone's report of their score on a test be uncritically accepted. Tests should be supervised and scored by a third party, ideally an individual who does not know the correct answers to test items. The supervisor should have no preexisting belief about the ability level of any particular test-taker. The absence of any preexisting supervisor assumptions would be most critical if the testing format were interactive—say, if the test required the supervisor to interview subjects. If the intended interpretation is that a test measures a preexisting ability, test-takers should get no preexposure to the sorts of items that appear on the test—other than an orienting instructional item or two.

CONCLUSION

Convincing evidence of lie detection wizardry has never been presented. In fact, no truly diagnostic procedure for identifying wizards has ever been reported. Thus, it is premature for government officials to rely on any "wizards" of lie detection in cases of extraordinary importance. It is likewise premature for forensic psychologists to base their research on the assumption that lie detection wizards do (or do not) exist. Rather than constructing research programs on any such assumption, forensic psychologists would be better advised to spend their time developing procedures that could in principle distinguish lie detection wizards from nonwizards.

References

Bond, C.F., Jr., & DePaulo, B.M. (In press). Accuracy of deception judgments. *Personality and Social Psychology Review.*

Ekman, P., & O'Sullivan, M. (1991). Who can catch a liar? *American Psychologist, 46,* 913-920.

Ekman, P., O'Sullivan, M., & Frank, M.G. (1999). A few can catch a liar. *Psychological Science, 10,* 263-266.

Etcoff, N., Ekman, P., Magee, J.J., & Frank, M.G. (2000). Lie detection and language comprehension. *Nature, 405,* 139.

Frank, M.G., & Ekman, P. (1997). The ability to detect deception generalizes across different types of high-stakes lies. *Journal of Personality and Social Psychology, 72,* 1429-1439.

Garrido, E., Masip, J., & Herrero, C. (2004). Police officers' credibility judgments: Accuracy and estimated ability. *International Journal of Psychology, 39,* 276-289.

Granhag, P.A., & Stromwall, L.A. (2004). *Deception detection in forensic contexts.* Cambridge, England: Cambridge University Press.

Howell, D.C. (2002). *Statistical methods for psychology* (5th edition). Pacific Grove, CA: Duxbury Press.

Kassin, S.M., & Fong, C.T. (1999). "I'm innocent!": Effects of training on judgments of truth and deception in the interrogation room. *Law & Human Behavior, 23,* 499-516.

Meissner, C.A., & Kassin, S.M. (2002). "He's guilty:" Investigator bias and judgments of truth and deception. *Law and Human Behavior, 26,* 469-480.

Nickerson, C.A.E., & Hammond, K.R. (1993). Comment on Ekman and O'Sullivan. *American Psychologist, 48,* 989.

Nunnally, J.C. (1978). *Psychometric theory* (Second edition). New York: McGraw Hill.

O'Sullivan, M. (2003). The fundamental attribution error in detecting deception: The boy-who-cried-wolf effect. *Personality and Social Psychology Bulletin, 29,* 1316-1327.

O'Sullivan, M. (2005). Emotional intelligence and deception detection: Why most people can't 'read' others, but a few can. In R.E. Riggio and R.S. Feldman (Eds.) *Applications of nonverbal communication* (pp. 215-253). Mahwah, NJ: Erlbaum.

O'Sullivan, M., & Ekman, P. (2004). The wizards of deception detection. In P.A. Granhag and L.A. Stromwall (Eds.) *Deception detection in forensic contexts* (pp. 269-286). Cambridge, U.K.: Cambridge Press.

O'Sullivan, M., Ekman, P., & Friesen, W.V. (1988). The effect of comparisons on detecting deceit. *Journal of Nonverbal Behavior,*

Rosenthal, R. (1994). On being one's own case study: Experimenter effects in behavioral research – 30 years later. In W. Shadish and S. Fuller *(Eds), The social psychology* of science (pp. 214-229). New York: Guilford Press.

Vrij, A. (2001). *Detecting lies and deceit: The psychology of lying and the implications for professional practice.* New York: Wiley.

Footnotes

[1] It is under the model based on student judges' lie detection accuracy that we must make the assumption outlined in the text. Under the model based on the accuracy of all earlier judges, we "predict" 29 wizards by assuming that 2,248 of the 12,000 professionals completed all of the lie detection tests. An alternative statistical analysis would treat as unknown the number of professionals who were invited to take all of the lie detection tests. Then it would use the chance probability of wizard-qualifying performances on the latter two tests to induce the number of professionals who in fact completed the test battery. Applying this alternative treatment in the context of the student judge research-based model, we "predict" 29 wizards if 114 of the 12,000 professionals completed all three tests. Obviously, our two statistical analyses yield different inferences. We ourselves regard the second analysis as more defensible—given that participants were (or were not) invited to complete the test battery based on their self-reports of a test outcome.

Published online: 13 January 2007

Journal of Experimental Social Psychology, 2004, 40, 29-40.

Maintaining lies: The multiple-audience problem[*1]

Charles F. Bond, Jr. , B. Jason Thomas and René M. Paulson

In an examination of lying in social context, undergraduates were videotaped while describing teachers. Each student described a teacher truthfully to one peer, described the teacher deceptively to a second peer, and was then required to describe the teacher to both peers as the latter sat side-by-side. Three experiments examined the psychology of this multiple-audience predicament. Results of an initial experiment show that students who are in the predicament appear deceptive. They appear deceptive whether they are lying or telling the truth. A second experiment replicates this finding, and suggests that the students' apparent deceptiveness is conveyed more strongly by audible than visible cues. In the interpersonal predicament created by multiple audiences, students offer equivocal, disfluent remarks, as a third experiment shows. Discussion centers on the challenge of maintaining lies in the context of multiple relationships.

> *Oh what a tangled web we weave when first we practice to deceive.*
> Sir Walter Scott's 1805 poem *Lay of the Last Minstrel*.

Long the stuff of poetry, deception has become a subject of scientific research. Having conducted hundreds of experiments on deception, investigators have clarified many facets of this social phenomenon. Still, scientists have not yet unraveled the most "tangled webs" that liars weave.

In the present paper, we examine an interpersonal predicament created by deception. We begin by noting that individuals are embedded in networks of on-going relationships. We distinguish between challenges that a liar confronts at the moment of deception and challenges that emerge for the liar over time. We study one of the emergent challenges, a challenge that reflects the liar's position in a social network.

Deception can be considered at different levels—at the level of the individual, the dyad, or a larger social unit. Individualistic treatments of deception focus on the liar: the liar's personality ([Riggio et al., 1988]), the liar's psychological state ([Zuckerman et al., 1981]), the liar's behavior ([DePaulo et al., 2003]), and facility at duping others ([Bond and Atoum, 2000]; [Bond et al., 1985]). Dyadic treatments emphasize one-on-one deception. They consider the liar's strategies for concealing the truth, the target's growing suspicions, and the moment-by-moment unfolding of the deceptive episode over time ([Buller and Burgoon, 1996]).

Although the individualistic and dyadic approaches have contributed to our understanding of deception, there are aspects of deceit that merit a broader focus. When the individual lies to an acquaintance, complications can ensue that reverberate through a wider social network. These are hard to capture by approaches that restrict themselves to the liar and to one-on-one deception.

Liars face many challenges. Some arise at the moment the lie is perpetrated, while others emerge over time. When perpetrating deception, a liar must: (1) construct a credible story, (2) seem spontaneous, (3) feign sincerity, and (4) mask emotional states that would be discrediting ([Ekman, 2001]). Although these challenges may sound formidable, they are challenges that most liars surmount. As hundreds of experiments show, people can make their lies virtually indistinguishable from truths. On videotape, liars appear sufficiently credible and composed to be judged nearly as honest as truth-tellers ([Vrij, 2000]). Indeed, liars are more often seen as truthful than deceptive ([Levine et al., 1999]). If we are to believe the research literature, it is easy to lie.

Deception may, however, become more challenging over time. Once the liar has duped a target, the deception becomes a part of the dyad's history, and there it will reside for so long as the relationship continues. Liars cultivate certain reputations—hoping to be seen as trustworthy and honest ([DePaulo, 1992]). On the individual's reputation for honesty will hinge the continuance of many relationships, as well as the prospects for future lies. In the wake of a successful deception, liars must be vigilant, lest their reputations for honesty be soiled. This is an emergent challenge of deception—to manage a reputational risk that the lie creates.

In the present article, we examine this challenge by confronting the liar with a predicament. Here students describe teachers. Each student gives a deceptive description of a teacher to one peer, a truthful description of that teacher to a second peer, and must then describe the teacher to both of these peers, as the latter sit side-by-side. We are interested in the student's apparent honesty when giving the final teacher description. At that juncture, the liar must negotiate a pathway through difficult terrain, in presenting the self to multiple audiences ([Fleming, 1994]). In three experiments, we examine this multiple-audience problem. Experiment I demonstrates that students appear dishonest when placed in the multiple-audience predicament. Experiment II assesses the role of visible and audible cues in the student's apparent dishonesty. Experiment III assesses the impact on the student's apparent dishonesty of some psychological factors: discomfort, complexity, and equivocation.

Experiment I

Liars sow the seeds for a self-presentational predicament when they tell different stories to different audiences. The risk is that in later interactions story inconsistencies will be unveiled. Faced with audiences who have heard mutually incompatible stories, liars may respond by reiterating one of their earlier tales. Story reiteration would be a shrewd response to the liar's predicament, in our view. Although audiences who have been offered different versions of the story might become suspicious ([Granhag and Strömwall, 2000]), story reiteration contains the self-presentational damage. Bystanders are given no reason to question the liar's veracity, nor does the liar tip off those who earlier heard the current tale. This would be a minimal effect of the multiple-audience predicament—to engender a story reiteration that implies deception only to a limited audience.

An initial Experiment tests for this minimal multiple-audience effect. It also probes for wider effects of the multiple-audience problem. Perhaps in this predicament, a liar's mendacity will be evident only to those who are privy to a conflicting tale, or maybe the liar will also appear deceptive to naïve onlookers. Perhaps students will be exposed as liars by the multiple-audience predicament only if the tale that they are telling is deceptive; or maybe they will appear deceptive in this predicament even if they are telling the truth. In addressing these issues, we hope to outline the breadth of the multiple-audience problem.

Method

Participants

Two hundred and forty-four undergraduates participated in Experiment I for extra credit in a psychology course. Of these 244 undergraduates, 48 were videotaped while lying and telling the truth; 196 judged the resulting videotape for deception.

Experimental arrangements

A videotape camera was positioned at one end of an experimental laboratory. Two chairs were located nearby—one 2 feet to the left and one 2 feet to the right of the camera. A third chair was located fifteen feet in front of the camera, facing the camera lens. Thus, a "T"-shaped configuration was formed.

Overview

Each of 48 research participants gave three teacher descriptions aloud. The first two descriptions concerned the same teacher. Some participants then described that teacher a third time; others described a different teacher. The third teacher description was given in the presence of two undergraduate peers. Some participants had given their earlier teacher descriptions in the presence of these two peers; others had given the earlier descriptions while alone.

Procedure

Students participated in the videotaping procedure individually. After giving informed consent, the participant listed on a written form two people who had taught them prior to college—a teacher they liked and a teacher they disliked. The participant was informed that as part of the experiment s/he would be speaking to two undergraduates. Participants were instructed to present themselves as honest and to convince the undergraduates that everything they said was true. The participant was then seated 15 feet in front of a videotape camera.

The experimenter consulted a randomization schedule, and instructed the participant to describe a teacher. The participant was instructed to give either: (1) a truthful description of the teacher they liked, (2) a deceptive description of the teacher they liked, (3) a truthful description of the teacher they disliked, or (4) a deceptive description of the teacher they disliked. For the deceptive description, participants were instructed to say either that they disliked the teacher they liked or that they liked the teacher they disliked.

Some of research participants gave this initial teacher description in the presence of an undergraduate peer. Others gave their teacher description in the absence of any peer. As participants were informed, their teacher descriptions were videotaped.

After this initial description, the participant was instructed to describe the same teacher a second time. This second description would be either truthful or deceptive. Participants who had earlier told the truth were instructed to lie. Those who had earlier lied were instructed to tell the truth. Participants who had been alone while giving the first teacher description were alone while giving this second description. Participants who had given the earlier teacher description in the presence of a peer gave this second description in the presence of a different peer. This second description was videotaped.

The participant then received some final instructions. One last time, the participant was to describe a teacher. Some participants were instructed to give a third description of the teacher described twice before. Other participants were instructed to describe the second teacher listed at the outset of the experiment—the one who had not yet been described. Some participants were instructed to lie; others were instructed to tell the truth. All participants gave this third teacher description in the presence of two undergraduate peers. For some participants, these same two individuals had been present at the earlier teacher descriptions—one at the first description; the other at the second description. Again, the description was videotaped. Afterwards, the participant was debriefed.

Experimental design

Each research participant gave three teacher descriptions. Of primary interest is the third description, given to two undergraduate peers. In a focal experimental condition, the participant had earlier given mutually inconsistent descriptions to these peers of the teacher now being described. Hereafter, we call this the *multiple-audience predicament*. For experimental comparison, there were other conditions. In one condition, the participant had earlier given mutually inconsistent descriptions to these two peers of a teacher other than the one now being described; in another condition, the participant had earlier been in the absence of peers while giving two mutually inconsistent descriptions of the teacher now being described; in a third condition, the participant had earlier been in the absence of peers while giving mutually inconsistent descriptions of a teacher other than the one now being described. Of the 48 student participants, 24 were assigned to the *multiple-audience predicament* and eight to each of the three non-focal conditions. Within each condition, half of the participants were instructed to lie when giving their third teacher description; the other half were instructed to tell the truth. For a diagram of the design, see Table 1. Note that a research participant's three teacher descriptions were offered in immediate succession, and that when describing a teacher to a peer, the participant would not be aware that they might later be required to describe that teacher again, or that the peer might be present at such a description.

Table 1. Experimental conditions over three trials

Experimental condition:	Trial 1	Trial 2	Trial 3
Peers present/ Relevant description	Describes Teacher 1 Peer 1 present	Describes Teacher 1 Peer 2 present	Describes Teacher 1 Both peers present
Peers present/ Irrelevant description	Describes Teacher 2 Peer 1 present	Describes Teacher 2 Peer 2 present	Describes Teacher 1 Both peers present
Peers absent/ Relevant description	Describes Teacher 1 No peers present	Describes Teacher 1 No peers present	Describes Teacher 1 Both peers present
Peers absent/ Irrelevant description	Describes Teacher 2 No peers present	Describes Teacher 2 No peers present	Describes Teacher 1 Both peers present

At trials 1 and 2, each participant lied once and told the truth once. Order of lying (vs. truth-telling) was counterbalancing within condition. For half of the research participants in each condition, the third teacher description concerned the teacher whom the participant liked; for the other half, it concerned the teacher whom the participant disliked.

Target impressions

The participant described a teacher to two undergraduate peers. Fourteen undergraduates served as peers over the course of 48 experimental sessions.

The two peers sat outside the laboratory except when needed. At appropriate times, the experimenter escorted peers into the laboratory, and seated them beside the videotape camera facing the research participant. The experimenter cued each teacher description with a generic instruction (e.g., "Could you please describe Mrs. B., your 10th grade English teacher?"), and waited behind a partition as the teacher was described. Peers, who were blind to the truthfulness of each description, sat passively when in the participant's presence. After observing a teacher description, peers returned to their seats outside the laboratory, where each independently indicated on a response form whether the description was the "truth" or a "lie." Research participants were forewarned that the peers would be trying to determine whether or not they were lying; and were instructed to try always to be judged as truthful. At 32 of the 48 experimental sessions, one peer saw the first teacher description and another saw the second description. Assignment of the two peers to the two descriptions was random.

Observer impressions

The students were videotaped while giving each teacher description. The camera recorded a frontal view of the student, who was seated in an armless swivel chair. The video captured the student's face and torso, down to the knees.

The resulting video footage was edited onto three videotapes. Each videotape depicted 48 teacher descriptions, one description from each of the 48 students. Tape 1 depicted each student's first teacher description; Tape 2, each student's second teacher description; and Tape 3 depicted each student's final teacher description.

For a judgment task, a separate set of undergraduates arrived at a classroom in small groups. After giving informed consent, the participants were told they would be seeing descriptions of teachers. Some of the descriptions would be truthful, and others would be deceptive. The participant's job was to watch each description and indicate on a written form whether the description was the "truth" or a "lie."

Participants then saw an audiovisual presentation of 48 teacher descriptions and made lie/truth judgments. Fifty-nine participants judged the teacher descriptions on Tape 1; 62 judged the teacher descriptions on Tape 2; and 75 judged the teacher descriptions on Tape 3. Each tape was presented in one of two different orders. After recording 48 binary lie/truth judgments, participants were debriefed and dismissed.

Results

Forty-eight undergraduates were videotaped while describing teachers, and their descriptions were judged for truthfulness. Preliminary analyses showed that a student's apparent truthfulness was not significantly affected by the order in which the student told lies and truths, by the order of the videotape presentation, or by the student's claimed feelings (of liking vs. disliking the teacher). These factors are ignored in the analyses below. The unit in each analysis is the student describing a teacher.

In the present study, we examine a predicament that can arise when the liar must describe a teacher to two peers. Here the focal experimental condition is one in which the student has earlier given those peers mutually incompatible descriptions of that teacher. We hypothesize that the students in this multiple-audience predicament will appear less truthful than those in three other conditions. Following the recommendations of [Rosenthal and Rosnow, 1985], we test this hypothesis with a single degree of freedom contrast; then probe for residual differences among the three other conditions with a diffuse test. Interactions with the focal comparison and with residual differences are also tested.

Target impressions

The student began by describing the same teacher twice. Thirty-two of the students gave the first description to one peer and the second description to another peer. From the earlier deception literature, we suspected that students would be successful at lying. They were. To the students' targets, deceptive teacher descriptions were no less believable than truthful descriptions: 53.11% of the deceptive descriptions and 56.25% of the truthful being judged as truthful; for the difference, $t(31)=.25$, *ns* (see Table 2).

Table 2. Experimental results

	Means				Pooled SD
	Multiple audience condition		Other conditions		
	Lie	Truth	Lie	Truth	
Experiment I					
Truth judgments (targets)	50.00%	50.00%	50.00%	83.33%	37.42
Truth judgments (observers)	51.99%	46.40%	63.06%	64.30%	17.79
Experiment II					
Truth judgments (Audiovisual)	50.00%	41.67%	63.75%	64.58%	18.75
Truth judgments (Audio-only)	47.33%	41.00%	61.33%	62.12%	16.89
Truth judgments (Video only)	48.75%	46.17%	62.71%	52.71%	19.65
Experiment III					
Comfort (-3 to +3)	.40	.03	.43	.64	1.02
Clarity (1 to 7)	3.06	3.00	3.68	3.34	.77
Affective intensity (0 to 3)	1.75	2.08	2.59	2.52	.77
Speech rate (words per minute)	176.02	174.12	205.20	205.24	39.21
Pauses (per minute)	2.18	2.93	1.05	1.39	1.75
Speech errors (per minute)	11.91	14.15	8.57	14.22	7.39

Of special interest is the third teacher description, given to two peers. We had imagined that the predicament might undermine students' ability to make targets believe their lies. It does not. Statistical analyses show no difference in targets' impression of students who lie while in the multiple-audience predicament vs. those who lie under other circumstances; *M*s=50.00% truth judgments to lies told in the predicament and 50.00% truth judgments to other lies. The multiple-audience predicament has a different effect: it undermines students' ability to convey the truth;

Ms=50.00% truthful target impressions of truths told in the predicament vs. 83.33% truthful target impressions of other truths; for the difference, $F(1,40)$=4.48, p<.05.

The multiple-audience predicament forced 24 of our student participants to describe a teacher to peers who had heard mutually incompatible characterizations of that teacher. One peer had earlier heard a characterization of the teacher that was consistent with the one now being offered; another had heard an inconsistent characterization. We anticipated that the student would make a less honest impression on the peer who had previously heard an inconsistent (rather than a consistent) teacher characterization. This expectation was not confirmed. Twelve of the 24 targets who had earlier heard an inconsistent teacher characterization judged the current description as truthful, as did 12 of the 24 targets who had heard a consistent characterization.

Observers' impressions

Having examined the impressions students conveyed to two live targets, we now analyze the impressions conveyed to naïve observers.

Again, we focus on the student's apparent truthfulness when giving the third of three teacher descriptions. Again, one might suppose that in the multiple-audience predicament students would appear dishonest only to people who had heard teacher characterizations that were discrepant from the one being offered. Results show that the multiple-audience predicament has a wider effect. To observers who have heard nothing about these teachers, students who are in the predicament appear less truthful than those in other conditions; Ms=49.19% vs. 63.68% truthful; for the difference, $F(1,44)$=8.41, p<.01. Students in the three non-focal conditions do not differ from one another in apparent truthfulness, $F(2,44)$=1.67, p>.20.

Each student gave two preliminary teacher descriptions. A multiple-audience effect also emerges from an analysis of the difference in percentage truth judgments to a student's final teacher description vs. these earlier descriptions. By this criterion, too, students who are in the multiple-audience predicament appear less truthful than those in other conditions, $F(1,44)$=12.18, p<.001; and there are no residual differences among the other conditions, $F(2,44)$=1.35, p>.25. For students in control conditions, the final teacher description appears more truthful than the earlier descriptions, M=11.15% more truthful, $t(44)$=3.12, p<.01. In the focal condition, the final teacher description appears no more truthful than earlier descriptions; in fact, M=−6.50% less truthful, $t(44)$=1.82, p<.07. Naïve judges cannot detect these students' lies. Overall, they judge 56.39% of deceptive teacher descriptions and 53.49% of truthful descriptions to be truthful; for the difference, $t(47)$=1.28, ns. The student's veracity does not interact with other factors (for the veracity × multiple-audience predicament interaction, $F(1,40)$=.43, ns).

Discussion

Liars can dupe targets, a vast literature shows. From the accumulated research, it might seem that deception is easy. However, existing studies are confined to the initial perpetration of a lie. Experiment I challenged liars to maintain their deceptions under difficult circumstances. This assignment proved to be vexing, and in the predicament created by multiple audiences, lies were exposed.

An aspect of these results merits emphasis. Prior to conducting Experiment I, we had entertained the notion that in the multiple-audience predicament liars would appear dishonest only to audiences who had heard them offer a discrepant tale. From Experiment I, we have learned that this notion is false. When describing a teacher to multiple audiences, students appear deceptive to peers who earlier heard them give a description similar to the one being offered, and they appear deceptive to observers who have never heard anything at all about the teacher.

Having documented these effects, we hoped to analyze the psychology of the multiple-audience problem. As an initial account of multiple-audience effects, let us propose a story-focus interpretation. According to this interpretation, the multiple-audience predicament encourages liars to focus on their stories. To reconcile tales they have told to multiple audiences, liars devote resources to story construction that they would otherwise invest in visible self-presentation. In doing so, liars leave themselves looking dishonest. Having withdrawn effort from a visible appearance of truthfulness, they look dishonest to the targets of their tales and to bystanders as well.

This interpretation is compatible with earlier research. Consistent with the story focus interpretation, earlier research implies that there is a trade-off between sounding honest and looking honest. Liars sound honest but look dishonest if they believe they can be heard but not seen ([Krauss et al., 1976]). People who are highly motivated to lie look dishonest but offer credible story content ([DePaulo and Kirkendol, 1989]). While assuming that there is a trade-off between sounding honest and looking honest, the story focus interpretation also presumes that images of truthfulness depend more heavily on visible than audible cues. This so-called *video primacy* is apparent in naïve judgments of mixed honest-sounding/dishonest-looking audiovisual segments ([Stiff et al., 1989]).

Experiment II

Impressions of dishonesty can be conveyed in different ways—by speech, by nonverbal actions, or by a combination of audible and visible cues.

To clarify the multiple-audience problem, we conducted a second experiment. Using the videotapes from Experiment I, we sought to determine whether liars would sound dishonest to naïve judges if they could not be seen; and whether they would look dishonest to naïve judges if they could not be heard.

Perhaps people respond to the multiple-audience problem by devoting resources to story reconciliation that would otherwise go to a visible self-presentation. If so, the multiple-audience predicament should make liars look dishonest to judges who cannot hear the liar's tale. However, it need not make liars sound dishonest to judges who cannot see them. With Experiment II, we hope to assess the impact of story focus on the liar's multiple-audience problem, as we isolate the media through which previously perpetrated lies come to be exposed.

Method

Participants

One hundred and thirty undergraduates participated in Experiment II to fulfill a course requirement. None of these individuals had participated in Experiment I.

Procedure

Participants arrived at a laboratory in small groups. After giving informed consent, participants learned that the experimenter would be presenting descriptions of teachers. Some of the teacher descriptions were truthful, and others were deceptive. The participant's job was to attend to each description and indicate on a written form whether it was the truth or a lie.

The experimenter then presented 48 teacher descriptions. Each of these had been given to two peers, as the final description offered by one of the students in Experiment I. Here participants judged the veracity of these 48 descriptions from one of three presentations. Forty of the subjects judged an audiovisual presentation; 40 judged a video-only presentation; and 50 judged an audio-only presentation of the 48 teacher descriptions. Within each Modality, the 48 teacher descriptions were presented in one of two different orders. After recording a binary lie/truth judgment to each teacher description, research participants were debriefed and dismissed.

Results

In Experiment I, students conveyed a truthful impression, unless they were addressing multiple audiences. To isolate the media by which this multiple-audience effect was carried, we conducted Experiment II. We wondered whether in an audiovisual airing, students in our focal experimental condition would again appear less truthful than students in other conditions. We also wondered whether similar results would be obtained in deception judgments made only from audio and only from video.

To analyze these data, we contrast the multiple-audience condition with the three non-focal conditions, and examine the interaction of this contrast with Impression Modality. For each such contrast and interaction reported below, we conducted a parallel test for residual differences among the three non-focal conditions. In no case did the three non-focal conditions differ significantly from one another; nor did residual differences significantly interact with Impression Modality or any other factor. For instance, residual differences in students' apparent truthfulness yields a main effect $F(2,44)=1.17$, *ns*.

Our focal contrast shows that students who are in the multiple-audience predicament appear less truthful to naïve judges than students in other conditions; and that this difference does not interact with the Modality by which impressions are conveyed, $F(1,44)=11.02$, $p<.005$ and $F(2,88)=2.14,ns$, respectively. When describing a teacher to peers who have heard conflicting descriptions of that teacher, students convey a deceptive impression in all three Modalities, appearing significantly less truthful than students in other conditions when judged from an audiovisual presentation ($F(1,44)=11.15$, $p<.005$), an audio-only presentation ($F(1,44)=10.82$, $p<.005$), and from a video-only presentation ($F(1,44)=4.28$, $p<.05$). In the multiple-audience predicament, students convey audiovisual, audio-only, and video-only impressions of truthfulness to 45.83, 44.17, and 47.54% of naïve judges; in other conditions, they convey audiovisual, audio-only, and video-only impressions of truthfulness to 64.17, 62.03, and 57.71% of these judges.

These patterns do not depend on whether the teacher description is truthful or deceptive, and the veracity of the description is not evident in any impression modality. ANOVAs reveal no significant main effect of description veracity or interactions involving that factor on the audiovisual impression, the audio-only impression, the video-only impression, or all impressions combined; for the largest F ratio involving description veracity, $p>.20$. Overall, students appear truthful to 51.38% of judges when telling the truth and to 55.65% of judges when lying; for the difference, $F(1,40)=.43$, ns.

According to the story focus interpretation, people devote resources to story reconciliation that would otherwise benefit a visible self-presentation. Results of Experiment II, however, indicate that the most truthful-sounding stories are constructed by individuals who look the most truthful; for the relationship between a storyteller's audio-only impression of truthfulness and video-only impression of truthfulness $r=+.53$, $p<.01$. No tension between audible and visible credibility is evident here.

Meditation of the audiovisual impression

We wondered whether our experimental effect on students' audiovisual impression was carried by audible cues, visible cues, or both. To assess this issue, we conducted two mediational analyses. Each was based on a three-step test recommended by [Baron and Kenny, 1986]. As those authors note, mediation of the multiple-audience effect will be demonstrated if (a) the multiple-audience predicament has a significant effect on students' audiovisual impression of truthfulness, (b) the predicament has a significant effect on a mediating variable, and (c) that mediating variable has a statistically significant partial effect on the audiovisual impression of truthfulness, when this dependent variable is regressed on both the mediating variable and the contrast which codes the predicament. Complete mediation, the authors note, will be demonstrated if the multiple-audience predicament has no partial effect on students' conveyed audiovisual truthfulness, once the mediating variable is controlled.

Tests of the first two criteria for mediation are reported above. Relative to students in other conditions, students in our focal condition convey a less truthful audiovisual impression, audio-only impression, and video-only impression. Thus, our independent variable (the multiple-audience predicament) has significant effects on the dependent variable, and on two potential mediators.

To check the third criterion for mediation, we conducted two multiple regression analyses. A first analysis shows that the video-only impression has a significant partial effect on the audiovisual impression of truthfulness, when controlling for the focal experimental comparison, standardized β=.62, p<.0001. Students who are in the predicament convey a less truthful audiovisual impression than those in other conditions, even when their video-only impression is controlled; $t(45)$=2.36, p<.05. The audio-only impression also has a significant partial effect on the audiovisual impression of truthfulness, when controlling for the multiple-audience comparison; standardized β=.84, p<.0001. Indeed, the multiple-audience predicament has no independent effect on the audiovisual impression when its effect on the audio-only impression is statistically controlled, $t(45)$=.81, ns. According to three-step tests ([Baron and Kenny, 1986]), both visible cues and audible cues play a role in mediating the multiple-audience effect on students' audiovisual impression of truthfulness. As correlations show, storytellers who convey a truthful audiovisual impression sound truthful (in audio-only) and look truthful (in video-only); simple rs=+.87 and +.69, respectively; each p<.01.

Audiovisual impressions of truthfulness may depend more heavily on audible than visible cues. To assess this latter assertion, we noted the difference (for each student) in the impression of truthfulness the student conveyed through audio-only vs. video-only. Analyzing this variable, we find that students who convey the most truthful audiovisual impression convey relatively more truthful audio-only impressions than video-only impressions, r=.30, p<.05 for the relationship between audiovisual truthfulness and the audio-only/video-only difference. We also regressed a student's audiovisual impression of truthfulness on the audio-only impression, the video-only impression, and our focal experimental contrast. The audiovisual impression of truthfulness shows a partial effect from the video-only impression (standardized β=+.31, p<.001), a larger partial effect from the audio-only impression (standardized β=+.69, p<.001), and no statistically significant partial effect from the multiple audience (standardized β=+.04, p>.25).

Discussion

Experiment II isolates the media by which the multiple-audience predicament makes liars appear deceptive. Liars sound deceptive when placed in the predicament, and they look deceptive too.

Experiment II contributes to our understanding of the psychology of the multiple-audience problem. Prior to conducting the Experiment, we had imagined that a story focus might contribute to the liar's multiple-audience problem. More specifically, our hypothesis was that people rise to the multiple-audience challenge by devoting resources to story construction that would otherwise benefit a visible self-presentation.

Experiment II does not support this reasoning. True, the multiple-audience predicament makes people look dishonest. However, people also sound dishonest in this predicament, and the multiple-audience effect on a person's audiovisual impression is strongly mediated by its impact on audible cues. Although it is possible that people make a special effort to sound credible when placed before multiple audiences, they do not construct credible-sounding stories. This predicament undermines audible credibility at least as much as visible credibility; and the most honest-looking individuals concoct the most credible-sounding tales. These results contradict the notion of a hydraulic relationship between audible and visible credibility.[1]

Not finding much support for a story focus interpretation, we considered three other factors that might inform our experimental effects: complexity, equivocation, and discomfort. Let us explain the relevance of these factors to the liar's multiple-audience problem.

The multiple-audience predicament challenges liars to spin a story that can reconcile two mutually contradictory tales. This is a cognitively taxing assignment, and its complexity may influence certain paralinguistic features of the liar's performance. As earlier research indicates, people pause frequently, speak slowly, and make many mistakes when they are giving cognitively complex speeches ([Knapp and Hall, 1992]). As other research shows, deception is often inferred from these paralinguistic complexity cues because they imply that the speaker is concocting a lie ([Vrij, 2000]). Thus, the multiple-audience predicament might in principle make liars appear dishonest by virtue of its cognitive complexity.

While challenging a liar's paralinguistic fluency, the multiple-audience predicament may also invite speech content that sounds dishonest. Multiple audiences create an avoidance-avoidance conflict for the liar. Anything said in the predicament may soil the liar's reputation by contradicting an earlier claim. Research shows that avoidance-avoidance conflicts encourage people to equivocate ([Bavelas et al., 1990]); and that people who equivocate sound deceptive ([Kraut, 1978]). Thus if liars respond to their multiple audiences by offering vague or ambivalent remarks, this strategy could explain why they appear dishonest.

Liars may also have non-strategic responses to the predicament. They may become uncomfortable in the presence of multiple audiences, imagining that their efforts at reputation maintenance are destined to fail. Discomfort could create a self-fulfilling prophecy, in which the expectation of looking dishonest makes the individual appear dishonest. This behavioral confirmation of anticipated suspicions would be ironic if, at the moment of the predicament, the truth were being told. Then observers would be subject to an Othello error in falsely perceiving deceit ([Bond and Fahey, 1987]). Consistent with this interpretation, deception is often inferred from signs of discomfort—like gaze aversion, self-manipulations, and postural shifts ([Vrij, 2000]).

To assess the impact of these various factors on the liar's multiple-audience problem, we conducted a third experiment.

Experiment III

In Experiment III, we investigate the role of complexity, equivocation, and discomfort in producing multiple-audience effects on an individual's apparent honesty. Again, tapes of students describing teachers are presented to naïve judges. Judges rate the students' comfort, the clarity of their teacher descriptions, and the students' feelings for their teachers. Raters score tapes of the teacher descriptions for several indices of complexity: speech rate, speech disturbances, and pauses.

Perhaps the multiple-audience predicament makes people appear deceptive because it makes them appear uncomfortable. If so, this discomfort should be evident to judges, and statistical analyses should show that discomfort mediates the multiple-audience effect on apparent truthfulness. Maybe the predicament makes people appear deceptive because it encourages them to equivocate. If so, students who are in the predicament should offer vague teacher descriptions. They should express little affect (or perhaps mixed affect) for the teacher—neither the strong positive feelings they had claimed to one audience nor the strong negative feelings they had claimed to the other. If statistical analyses reveal that vagueness and affective neutrality mediate the multiple-audience effect, an equivocation explanation will be supported. Perhaps the multiple-audience predicament makes people appear dishonest because it poses a cognitive challenge. If so, we would expect teacher descriptions offered to multiple-audiences to exhibit slow speech rates, high numbers of speech disturbances, and frequent pauses. Descriptions that have these paralinguistic features should be judged as dishonest, and regression analyses should show that the multiple-audience effect on an individual's apparent truthfulness is mediated by its effect on complexity cues.

While allowing us to assess the impact of discomfort, equivocation, and complexity in creating the liar's multiple-audience problem, Experiment III also provides a check on the validity of an experimental manipulation. In Experiment I, we instructed some research participants to lie, and claim to like a teacher they disliked or claim to dislike a teacher they liked. Discovering that multiple-audience effects are not much affected by these experimental instructions, we have inferred that this interpersonal predicament has similar effects on liars as truth-tellers. However, there is another possibility. [Bavelas et al., 1990] question the validity of experimental manipulations of deception. These authors doubt that research participants lie when instructed to lie, and challenge researchers to provide independent evidence of compliance with experimental deception instructions.

In Experiment III, naïve judges rate our Experiment I research participants' feelings for their teachers. This allows us to check our Experiment I deception manipulation. If Experiment I research participants lied when instructed to lie, judges should infer that these participants like teachers whom the participants in fact dislike, and that they dislike teachers whom the participants like. By monitoring compliance with deception instructions, we assess one explanation for the generality of multiple-audience effects.

Method

Ninety-nine undergraduate psychology students participated in Experiment III for extra credit. None of these individuals had participated in the earlier Experiments.

Procedure

Participants arrived at a laboratory in small groups. After giving informed consent, participants learned that the experimenter would be presenting descriptions of teachers. The participant's job was to render a judgment of each description.

The experimenter presented 48 teacher descriptions. These had been targeted to two peers, as the third teacher descriptions of Experiment I. Participants made one of three judgments to these descriptions: 31 judged the student's comfort, 36 judged the clarity of the student's description, and 32 judged the student's feelings for the teacher.

Comfort judgments were made from an audiovisual presentation, on a scale that ranged from −3 (the student is extremely uncomfortable) to +3 (the student is extremely comfortable). Clarity and affect judgments were made from an audio-only presentation—clarity on a scale that ranged from 0 (the description is not at all clear) to 6 (the description is perfectly clear), and affect on a scale that ranged from −3 (the student feels totally negative about the teacher) through 0 (mixed feelings) to +3 (the student feels totally positive about the teacher). Each judgment was made from one of two different orders of the 48 teacher descriptions. After recording 48 judgments, research participants were informed that some of the descriptions had been deceptive. The veracity of the descriptions had not been mentioned earlier.

Behavior codings

We had raters code several aspects of the 48 final teacher descriptions from Experiment I. Two raters, who were unaware of each research participant's experimental condition, independently noted the length of each description (in seconds), the number of words in the description, the number of unfilled pauses in the description, and the number of speech disturbances in the description. Speech disturbances included stuttering, mispronunciations, repetitions, self-corrections, ahs, and uhs.

Results and discussion

Preliminary analyses revealed that there was strong inter-judge reliability in ratings of comfort, clarity, and affect: Cronbach's α=.93, .93, and .99, respectively; and moderate to strong inter-rater reliability in coding behaviors: effective r=.99, .72, and .75 for two independent judgments of number of words, number of unfilled pauses, and number of speech disturbances in each teacher description, respectively. Two independent timings of the duration of each description (in seconds) yielded an effective r=.99. Below we analyze the mean of the two judgments of each behavior.

Manipulation check

In Experiment I, we instructed some research participants to lie by claiming to like a teacher they disliked or claiming to dislike a teacher they liked. Having solicited naïve judgments of how much these participants like their teachers, we can assess compliance with our Experiment I instructions. The relevant analysis is a two-way Participants' Veracity Instructions (Lie vs. Tell the Truth) × Participants' Actual Feelings for Teacher (Like vs. Dislike) ANOVA on judged liking. Results show a very strong two-way interaction, $F(1,44)=226.92$, $p<.0001$ that accounts for 83.46% of the variance in judged liking. Means indicate that participants complied with instructions. Students who were instructed to tell the truth convey more positive feelings when describing a teacher they like, rather than a teacher they dislike; $Ms=2.16$ vs. -2.24, $F(1,44)=116.16$, $p<.0001$. Students who were instructed to lie about their feelings convey more negative feelings when describing a teacher they actually like, rather than a teacher they actually dislike, $Ms=-1.90$ vs. $+2.38$; $F(1,44)=110.42$, $p<.0001$.

Discomfort, equivocation, and complexity

To investigate the role of discomfort, equivocation, and complexity in our results, we analyzed each variable with a contrast between students who were in the multiple-audience predicament vs. students who were in other conditions. In analyses parallel to the ones reported below, there are no statistically significant residual differences among the three control conditions on any variable. Relevant means appear in Table 2.

People may feel uncomfortable when forced to reconcile earlier stories; and this discomfort may be palpable to on-lookers. To assess this possibility, we noted each student's apparent comfort to the current judges. Although students appear a bit less comfortable in the multiple-audience predicament than in other conditions (M comfort ratings $=.22$ vs. $.54$, respectively), this difference is not statistically significant, $F(1,44)=1.17$, ns. The veracity of the student's description has no significant impact on the student's apparent comfort, main effect $F(1,40)=.03$, ns; and there is no evidence that truth-tellers who are facing multiple audiences experience any special discomfort.

Although discomfort may not explain the multiple-audience effect, students who appear uncomfortable do appear dishonest. For the pooled within-cell correlations of apparent discomfort with the Experiment II audiovisual, audio-only, and video-only impressions of truthfulness, $rs=-.55$, $-.51$, and $-.50$, respectively; each $p<.001$.

People may equivocate in front of multiple audiences. There is some support for this hypothesis. In an audio-only presentation, students in the focal experimental condition convey vaguer teacher descriptions than students in other conditions, $Ms=3.03$ vs. 3.51 on a scale that ranges from 1 (not at all clear) to 7 (perfectly clear), $F(1,44)=4.83$, $p<.05$. The vaguer the student's description, the more deceptive the description appears, pooled within-cell r between judged vagueness and the Experiment II audiovisual impression of truthfulness $=-.42$, $p<.01$. Deceptive descriptions sound neither more nor less vague than truthful descriptions; $F(1,40)=1.16$, ns.

Having claimed positive feelings for a teacher to one peer and negative feelings for that teacher to a second peer, liars may respond to the dilemma of addressing both peers by claiming little (or mixed) affect for the teacher. To assess this hypothesis, we expressed judgments of the student's feelings for the teacher as an absolute deviation from the midpoint of a 7-point scale (that midpoint being labeled "mixed feelings"). Results show that students who are in the multiple-audience predicament convey less affect for their teachers than students in the other conditions, Ms=2.02 vs. 2.62, $F(1,44)$=8.01, p<.01. Conveyed affect is not, however, related to a student's apparent truthfulness; pooled within-cell r between affect and the Experiment II audiovisual impression of truthfulness =.22, ns; and the veracity of a teacher description is unrelated to its affective intensity, $F(1,40)$=.01, ns.

The multiple-audience predicament may disrupt a speaker's fluency by posing a cognitive challenge, and paralinguistic complexity indicators may be construed as signs of on-the-spot message fabrication. To assess this interpretation, we examined three paralinguistic complexity cues: slow speech rate, numerous pauses, and frequent speech disturbances. Results support the complexity interpretation.

An analysis on speech rate shows that who are in the multiple-audience predicament speak more slowly than those in other conditions; Ms=175.07 vs. 205.22 words per minute; $F(1,44)$=7.24, p<.01; and that people who speak slowly sound deceptive; pooled within-cell or between speech rate and the Experiment II audio-only judgment of deceptiveness = $-$.65, p<.001. These results are consistent with the complexity interpretation, as is the pattern of results on a second variable: unfilled pauses. Students who are in the multiple-audience predicament pause more frequently than those in other conditions, Ms=2.55 vs. 1.22 pauses per minute, $F(1,44)$=6.84, p<.02; and those who pause frequently sound deceptive; pooled within-cell r between pause rate and Experiment II audio-only judgment of deceptiveness =+.60, p<.001. Results for speech errors are not as clear-cut. Although students who are in the multiple-audience predicament may commit a few more speech errors than those in other conditions (Ms=13.03 vs. 11.39 errors per minute), the difference is not statistically significant, $F(1,44)$=.54, ns.

Mediation of impressions

Finding suggestions that equivocation and complexity may contribute to the liar's multiple-audience problem, we conducted some mediational analyses.

The multiple-audience predicament reduces the clarity of a student's teacher description and the intensity of affect the student claims. To assess the role of equivocation in mediating the multiple-audience effect, we again pursued the logic outlined by [Baron and Kenny, 1986]. For the key step in this analysis, we regressed the Experiment II audio-only impression of truthfulness on the contrast coding our multiple-audience predicament, as well as our two indicators of equivocation. Results show that audio-only impressions of truthfulness are subject to a partial effect for equivocation. When clarity and affective intensity are entered as a two-predictor block to an equation that already includes the multiple-audience contrast, change-in-R^2=.12, $F(2,44)$=3.72, p<.05 (for the partial effects of vagueness and neutrality on apparent truthfulness, standardized β=$-$.37 and +.03, respectively). However, students who are in the multiple-audience predicament continue to sound less truthful than those in other conditions, even when our two indicators of equivocation are controlled (for the partial effect of the predicament, standardized β=+.33,

$t(44)=2.44$, $p<.05$). From these results, it appears that equivocation explains only a part of the liar's multiple-audience problem.

When placed in the multiple-audience predicament, students speak slowly and pause frequently. For a second mediational analysis, we regressed the Experiment II audio-only impression of truthfulness on speech rates and pause rates, as well as the multiple-audience contrast. Results show that these two complexity indicators have a partial effect on apparent truthfulness. When added as a two-predictor block into a regression equation that already includes the multiple-audience contrast, they produce a change-in-$R^2=.53$, $F(2,44)=16.04$, $p<.0001$ (for the partial effects of speech rate and pause rate on apparent truthfulness, standardized $\beta=-.37$ and $+.30$, respectively). Controlling for these two indicators of speech complexity, students who are in the multiple-audience predicament do not sound significantly less truthful than those in other conditions (for the partial effect of the predicament, standardized $\beta=+.18$, $t(44)=1.65$, $p=.11$). Complexity strongly mediates the multiple-audience effect.

To assess the relative contribution of equivocation and complexity to the liar's multiple-audience problem, we conducted one final set of regression analyses. These show that equivocation has no partial effect on a student's apparent truthfulness, once we control for the multiple-audience predicament and complexity. Entering vagueness and affective neutrality as a two-predictor block into a regression equation that already includes speech rate, pause rate, and the multiple-audience contrast, equivocation produces a change-in-$R^2=.04$, $F(2,42)=1.97$, $p>.15$. However, complexity has a partial effect on a student's apparent truthfulness, once we control for the multiple-audience predicament and equivocation. Entering speech rate and pause rate as a two-predictor block into an equation that already includes vagueness, affective neutrality and the multiple-audience contrast, complexity produces a change-in-$R^2=.21$, $F(2,42)=10.38$, $p<.0001$. The multiple-audience predicament has no partial effect on a student's apparent truthfulness, once vagueness, affective neutrality, speech rate, and pause rate are controlled, standardized $\beta=+.15$, $t(42)=1.29$, $p>.20$. This pattern of results favors a complexity explanation for the multiple-audience effect. Analyses of audiovisual impressions of truthfulness yield a similar pattern.

General discussion

Always tell the truth. Then you don't have to remember anything—Mark Twain

In three experiments, we have examined an interpersonal predicament created by deception. In this predicament, people have difficulty maintaining their lies because they sound and look deceptive. When facing multiple audiences, people are disfluent and equivocate. Of several factors investigated, paralinguistic cognitive complexity cues most clearly explain why people appear deceptive in the multiple-audience predicament.

These results invite comparison with earlier research. Reviewing the literature on subjective indicators of deception, [Vrij, 2000] tallied some pertinent findings. People infer deception from speech errors (in 13 of 18 studies), from hesitations (in 14 of 19 studies), and from slow speaking rate (in six of 12 studies). These are not, however, reliable cues to deceit. In fact, liars and truth-tellers show no general difference in their tendency to make speech errors, hesitate, or speak slowly, a comprehensive meta-analysis reveals ([DePaulo et al., 2003]). Although people intuit that lying is cognitively difficult, it need not be so. Under challenging circumstances like the multiple-audience predicament, truth-telling can be just as difficult. Then mistaken intuitions promote misperceptions of deceit (cf. [Bond and Fahey, 1987]).

Although the initial act of deception may be easy, lies initiate an on-going challenge. To manage reputational risks across a network of acquaintances, several skills are required. Here the liar's predicament arose in an experimental setting, over a brief time frame. Outside the laboratory, longer intervals will elapse between the initial perpetration of a lie and its awkward resurfacing. In the real time of the multiple-audience problem, liars may find themselves groping to ascertain what was said to whom, and who remembers how much. The challenges thereby posed may dwarf any we have seen. Here the predicament arose from little lies—stories that experimental participants were instructed to tell. Most of the lies of everyday life are little ([DePaulo et al., 1996]), and most multiple-audience predicaments may be little too. Having been polite to a series of one-on-one interaction partners, individuals may find themselves in a predicament of the sort we studied. Other multiple-audience predicaments may involve high stakes ([Ekman, 2001]). These would be quite different.

The current work has limitations. To isolate factors that impede the maintenance of lies, we created an experimental analogue of the multiple-audience predicament. Additional work will be needed to establish the external validity of our conclusions, and to understand liars' predicaments in their social and motivational context. Other work will be required to address issues of internal validity. Here we analyzed observational evidence to infer that cognitive complexity explains the liar's multiple-audience problem. This explanation should be regarded as tentative until liars can be placed in predicaments where cognitive complexity has been experimentally controlled. Could liars master the multiple-audience problem if given more time to prepare? Could they avoid the problem altogether if apprised of its possibility beforehand? Future research will be needed to answer these questions.

In the moment of the multiple-audience predicament, the liar has limited options, and some of these have been discussed. The liar can reiterate an earlier story, feigning ignorance of other versions; the liar can offer comments so vague that they contradict nothing. There are other options too. The liar may concoct yet another story that subsumes all earlier versions, or offer up a new set of comments that complement previous tales while avoiding inconsistencies. Whatever the liar says in a multiple-audience predicament, confrontations by audience members may ensue. Then we would expect the liar to issue denials, excuses, accounts, and apologies of the usual sort ([Leary, 1995]). Earlier stories will be repudiated, and a renewed commitment to honesty avowed.

In maintaining their deceptions, people face many challenges, of which the multiple-audience problem is just one. In analyzing the problem, we begin to appreciate the complexities of social life, and to untangle one of the webs that liars weave.

References

Baron and Kenny, 1986. R.M. Baron and D.A. Kenny, The moderator–mediator variable distinction in social psychological research: Conceptual, strategic, and statistical considerations. *Journal of Personality and Social Psychology* **51** (1986), pp. 1173–1182.

Bavelas et al., 1990. J.B. Bavelas, A. Black, N. Chovil and J. Mullett, Equivocal communication. , Sage, Newbury Park, CA (1990).

Bond and Atoum, 2000. C.F. Bond, Jr. and A.O. Atoum, International deception. *Personality and Social Psychology Bulletin* **26** (2000), pp. 385–395.

Bond and Fahey, 1987. C.F. Bond, Jr. and W.E. Fahey, False suspicion and the misperception of deceit. *British Journal of Social Psychology* **26** (1987), pp. 41–46.

Bond et al., 1985. C.F. Bond, Jr., K.N. Kahler and L.M. Paolicelli, The miscommunication of deception: An adaptive perspective. *Journal of Experimental Social Psychology* **21** (1985), pp. 331–345.

Buller and Burgoon, 1996. D.B. Buller and J.K. Burgoon, Interpersonal deception theory. *Communication Theory* **6** (1996), pp. 203–242.

DePaulo, 1992. B.M. DePaulo, Nonverbal behavior and self-presentation. *Psychological Bulletin* **111** (1992), pp. 203–243.

DePaulo et al., 1996. B.M. DePaulo, D.A. Kashy, S.E. Kirkendol, M.M. Wyer and J.A. Epstein, Lying in everyday life. *Journal of Personality and Social Psychology* **70** (1996), pp. 979–995.

DePaulo and Kirkendol, 1989. B.M. DePaulo and S.E. Kirkendol, The motivational impairment effect in the communication of deception. In: J.C. Yuille, Editor, *Credibility assessment*, Kluwer Academic Publishers, Dordrecht (1989), pp. 51–90.

DePaulo et al., 2003. B.M. DePaulo, J.J. Lindsay, B.E. Malone, L. Muhlenbruck, K. Charlton and H. Cooper, Cues to deception. *Psychological Bulletin* **129** (2003), pp. 74–112.

Ekman, 2001. P. Ekman, Telling lies: Clues to deceit in the marketplace, politics, and marriage. , Norton Press, New York (2001).

Fleming, 1994. J.H. Fleming, Multiple-audience problems, tactical communication, and social interaction: A relational-regulation perspective. In: M.P. Zanna, Editor, *Advances in experimental social psychology* **vol. 26**, Academic Press, New York (1994), pp. 215–291.

Granhag and Strömwall, 2000. P.A. Granhag and L.A. Strömwall, Effects of preconceptions on deception detection and new answers to why lie-catchers often fail. *Psychology, Crime, and Law* **6** (2000), pp. 197–218.

Knapp and Hall, 1992. M.L. Knapp and J.A. Hall, Nonverbal communication in human interaction. (third ed.), Harcourt Brace, Fort Worth (1992).

Krauss et al., 1976. Krauss, R. M., Geller, V., Olson, C. (1976). Modalities and cues in the detection of deception. Paper presented at the annual meeting of the American Psychological Association, Washington, DC

Kraut, 1978. R.E. Kraut, Verbal and nonverbal cues in the perception of lying. *Journal of Personality and Social Psychology* **36** (1978), pp. 380–391.

Leary, 1995. M.R. Leary, Self-presentation: Impression management and interpersonal behavior. , Brown & Benchmark, Madison, WI (1995).

Levine et al., 1999. T.R. Levine, H.S. Park and S.A. McCornack, Accuracy in detecting truths and lies: Documenting the "veracity effect". *Communication Monographs* **66** (1999), pp. 125–144.

Riggio et al., 1988. R.E. Riggio, C. Salinas and J. Tucker, Personality and deception ability. *Personality and Individual Differences* **9** (1988), pp. 189–191.

Rosenthal and Rosnow, 1985. R. Rosenthal and R.L. Rosnow, Contrast analysis: Focused comparisons in the analysis of variance. , Cambridge University Press, New York (1985).

Stiff et al., 1989. J.B. Stiff, G.R. Miller, C. Sleight, P.A. Mongeau, R. Garlick and R.G. Rogan, Explanations for visual cue primacy in judgments of honesty and deceit. *Journal of Personality and Social Psychology* **56** (1989), pp. 555–564.

Vrij, 2000. A. Vrij, Detecting lies and deceit: The psychology of lying and the implications for professional practice. , Wiley, West Sussex, UK (2000).

Zuckerman et al., 1981. M. Zuckerman, B.M. DePaulo and R. Rosenthal, Verbal and nonverbal communication of deception. In: L. Berkowitz, Editor, *Advances in experimental social psychology* **Vol. 14**, Academic Press, New York (1981), pp. 1–59.

Notes

*1 We are grateful to Gary Boehm and Claudia Camp for comments on an earlier draft.

[1] A reviewer noted a limitation of Experiment II. Although Experiment II shows that people do not *sound* honest when placed in a multiple-audience predicament, the *content* of their stories might nonetheless be highly credible. To assess this possibility, future researchers may wish to solicit deception judgments from *transcripts* of stories given in a multiple-audience predicament (cf. [DePaulo and Kirkendol, 1989]).

Received 2 December 2002;
Revised 24 April 2003.
Available online 31 July 2003.

Journal of Experimental Social Psychology
Volume 40, Issue 1, January 2004, Pages 29-40

Personality and Social Psychology Review, 2006, Vol. *10,* No. *3,* 214-234.

Accuracy of Deception Judgments

Charles F. Bond, Jr.
Texas Christian University

Bella M. DePaulo
University of California at Santa Barbara

We analyze the accuracy of deception judgments, synthesizing research results from 206 documents and 24,483 judges. In relevant studies, people attempt to discriminate lies from truths in real time with no special aids or training. In these circumstances, people achieve an average of 54% correct lie/truth judgments, correctly classifying 47% of lies as deceptive and 61% of truths as non-deceptive. Relative to cross-judge differences in accuracy, mean lie/truth discrimination abilities are non-trivial, with a mean accuracy d of roughly .40. This produces an effect that is at roughly the 60th percentile in size, relative to others that have been meta-analyzed by social psychologists. Alternative indices of lie/truth discrimination accuracy correlate highly with percentage correct, and rates of lie detection vary little from study to study. Our meta-analyses reveal that people are more accurate in judging audible than visible lies, that people appear deceptive when motivated to be believed, and individuals regard their interaction partners as honest. These results may reflect a double standard in evaluating deceit.

Deception entered Western thought in a telling guise when the author of *Genesis* placed a serpent in the Garden of Eden. By lying, the serpent enticed Eve into committing the original sin. Thus deception was enshrined as the ultimate source of evil.

Lying has always posed a moral problem. Aristotle wrote that "falsehood is in itself mean and culpable"; St. Augustine believed that every lie is a sin; and Kant regarded truthfulness as an "unconditional duty which holds in all circumstances." Others take a more permissive stance. Aquinas countenanced lies told in the service of virtue, while Machiavelli extolled deceit in the service of self. For background on these ethical matters and a contemporary position, see Bok (1989).

Having been a moral issue for millenia, deception came also to be viewed as a legal challenge. Since Diogenes, many had suspected that lying was commonplace and could have pernicious influences on human affairs. The chore of truth finding fell to the legal system, and procedures for lie detection were devised. Over the centuries, authorities employed a number of unsavory means to extract legal "truths" (Trovillo, 1939). Modern sensibilities inspired some of the current techniques: religious oaths, cross-examinations, threats of incarceration. Technological developments have had an impact too. The polygraph, the psychological stress evaluator, brain fingerprints, EEGs – these have been promoted for their ability to divine deception. Yet in the first decade of the 21st century, American jurisprudence entrusts lie detection to ordinary citizens. U.S. courts bar technological aids to lie detection and deception experts too. Witnesses must appear in person before jurors who are the "sole judges" of the witness's believability. American jurors are instructed to judge the person's truthfulness by considering his or her "demeanor upon the witness stand" and "manner of testifying" (Judicial Committee on Model Jury Instructions for the Eighth Circuit, 2002; p. 53). According to an official view, this system of lay judgment solves the legal problem of deception because "lie detecting is what our juries do best" (Fisher, 1997).

A moral problem for millenia and a legal problem for centuries, deception has more recently become a research problem. How successful are people at deceiving others? How likely are they to believe others' fibs? What accounts for liars' successes and failures? When and why are people duped? These questions are of moral and legal interest. The ethics of lying would be moot if people were rarely duped. Current legal practices would be called into question if ordinary people could not spot deception when they saw it.

In the current article, we summarize research on 4435 individuals' attempts to dupe 24,483 others. We offer quantitative measures of deceptive success and identify conditions under which people are more and less gullible. As a background for our statistical synopses, we summarize some earlier characterizations of deception, sketch a new framework for understanding this subject, and consider earlier research reviews.

Characterizations of Deception

"No mortal can keep a secret. If his lips are silent, he chatters with his finger-tips; betrayal oozes out of him at every pore."   Freud (1905)

With this quotation, Ekman and Friesen (1969) open a pioneering article on the psychology of deception. Where Freud had analyzed verbal slips to self-deception, Ekman and Friesen describe nonverbal signs of individuals' attempts to deceive one another. These authors discuss lies that involve high stakes and strong emotion. In their view, liars face challenges. They must guard against nonverbal "leakage" of feelings they are trying to conceal and must hide their own affective reactions to the act of lying, such as guilt, anxiety, and shame. People find it especially difficult to lie in certain situations: when the possibility of deception is salient to both actor and target, when the target can focus on detecting deception without concern for his/her own behavior, and when the actor and target have antagonistic interests (the actor wishing to perpetrate deceit and the target to uncover it).

Ekman and Friesen (1969) offer a theory about the anatomical locus of nonverbal deception cues. They predict that people are most likely to show deception in the legs and feet, less likely to show it in the hands, and least likely to show deception in the face. These predictions follow from a communicative analysis: relative to the face, the feet and legs have a weak sending capacity, generate little internal feedback, and occasion few reactions from others. Thus, people have more ability and motivation to control the face than the feet and legs. By this logic, people have intermediate ability and motivation to control the hands.

Thirty-two years later, Ekman (2001) emphasizes the ambiguity of nonverbal deception cues. There being no foolproof sign of deceit, many inferences of deception are mistaken. In trying to spot lies, people must avoid untoward influences of their own suspicions as well as misinterpretations of others' idiosyncrasies. Ekman attributes failures at lie detection to many factors: poor evolutionary preparation, socialization to overlook lies, the psychological benefits of trust, and inadequate feedback from errors.

Ekman's work has been influential. It has encouraged nonverbal analyses that aim to expose deceit. Inspired by Ekman's early work, Miller and Stiff (1993) enumerate cues to deception and cues to judgments of deception, then attribute failures at spotting deception to differences in the two sets of cues. Pursuing Ekman's emphasis on high-stakes deceit, forensic psychologist Vrij (2000) discusses the implications of experimental findings for professional lie catchers.

Buller and Burgoon (1996) propose a theory for face-to-face deceptive interactions. In order to dupe others, people must craft a verbal deception, bolster it with ancillary strategic messages, and suppress discrediting behaviors. Meanwhile, the targets of face-to-face deceit must manage behavioral signs of suspicion. Burgoon and Buller (1996) trace the unfolding of deceptive exchanges over time. Theoretically, receivers are more likely to perceive a person as truthful if they are interacting with that person – rather than seeing the person on videotape. Theoretically, deceivers should be more likely to engage in strategic activity and less likely to engage in non-strategic activity in interactive contexts. In interactive contexts, deceivers react to signs of suspicion, and targets react to indications that their suspicions have been surmised.

Critical of Buller and Burgoon's approach (DePaulo, Ansfield, & Bell, 1996), DePaulo and colleagues favor a self-presentational perspective on deception (DePaulo, 1992; DePaulo, Kashy, Kirkendol, Wyer, & Epstein, 1996; DePaulo, Lindsay, Malone, Muhlenbruck, Charlton, & Cooper, 2003). In this view, lying is a part of everyday life. People tell lies to avoid embarrassment and make positive impressions. They fib on the spur of the moment without compunction, telling polite lies of little consequence. Some everyday lies are scripted and require less cognitive effort than meticulously truthful statements. Occasionally, people tell lies to hide transgressions. Most of these serious lies involve a self-presentational stake: the liar's reputation. In this view, the signs of deception are subtle, and social norms encourage people to accept others' representations at face value.

A Double Standard

Having reviewed some earlier characterizations of deceit, let us offer a new framework for understanding this subject. We believe that there is a double standard in evaluating deception.

Our framework begins by noting that people regard truth telling as unexceptional. They accept most statements at face value, rarely inquiring into the authenticity of what they hear. People come to regard an assertion as *truthful* only after entertaining the possibility that it was deceptive. Then they see truthfulness as a virtue. People are proud of themselves for speaking the truth. People who are told the truth praise truth tellers, and psychologists praise them too. No doubt, there are limits to the morality of truthfulness. Truths are seen as most virtuous when they oppose the truth teller's interest. Occasionally, people volunteer truthful observations that hurt others, and these are ethically dubious. In most cases, however, truth telling is non-problematic. Problems arise not from truth telling but from deception.

There are two perspectives on deception. One is the perspective that people hold when they themselves are lying; a second is the perspective they bring to others' lies (Gordon & Miller, 2000). As deceivers, people are practical. They accommodate perceived needs by lying. Of course, deceivers rarely regard their own falsehoods as *lies* but as something more innocuous. People may lie in the interest of impression management (DePaulo et al, 2003) or for more tangible ends. They exaggerate, minimize, and omit. They give misleading answers to questions. Regarding half-truths and self-editing as necessities of social life, deceivers see deception as similar to these sanctioned practices. Animated by momentary exigencies, offered in passing, lies occasion little anxiety, guilt, or shame (DePaulo, Kashy, Kirkendol, Wyer, & Epstein, 1996). They are easy to rationalize. Yes, deception may demand construction of a convincing line and enactment of appropriate demeanor. Most strategic communications do. To the liar, there is nothing exceptional about lying.

If pragmatic about their own deceptions, people become moralistic when they consider others' lies (Saxe, 1991). Then deception is wrong and reflects negatively on the deceiver. Indeed, people view duplicity as one of the gravest moral failings. In their ratings of 555 personality trait terms, college students rate as *least* desirable the trait of being a *liar* (Anderson, 1968). Social logic assumes that honest people always act honestly (Reeder, 1993); thus, to label a statement a *lie* is to imply that the person who made that statement is a *liar* (O'Sullivan, 2003). This is a serious accusation. People have a prescriptive stereotype of the liar -- stricken with shame, wracked by the threat of exposure, liars leak signs of their inner torment. They fidget, avoid eye contact, and can scarcely bring themselves to speak – a worldwide stereotype holds (Global Deception Research Team, 2004). The stereotypic reasons for lying are nefarious too – terrorists lying to further their murderous plots, charlatans scheming to bilk the innocent, husbands cheating on their faithful wives. As old as the Garden of Eden, this moralistic perspective on deceit underlies current psychological thought.

Let us sketch a few implications of the double standard in evaluating deception. People hold a stereotype of the liar – as tormented, anxious, and conscience-stricken. Perceivers draw on this stereotype when considering a target's veracity. Targets who most resemble the stereotype are most likely to be regarded as *liars*; those who least resemble it are most likely to be believed. Factors that influence a person's likelihood of appearing tormented, anxious, or conscience-stricken should affect the person's judged truthfulness. One such factor would, we suspect, be the stakes surrounding a speaker's credibility. Most lies are little. When telling white lies of the sort often studied by researchers, people have no reason to appear tormented. Thus, they should often be judged truthful. Occasionally, the stakes of being believed are big. When facing huge stakes, people who ruminate over their credibility may come to match the liar stereotype. Then they would be judged deceptive.

In the current article, we consider veracity judgments in light of the double standard for evaluating deception. We do not confine attention to momentous lies or evil deceit of the sort most would associate with *others'* deception. Rather, we consider all falsehoods that have been studied and hope to use the accumulated literature to learn about people's successes in engineering various forms of deception. We will credit people for their successes at perpetrating deceit, while noting some unintended consequences of observers' moralistic stance.

Research on Detection Accuracy

To understand deception, researchers conduct experiments. They arrange for people to lie and tell the truth, and for others to judge the veracity of the resulting statements. For convenience, we will be calling the peoples who lie in these experiments *senders*, the truthful and deceptive statements *messages*, and the people who judge these messages *receivers*. We are interested in receivers' accuracy in judging senders' veracity. We will not be reviewing all attempts at lie detection. Rather, we confine attention to receivers who must judge deceit without the aid of polygraphs, fMRIs, or other physiological devices; receivers who judge deception from a brief encounter with an unfamiliar sender in real time. These deception judgments are based on verbal content and the liar's behavior. Here we review earlier summaries of this research.

Often, lie detection abilities are expressed on a familiar scale: percentage correct. In relevant experiments, receivers classify messages as either lies or truths; hence across messages, the percentage of messages a receiver correctly classifies can be used as an index of his/her detection ability. Ordinarily, half of the messages a receiver encounters are truths, and half are lies; hence by guessing a receiver could expect to achieve 50% correct classifications.

Kraut (1980) offered a statistical summary of results from 10 such experiments. Finding a mean accuracy rate of 57%, Kraut concluded that "the accuracy of human lie detectors is low." In a summary of 39 studies published after 1980, Vrij (2000) replicated Kraut's finding, discovering that receivers of more recent research achieve an average of 56.6% accuracy. Along with narrative reviews of the research literature, these statistical summaries have inspired a consensus -- "it is considered virtually axiomatic . . . that individuals are at best inaccurate at deception detection" (Hubbell, Mitchell, & Gee, 2001).

Although it may be "virtually axiomatic" that people are poor at detecting deception, we are reluctant to accept this conclusion on the basis of existing work. We agree that in 50 (or so) pertinent studies people achieve 50-60% correct when classifying messages as lies or truths. However, meta-analyses of percentage correct omit evidence relevant to ascertaining the accuracy of deception judgments. In the omitted experiments, receivers rate the veracity of lies and truths on multi-point rating scales. There accuracy is not gauged in terms of percentage correct – but as a difference between the rated veracity of truths vs. the rated veracity of lies.

Three statistical summaries of lie detection accuracy have incorporated rated-veracity results. They quantify the degree to which lies can be discriminated from truths by a standardized mean difference (d): the mean difference between obtained and chance accuracy in a study divided by a standard deviation from that study. Applying this metric to the results of 16 early studies, DePaulo, Zuckerman, and Rosenthal (1980) calculated a median d of .86 standard deviations. Twenty years later, Mattson, Allen, Ryan, and Miller (2000) found an average difference between the judged veracity of lies and truths of $d = 1.07$ standard deviations in 7 studies of organizational deception. Assessing the accuracy of deception judgments in various media, Zuckerman, DePaulo, and Rosenthal (1981) found that receivers who have access to speech regard lies as less credible than truths with a mean $d = 1.14$.

How strong are the levels of lie detection found in these rated-veracity reviews? To answer this question, it may be helpful to consider results found in other lines of research. From a large-scale compilation, Richard, Bond, and Stokes-Zoota (2003) developed empirical guidelines for evaluating effect sizes. These scholars describe a d of .20 as small, a d of .40 as medium, and a d of .60 as large because these values would be larger than the average standardized mean differences found in 30%, 50%, and 75% of 474 social psychological research literatures the scholars reviewed. Compared to these reference values, people would seem to have a strong ability to detect deception. The median d of .86 standard deviations found by DePaulo, Zuckerman, and Rosenthal (1980) would place lie detection accuracy at roughly the 85th percentile in size, relative to 474 social psychological effects (Richard, Bond, & Stokes-Zoota, 2003). The ability to detect audible lies (mean $d = 1.14$ standard deviations: Zuckerman, DePaulo, and Rosenthal, 1981) is even better -- ranking at the 95th percentile of 474 social psychological effects.

While amassing evidence on receivers' accuracy in discriminating lies from truths, scholars have been interested in a more general judgmental tendency – a bias to perceive messages as truthful. By virtue of the bias, truthful messages are more often detected than deceptive messages. Summarizing 15 studies, Zuckerman, DePaulo, and Rosenthal (1981) express this accuracy difference in standard deviation units and find a mean $d = .86$. Vrij (2000) summarizes 9 percentage-correct studies to find a strong truth bias – a mean of 61.5% truth judgments, 67% accuracy for truths and 44% accuracy for lies.

The Present Review

Given the moral and legal significance of deception, it is important to know how often people are duped. Although previous work provides some hints about people's success in deceiving others, the work has limitations. The largest review to date is based on 39 research studies. Here we summarize evidence from 206 studies. Some of the previous reviews express the accuracy of deception judgments as a standardized mean difference while others gauge accuracy in terms of percentage correct. Each of these measures has limitations. Standardized mean differences can be hard to interpret (Bond, Wiitala, & Richard, 2003), and meta-analyses of percentage correct cannot include results on rating scale judgments of deception.

Here we assess the accuracy of deception judgments in terms of percentage correct, the standardized mean difference, and with some indices that statisticians favor – the log odds ratio and d' (Swets, 1996). Perhaps the pattern of results across various measures of accuracy can help resolve a tension in earlier meta-analytic results – between the strong detection abilities implied by standardized results and an "axiom" of inaccurate lie detection in percentage correct (Hubbell, Mitchell, & Gee, 2001).

Some have thought that detection performances vary "only slightly" across situations (Kalbfleisch, 1990); while others have concluded that performance variance across situations is "considerable" (Miller & Stiff, 1993). Here we provide the first test to date of the possibility that there is no variance in detection performances across situations. Assuming that there is such variance, we will provide the first estimates to date of the magnitude of these situational differences. We will also have the opportunity to document the impact of various factors on the accuracy of deception judgments, like the medium in which deception is attempted, the liar's motivation, and the judge's expertise. The evidence may have implications for theories of deception, including our double standard framework.

METHOD

Literature Search Procedures

To locate relevant studies, we conducted computer-based searches of *Psychological Abstracts*, *PsycInfo*, *PsycLit*, *Communication Abstracts*, *Dissertation Abstracts International*, *WorldCat*, and *Yahoo* through August of 2005 using the keywords *deception*, *deceit*, and *lie detection*; searched the *Social Sciences Citation Index* for papers that cited key references (*e.g.,* Ekman & Friesen, 1974); examined reference lists from previous reviews (DePaulo et al. 1985a; Zuckerman et al., 1981; Zuckerman & Driver, 1985), and reviewed the references cited in more than 300 articles on the communication of deception from our personal files plus all references cited in every article we found. We sent letters requesting papers to scholars who had published relevant articles.

Criteria for Inclusion and Exclusion of Studies

Our goal was to summarize all English-language reports of original research on the accuracy of judgments of lies and truths available to us prior to September 2005. To be included in this review, a document had to report a measure of accuracy in discriminating lies from truths.

We excluded studies in which individuals judged only lies and those in which individuals judged only truths. We excluded studies in which judges received experimental training or instructions about how to detect deception, studies in which judges received attention-focusing instructions, studies in which senders and receivers knew one another prior to the study, and studies in which individuals could incorporate into their judgments systematic aids to lie detection (e.g., polygraph records, CBCA, or behavior codings from repeated viewings of a videotape). We excluded reports that were not in English, judgments for lies and truths told by senders who were less than

17 years old, as well as judgments made by receivers who were less than 17. We excluded reports in which senders role-played an imagined person in an imagined situation. We also excluded all results on implicit deception judgments (implicit judgments having recently been meta-analyzed by DePaulo *et al*, 2003), and on judgments of affect (even affects that people were trying to conceal). We uncovered 206 documents that satisfied our inclusion criteria. For a listing of these documents, see Appendix A.

Identifying Independent Samples

Research studies in this literature exhibit two forms of interdependence: sender interdependence and receiver interdependence. Senders are interdependent when the lies and truths told by a given sample of senders are shown to multiple samples of judges. Receivers are interdependent when researchers report multiple measures of lie/truth accuracy for a given sample of judges. The unit of aggregation in the current meta-analysis is the receiver sample. The primary analyses below extract one measure of lie/truth discrimination accuracy from each independent sample of judges – even in those cases where several samples are judging the same lies and truths. For these analyses, our data set consists of 384 independent samples. To assess the impact of moderator variables, we disaggregated receiver samples to reflect within-receiver experimental manipulations.

Variables Coded From Each Report

From each report, we sought information about the following variables: a) number of senders, b) number of receivers, c) percentage correct, d) percentage truth, e) an accuracy standardized mean difference, f) sender motivation, g) receiver motivation, h) sender preparation, i) sender interaction, j) receiver expertise, k) judgment medium, and l) baseline exposure. For our coding of these variables in each of 384 receiver samples, see Appendix B.

Let us explain these variables. The *number of senders* and *number of receivers* were coded from each document. From each document that reported results on dichotomous lie-or-truth classifications, we noted *percentage correct* – more precisely, the unweighted average of the percentage of truthful messages correctly classified and the percentage of deceptive messages correctly classified. Of our 384 receiver samples, 343 judged 50% lies and 50% truths. In these cases, the unweighted average was the overall percentage correct. Whenever authors reported the overall percentage of messages classified as truthful, this *percentage truth* judgments was coded. From each document that reported results on rating-scale veracity judgments, we noted an *accuracy standardized mean difference* -- defining d as the mean veracity rating of truths minus the mean veracity rating of lies divided by a standard deviation. As Kalbfleisch (1990) notes, deception researchers' reporting of standard deviations poses challenges for meta-analysts. Whenever possible, we used as our standard deviation a pooled within-message standard deviation across receivers. In such cases, we would note the variance across receivers in judgments of the veracity of truthful messages and the variance across receivers in judgments of the veracity of deceptive messages, before taking the square root of the average of these two variances. When necessary, we used other standard deviations – for example, the standard deviation across receivers in the difference between the mean rated veracity of truths and the mean rated veracity of lies.

The other variables of interest to us are categorical. People can try to detect lies over various media. Here we coded *deception medium* by noting whether a given sample of receivers was trying to detect lies over a video medium, an audio medium, an audiovisual medium, or some other medium. We coded *sender motivation* by noting whether participants had any special motivation to succeed at deception. Our coding of *sender preparation* reflected whether the senders in a study had any time to prepare their lies and truths. We coded whether or not receivers got a *baseline exposure* to the sender before making deception judgments.

In some studies, senders are interacting with others as they lie and tell the truth; in other studies, they are not. For purposes of coding *sender interaction,* we regarded senders as not interacting if when lying they were alone or in the presence of a passive observer. We deemed all other senders to be interacting, and noted whether or not the interaction partner was the receiver (e.g., the person who was judging deception). Most of the receivers in this literature are college students. Others are people whose occupations are thought to give them special expertise at lie detection. We noted this variable of *receiver expertise.*

We coded the status of the report as published or unpublished. In some instances, the same data are reported in two places – say, a dissertation and a journal article. In such cases, we have listed the more accessible report in the References below. Occasionally, results from a given study are more fully reported in one document than another. Then we used the more complete reporting even if it was from the less accessible document.

Reliability of Coding

For a reliability check, the two authors independently coded 24 of the documents in Appendix A. These were selected at random, subject to the restriction that no individual appear as an author on more than two documents. The 24 documents we selected in this manner contribute 46 independent receiver samples to our meta-analysis, and it is on these 46 receiver samples that reliability data are available. The following quantitative variables were checked: number of senders, number of receivers, percentage correct, percentage truth, and accuracy d. Reliabilities on these variables were uniformly high; lowest Pearson's $r = .894$ for 10 accuracy ds. We also checked coding of the following categorical variables: sender motivation, receiver motivation, sender preparation, sender interaction, judgment medium, and baseline exposure. For the percentage agreement on each of these variables, see Table 1.

RESULTS

Characteristics of the Literature

We found 206 documents that satisfied our criteria – 133 that were published and 73 that were unpublished. The earliest document was dated 1941, and the latest was published in 2005. Half of these documents were dated 1994 or earlier.

Table 1

Characteristics of the Research Literature

Quantitative Variables

Variable	*Minimum*	*Maximum*	*Mean*	*Median*	*s*
Number of Senders	1	200	22.45	16.00	22.63
Number of Receivers	1	816	63.65	41.50	70.56
Messages per Receiver	1	416	31.89	16.00	44.50
Message Duration (sec.)	2	1200	110.63	52.00	173.16

Categorical Variables

Variable	# (%) of Receiver Samples		Coding Agreement
Deception Medium			91.3%
Video	47	(12.2%)	
Audio	42	(10.9%)	
Audiovisual	262	(67.4%)	
Other	22	(4.9%)	
Within-receiver manipulation	11	(4.4%)	
Sender motivation			89.5%
No motivation	214	(55.7%)	
Motivation	153	(39.8%	
Within-receiver manipulation	17	(4.4%)	
Sender preparation time			81.1%
None	196	(51.0%)	
Some	165	(43.0%)	
Within-receiver manipulation	23	(6.0%)	
Baseline exposure			91.3%
No exposure	360	(93.7%)	
Exposure	20	(5.2%)	
Within-receiver manipulation	4	(1.1%)	
Sender interaction			100%
None	127	(33.1%)	
Interaction with receiver	33	(8.6%)	
Interaction with another	224	(58.3%)	
Receiver expertise			100%
Not expert	338	(88.0%)	
Expert	46	(12.0%)	

The documents reported results on 24,483 receivers' deception judgments of 6651 messages offered by 4435 senders. There were 177 independent samples of senders, and 384 independent samples of receivers. One hundred and ten of the sender samples were judged by only a single receiver sample; at the other extreme, one sample of senders was judged by 13 independent receiver samples.

In 277 receiver samples, participants classified messages as lies or truths; in 92 samples, they judged messages on multi-point rating scales; and in 15 samples, receivers made lie-or-truth classifications as well as multi-point ratings. For some other characteristics of this literature, see Table 1.

In a typical research study, 41 receivers made judgments of 16 messages – one message offered by each of 16 senders. The typical message lasted 52 seconds. In most cases, the judgment medium was audiovisual, and receivers had no baseline exposure to the sender. Although about 55% of the sender samples had no particular motivation to succeed when lying, over 40% were motivated. Receivers were rarely motivated; barely 12% of the receiver samples had any special incentive to succeed at lie detection. In a little over half of the samples, receivers were judging senders who had had time to prepare their lies; in about 65% of the samples, receivers judged senders who were interacting as they lied. Although only 12% of the receiver samples could claim any occupational expertise in detecting deception, this was nonetheless 2842 experts.

Percentage Correct

In 292 samples, receivers classified messages as lies or truths. From each such sample, we noted the mean percentage correct lie/truth classifications. These are shown on the right side of Figure 1 as a stem-and-leaf display. As can be determined from the display, over three-fourths of these means are greater than 50% and less than one in seven is greater than 60%. Across all 292 samples, the unweighted mean percentage correct lie/truth classifications is 53.98%. The highest mean percentage correct attained in any sample is 73%, and the lowest is 31%. Means at the first, second, and third quartile are 50.07%, 53.90% and 58.00%.

Further insight into lie/truth discrimination abilities can be gleaned from Figure 2, which displays the mean percentage correct lie/truth classifications in a study as a function of the total number of judgments on which the mean was based. The latter was determined by multiplying the number of receivers in a sample by the number of judgments each receiver rendered. Note, for example, the right-most point in the plot. This represents the mean lie/truth discrimination accuracy of 54.30% observed by DePaulo and Pfeiffer (1986) in 10,304 dicomotous lie/truth judgments (64 judgments made by each of 161 receivers).

Figure 2 display exhibits a funnel pattern (Light, Singer, & Willett, 1994) with high variability among means based on small numbers of judgments and low variability among means based on large numbers of judgments. This pattern suggests that the studies are estimating a common value and that small sample sizes account for much of the variability toward the left of the plot.

Figure 1

Stem and leaf plots

Mean percentage truth judgments		*Mean percentage correct lie/truth judgments*
(k = 207)		*(k = 292)*
Leaves	*Stem*	*Leaves*
0	**9**	
	8	
666	**8**	
	8	
322	**8**	
110	**8**	
98	**7**	
76	**7**	
5544	**7**	
2	**7**	3
110000	**7**	11
98888888	**6**	
7777	**6**	667777
55555554	**6**	444455
333222	**6**	22222222333
1111000000000	**6**	0000000000000111111
9999999988888888	**5**	8888888888888888899999999999999999
7777777777777666666	**5**	666666667777777777777777777
555555544444444444	**5**	4444444444444444444444444455555555555555555555555
3333333333333333322222222222222	**5**	22222222222222223333333333333333333
1111100000000	**5**	0000000000000000000000111111111111111111111111
99999988888	**4**	888888888889999999999999
7777666666666666666666	**4**	6666666777777777777777
5544	**4**	4455555
33222	**4**	2222
	4	0011
9	**3**	99
	3	7
55	**3**	5
	3	
10	**3**	1
9	**2**	
77	**2**	

Figure 2

Mean Percent Correct by Number of Judgments

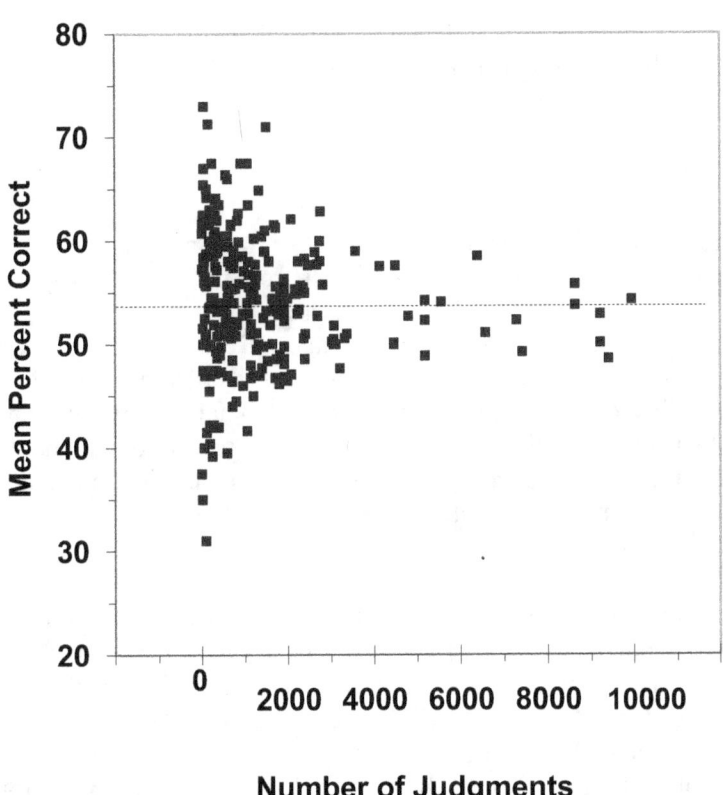

Number of Judgments

A formal analysis of between-study differences begins by noting that the observed standard deviation in mean percentage correct is only 6.11% (that is, variance = 37.33%). Statistically, results would vary some from study-to-study merely by virtue of different investigators examining different receivers. Random-effects techniques can be used to separate between-study variance due to sampling variability from true variance (Hedges & Vevea, 1998). Using a weighted method of moments technique, we infer that receiver sampling error accounts for 45.29% of the observed between-study variance in mean percentage correct, and that the true standard deviation across studies in mean percentage correct is only 4.52%.

For other analyses of mean percentage correct, we used procedures outlined by Bond, Wiitala, and Richard (2003). These require an estimate of the standard deviation in percentage correct in each study. Whenever a standard deviation was reported (or could be calculated), we used it.

Otherwise, we imputed the standard deviation across the receivers in a sample from the binomial distribution, using the mean sample percentage correct as well as the number of judgments made by each receiver in that sample.

These weighted techniques reveal a mean of 53.46% correct lie/truth classifications; 95% confidence interval = 53.31-53.59%. This mean is significantly greater than 50%, $t(7994) =$ 39.78, $p < .0001$. Between-study variability (though small in size) is greater than would be expected by chance, $F_w(283,3658) = 12.61$, $p < .0001$.

Standardized mean differences

Having found that dichotomous lie-or-truth classifications are correct slightly more than half of the time, we next wished to gauge receivers' ability to distinguish lies from truths on multi-point rating scales. In relevant studies, accuracy is operationalized as the mean honesty rating of truthful messages minus the mean honesty rating of deceptive messages. Because different rating scales are used in different studies, it is necessary to standardize these results before summarizing them. To do so, we divide the mean difference in a study between the rated honesty of truths and lies by a standard deviation from that study. Earlier meta-analyses gave us reason to imagine that rating-scale lie/truth discrimination might be sizeable – yielding mean differences in the range of .86 standard deviations (DePaulo, Zuckerman, & Rosenthal, 1980) or 1.14 standard deviations (Zuckerman, DePaulo, & Rosenthal, 1981).

We found 107 samples of receivers who rated deceptive and truthful messages on multi-point scales. For each of these samples, we computed a standardized difference between means (d). The unweighted mean d was .35 ($s = .47$). The ds at the first, second, and third quartile were .09, .31, and .67. By fixed-effects methods (Lipsey & Wilson, 2001), the weighted mean d for lie/truth discrimination is .34; 95% confidence interval = .31 to .38. There is statistically significant heterogeneity in the size of these Cohen's ds, $Q(106) = 458.74$, $p < .01$. Receiver sampling error accounts for 21.92% of the observed variance in effect-sizes, and the true standard deviation in these standardized mean differences is .37. It is noteworthy that the level of lie/truth discrimination we find in 107 studies of rated veracity (mean $d = .35$) is less than half as large as the levels reported in earlier rating reviews (where ds exceeded .85).

Existing summaries led us to suspect that lies might be better discriminated from truths when the discrimination was attempted on multi-point rating scales rather than with dichotomous classifications. To assess this suspicion, we also computed a standardized mean difference for each study in which participants made lie-or-truth classifications. In such cases, the relevant measure is the mean percentage of truthful messages classified as truths minus the mean percentage of deceptive messages classified as truths divided by a standard deviation.

The dichotomous standardized mean differences yielded a weighted mean of .42 in 216 samples from which they could be computed. Values at the first, second, and third quartile were .02 .50 and 1.04. For 61 other samples, no standard deviation in percentage correct lie/truth classifications was reported. There we used the binomial distribution to impute a within-message standard deviation across receivers, and found a weighted mean d of .40.

As these computations indicate, the standardized mean difference in the perceived truthfulness of truths and lies is smaller when receivers use rating scales, rather than when they make lie-or-truth classifications, weighted mean ds = .34 vs. 41; for the difference, $Q(1) = 8.86$, $p < .05$. Combining together lie/truth discrimination results from all 384 receiver samples, we find weighted and unweighted mean ds of .39 and .49, respectively. The median d is .39. Standardized mean differences can be converted to Pearson product-moment correlation coefficients. If we convert each d to an r and cumulate the latter in the usual way, we find an unweighted mean accuracy $r = .19$ and r corresponding to the weighted Fisher's $Z = .21$.

Here lie/truth discrimination abilities produce a weighted mean d of approximately .40. This is considerably smaller than the ds of .86, 1.07, and 1.14 reported in earlier rated-veracity reviews. Even so, the ability to discriminate lies from truths at this level should not be dismissed. Many widely cited effects in social psychology are smaller than this one. Indeed, our d of .39 (or r of .21) would rank above the 60th percentile in size, relative to 474 social psychological effects compiled by Richard, Bond, and Stokes-Zoota (2003).

Percentage Judged True

Deception judgments can have large consequences whether or not they are correct. Thus, it is important to understand factors that may bias the judgments in one direction or another. Vrij (2000) reviewed evidence for a truth bias – receivers' tendency to err in the direction of judging messages as true.

Researchers reported the percentage of messages receivers classified as true in 207 receiver samples. These are displayed on left side of the stem-and-leaf plot in Figure 1. As Figure 1 shows, the percentage of truth classifications is higher than the percentage of correct classifications, and the percentage of truth classifications is more variable. Percentage truth classifications show an unweighted mean of 56.86% and weighted mean of 55.23%. Each of these values is significantly greater than 50%; for the weighted mean, $t(6914) = 46.85$, $p < .0001$. The 95% confidence interval for the weighted mean percentage judged true extends from 54.99% to 55.46% and the true standard deviation across studies in this percentage is 8.13.

Senders succeed in conveying more honesty than dishonesty in these studies. However, the bias thus introduced into receivers' judgments (of roughly 56% truth judgments) is smaller than the 61% truth judgments reported in a tabulation of 9 studies (Vrij, 2000). Across studies, there is no relationship between the percentage of truth judgments receivers rendered and the percentage of correct lie/truth classifications they achieved, $r = -.008$.

Stimulus Accuracy

Because an overall accuracy score is computed by averaging the percentage of correct classifications of truthful messages with the percentage of correct classifications of deceptive messages, it may seem informative to analyze separately the two component scores. We will be regarding these two scores as indices of *stimulus accuracy* for truthful messages and *stimulus accuracy* for deceptive messages, respectively.

In 207 receiver samples, percentage accuracy rates could be determined for truthful messages and deceptive messages separately. These are the same 207 samples used in our previous tabulation of the truth bias. Unweighted analyses reveal that people correctly classify 61.34% of truthful messages as truthful and 47.55% of deceptive messages as deceptive.

There is variability from study to study in the percentage correct classification of deceptive messages as well as truthful messages (each $s = 12.51\%$). The greater the percentage of lies in a study that are correctly classified, the *lower* is the percentage of truths in that study correctly classified; for the cross-study relationship, $r = -.53, p < .0001$. Across studies, accuracy at detecting lies shares little variance with accuracy at detecting truths. Any shared accuracy variance is overwhelmed by cross-study differences in suspicion.

Response Accuracy

The questions of whether people can identify truths as truths and lies as lies, and of differential rates of success, are important ones. But they tell only part of the story about accuracy at detecting deception. Left unanswered are two parallel questions. Given that a person has judged a statement to be truthful, what is the likelihood that the statement was in fact truthful? And, given that a person has judged a statement to be a lie, what is the likelihood that it was actually a lie? To address these questions, we determined the *response accuracy* of a receiver's truth judgments and the receiver's lie judgments – defining them as the percentage of truth (and of lie) judgments that were correct. Recognizing that response accuracy scores could depend heavily on the baseline percentages of truthful and deceptive messages judged, we restricted our analyses of these measures to receivers who judged an equal number of deceptive and truthful messages. Unweighted means on the relevant 187 samples indicate that judgments of truthfulness are *less* likely to be accurate than are judgments of deceptiveness, unweighted means = 54.12% vs. 55.84%, $t(187) = 5.12, p < .01$. There are cross-study differences in the response accuracy of lie and truth judgments ($s = 7.75$ and 5.84, respectively). Interestingly, the greater the response accuracy of truth judgments in a study, the greater is the response accuracy of lie judgments in that study, and this relationship is strong, $r = .80, p < .0001$.

Other Accuracy Measures

All of the measures of accuracy that we have considered so far have limitations. Stimulus accuracy measures can be inappropriately affected by variations in judgmental bias, while response accuracy measures can be artifactually affected by variations in deception baserate. In light of these limitations, we analyzed this research literature with several alterative measures of lie/truth discrimination accuracy – including the log odds ratio and d'. These measures have a theoretical advantage over percentage correct, as they are statistically independent of variations in judgmental bias and baserate. We had imagined that these alternative measures might provide distinctive information about people's average ability to detect lies and give us new insights into cross-study differences in lie detection. They did not.

For one set of analyses, we used methods described in Fleiss (1994) to compute a detection accuracy odds ratio. This was a ratio of the odds that a truthful message was judged to be the truth (rather than a lie) divided by the odds that a deceptive message was judged to be the truth (rather than a lie). Aggregating log odds ratios across the 207 samples in this literature for which requisite data are available, a back-transformation of the mean indicates that the odds of judging a truthful message as the truth is 1.46 times as great as the odds of judging a deceptive message to be the truth (95% CI = 1.41 - 1.51). The back-transformed mean odds of truth detection is 1.65, and the corresponding mean for lie detection is .91. These imply means of 62.30% and 47.53% correct judgments to truthful messages and deceptive messages, respectively – quite close to the stimulus accuracy means of 61.34% and 47.55% directly computable from these samples.

Encouraged by signal detection theorists (*e.g.*, Swets, 1996), we used a binormal method to calculate d' from each of 207 receiver samples. Here d' represents a mean difference in apparent honesty between deceptive and truthful messages. The mean d' in these studies is .24; the median is .22. Although a given d' can correspond to a number of different percentage correct lie/truth classifications, the maximum percentage correct would occur if the percentage correct judgments of deceptive messages equaled the percentage correct judgments of truthful messages (Walter, 2001). For the mean d' of .24 in this literature, this maximum is 54.79% -- quite close to the mean of 54.45% correct directly computable from these samples.

Calculations with the odds ratio and d' corroborate the general conclusion we reached from analyzing percentage correct -- that in the typical research setting lies are discriminated from truths at levels that are slightly better than would be attained by flipping a coin. To determine whether these alternative accuracy measures might give us distinctive information about cross-study differences in lie/truth discrimination, we computed some correlation coefficients across the relevant 207 receiver samples. Results reveal that the three accuracy measures we have been discussing are very highly inter-correlated. As an index of cross-study accuracy differences, percentage correct is virtually interchangeable with the log odds ratio (r = .979) and d' (r = .988). The latter two measures are barely distinguishable, r = .999. These results should be heartening to the many researchers who have been measuring lie detection accuracy as percentage correct.

Determinants of Accuracy

Thus far, our analysis indicates that individuals have some ability to detect deception. On the average, judges achieve about 54% lie/truth discrimination accuracy. As a percentage, lie/truth discrimination abilities seem poor; but when scaled by cross-judge standard deviations, these abilities appear non-negligible. These are typical results over a variety of receiver samples, sender samples, deception media, types of lies, and contexts. Perhaps under certain conditions judges show high percentage lie/truth discrimination rates; perhaps under other conditions, they show trivial standardized discrimination performances. To assess these possibilities, we now examine various subsets of the research literature on deception judgments. We hope to determine how deception judgments are influenced by six factors: 1) deception medium, 2) motivation, 3) preparation, 4) baseline exposure, 5) interaction, and 6) receiver expertise.

Each of these factors will be assessed in its impact on three different indices of judgment: 1) percentage truth classifications, 2) percentage correct lie/truth classifications, and 3) a standardized difference between the perceived veracity of truths and the perceived veracity of lies. Indices 1) and 2) were coded from studies in which individuals made dichotomous lie/truth classifications and were analyzed with the raw techniques of Bond, Wiitala, and Richard (2003). Index 3), which included results from both lie-or-truth classifications and veracity ratings, was analyzed with standardized fixed effects techniques (Lipsey & Wilson, 2001).

To infer the effects of each factor we consider three forms of evidence: within-study comparisons, between-study comparisons, and statistically adjusted comparisons. We aggregate *within-study comparisons* for each moderator variable that has been examined within studies. Summaries of relevant experiments provide us with controlled evidence of the impact of moderator variables. Unfortunately, the number of experiments that manipulate a given factor is limited, as is the range of conditions under which it has been examined. Thus, we also assess effects using *between-study comparisons*. We assess the effect of a person's motivation to lie, for instance, from a comparison of effect-sizes in studies where participants were motivated to lie with effect-sizes in studies where they were not motivated. Although we can base between-study comparisons on impressive amounts of data, the studies at one level of a moderator variable may differ in any number of ways from the studies at another level. In light of these potential confounds, we also make *statistically adjusted comparisons*. They gauge the impact of a given moderator variable from a multiple regression analysis that adjusts for the impact of other variables. In particular, our statistically adjusted comparisons of percentage truth classifications and percentage correct lie/truth classifications document the partial effect of a given moderator variable from an inverse variance-weighted multiple regression equation that includes as regressors the six factors enumerated above (deception medium, motivation, preparation, baseline exposure, interaction, and receiver expertise), as well as a control variable indicating whether or not messages were edited prior to presentation. Our statistically adjusted comparisons of ds reflect results from an inverse variance-weighted multiple regression equation that includes the seven regressors just mentioned, as well as an eighth variable that indicates whether deception judgments were rendered as lie-or-truth classifications or on multi-point rating scales.

Let us remind the reader of a framework we bring to deception judgments. In our view, people are harsher in evaluating others' lies than their own. They stereotype liars as conscience-stricken souls. When asked to judge deception, people consult this stereotype and assess its fit to the person at hand. In general, they are reluctant to label an assertion as deceptive when this judgment would imply that the person offering the assertion was a *liar*. The inaccurate stereotype and unwanted dispositional implication may help explain why receivers' judgments are so often inaccurate -- (more specifically) why so many deceptive messages are misclassified as truthful. Our double-standard hypothesis also provides a framework for interpreting the effects of various factors on deception judgments, effects which we now consider.

Deception Medium. Deception can be judged over various media. Some may invite application of a stereotype for inferring deceit, while others encourage reflection. The video medium, we suspect, should encourage use of a liar stereotype. Indeed, if forced to judge deceit from nothing more than a video image, observers have recourse to little other than their stereotypes. Access to verbal content gives judges the option of analyzing issues of veracity in a more thoughtful fashion. Thus, it is of interest to compare detection rates for lies that can only be seen vs. those that can be heard.

Having sketched the relevance of our double-standard framework for interpreting deception attempts in different media, let us mention another theoretical perspective. According to Ekman and Friesen (1969), people should be most successful in their attempts at facial deceit and least successful in lying with the body because they are most motivated and able to control the face.

To assess the impact of deception medium, we identified fifty studies that experimentally manipulated this factor and extracted from these studies 177 pair-wise comparisons of lie/truth discrimination accuracy in one medium vs. another medium. Ninety eight of the comparisons were made on percentage correct lie/truth classifications and 79 on rating scales. Converting each comparison to a standardized mean difference, we conducted a fixed-effects meta-analysis. Results show that lie/truth discrimination accuracy is lower if judgments are made in a video rather than an audiovisual or audio medium (for comparison of video to audiovisual and audio lie/truth discrimination, weighted mean ds = -.44 and -.37, Zs = -15.72 and –9.51 in 58 and 34 experimental comparisons, respectively; each $p < .0001$). In fact, lie/truth discrimination from video presentations is inferior to discriminations made from written transcripts, weighted mean d = -.28, Z = -4.16, $p < .001$ in 10 experimental comparisons. The levels of lie/truth discrimination achieved from transcript, audiovisual, and audio presentations do not differ from one another.

We tabulated analogous evidence of receivers' general tendency to perceive messages as truthful. Results show that messages are perceived as less truthful if judged from a video than an audiovisual or audio presentation, weighted mean d = -.29 and -.34, Zs = -4.26 and –5.79 in 14 and 15 experimental comparisons, respectively; each $p < .0001$). Messages conveyed in transcripts are judged as less truthful than audiovisual messages and as somewhat more truthful than those presented in video, weighted mean ds = -.32 and +.20, Z = -3.31, $p < .01$ and Z = 1.94, $p = .06$, in five and four experimental comparisons, respectively. In perceived truthfulness, audio-based messages do not differ significantly from audiovisual or transcript messages; each $p > .10$.

To complement these within-study comparisons, we examined medium differences across all of the studies in the research literature. In 195 samples, we have data on percentage truth classifications to messages conveyed in one of three media: video-only, audio-only, or audiovisual. Relevant results appear at the top of Table 2 and suggest that there is a truthfulness bias in judging messages that can be heard. Both audio-only and audiovisual presentations received more than 50% truth judgments. As the within-study comparisons indicated, video-only presentations are less often judged truthful. Medium effects on lie/truth discrimination appear in the bottom two-thirds of the table. Corroborating the within-study evidence, these comparisons show that discrimination is poorer for video-only messages than for messages presented in an audio-only or audiovisual medium.

Table 2

Deception in Three Media: Within and Between Studies

Within Studies

Comparison	k	Weighted mean accuracy d (95% CI)[1]	
Video vs. Audio	34	-.371 (± .076)	Audio is more accurate
Video vs. Audiovisual	58	-.438 (± .053)	Audiovisual is more accurate
Audio vs. Audiovisual	47	-.056 (± .057)	

Between Studies

Total Truth classifications

	k	Raw M[2] (95% CI)	Adjusted M
Video	24	52.18% (± .54)	52.16%
Audio	24	58.78% (± .64)	63.38%
Audiovisual	147	56.32% (± .27)	56.20%
For the difference		$F_w(2,4683) = 174.05$, $p < .001$	

Correct L/T classifications

	k	Raw M (95% CI)	Adjusted M
Video	37	50.52% (± .42)	50.35%
Audio	36	53.01% (± .43)	53.75%
Audiovisual	212	54.03% (± .22)	53.98%
For the difference		$F_w(2,5348) = 118.38$, $p < .001$	

Accuracy d

	k	Raw M (95% CI)	Adjusted M
Video	53	.077 (± .057)	.097
Audio	56	.419 (± .053)	.376
Audiovisual	278	.438 (± .022)	.448
For the difference		$Q(2) = 132.17$	$Q(2) = 140.04$
		$p < .001$	$p < .001$

[1] Note: For within-study comparisons here and elsewhere, positive ds imply that lie/truth discrimination was higher in the condition listed first in the comparison; negative ds imply that it was higher in the condition listed second. In cases where the comparison is statistically significant (at $p < .05$), the condition that shows higher accuracy is noted in the Table.
[2] Note: Percentages here and in later Tables are precision weighted in the manner described by Bond, Wiitala, and Richard (2003).

From our double-standard framework, we interpret these results as follows – that the usual stereotype of a *liar* is largely visual, hence is most strongly evoked by video images of people speaking. Those who can be viewed as tormented are judged to be lying; but apparent torment reflects many factors other than deceit.

Ekman and Friesen (1969) hypothesized that there are more deception cues in the body than the face. To examine this possibility, we divided the video-based deception attempts into ones that provided the receiver with cues from only the face ($k = 15$), only the body ($k = 9$), or the face plus the body ($k = 29$). Results provide only partial support for the Ekman and Friesen (1969) formulation. Consistent with that formulation, attempts at lie detection are unsuccessful when receivers see only the sender's face; however, detection efforts are similarly unsuccessful when receivers see only the liar's body (weighted mean accuracy $d = .01$, $-.15$, and $+.12$ for face, body, and both, respectively).

Motivation. Deception studies are criticized when research participants have no incentive to be believed. Critics note that a lack of motivation may influence participants' believability. To address this issue, we divided the research literature into studies in which participants had little (or no) motivation to be believed and those in which they had higher motivation.

DePaulo and her colleagues (*e.g.*, DePaulo, Stone, & Lassiter, 1985) have hypothesized that senders are undermined by their efforts to get away with lying. In DePaulo's *motivational impairment hypothesis*, the truths and lies of highly motivated senders will be more easily discriminated than those of unmotivated senders unless receivers have access to nothing but a transcript of the sender's remarks.

For a controlled assessment of this hypothesis, we identified 20 studies that experimentally manipulated sender motivation, extracted from those studies 42 distinguishable motivation effects on lie/truth discrimination, and measured each effect as a standardized mean difference. Consistent with the motivational impairment hypothesis, experimental evidence shows that lies are easier to discriminate from truths if they are told by motivated rather than unmotivated senders (for impact of motivation, weighted mean $d = .171$, $Z = 7.10$, $p < .0001$).

The double-standard hypothesis has a different implication for understanding the impact of motivation on deception judgments. People who are afraid of being disbelieved may come to resemble the stereotypic liar. If so, they are likely to be judged deceptive. From this perspective, it should matter little whether or not a highly motivated speaker is lying. What matters is the speaker's fear of being disbelieved. High motivation would rarely make a person feel guilty or ashamed for lying; indeed, high stakes should make it easy to rationalize deceit.

For between-study evidence relevant to this perspective, see the top third of Table 3. Consistent with the double-standard hypothesis, motivation to be believed reduces a speaker's apparent honesty. Perhaps motivation makes people resemble a *visible* stereotype of the liar. If so, motivational effects on credibility might be most apparent on video-based judgments. To assess this possibility, we examined the impact of motivation on lie- and truth-tellers' believability in video, audio, and audiovisual media. Between-study comparisons reveal that motivation significantly reduces senders' video and audiovisual appearance of truthfulness. For example, unmotivated and motivated senders are classified as truthful by 54.44% and 46.84% of receivers who see them in video-only presentations; $t'(95) = 7.17$, $p < .001$. However, motivation has no effect on how truthful a sender *sounds*; $t'(137) = 1.31$, *n.s.*

The bottom two-thirds of Table 3 displays between-study evidence on sender motivation and lie/truth discrimination. Here it does not appear that motivation makes liars easier to detect.

Table 3

Motivated and Unmotivated Deception Within and Between Studies

Within Studies

Comparison	*k*	Weighted mean accuracy *d* (95% CI)
Motivated vs. Unmotivated	42	.171 (± .047) Motivated is more accurate

---

Between Studies

Total Truth classifications

	k	Raw M (95% CI)	Adjusted M
No motivation	130	57.24% (± .28)	57.19%
Motivation	85	53.43% (± .15)	55.66%
For the difference		$t'(1021) = 8.07$, $p < .001$	

Correct L/T classifications

	k	Raw M (95% CI)	Adjusted M
No motivation	177	53.36% (± .21)	53.43%
Motivation	125	53.85% (± .27)	53.27%
For the difference		$t'(506) = 1.01$	

Accuracy *d*

	k	Raw M (95% CI)	Adjusted M
No motivation	231	.462 (± .026)	.396
Motivation	170	.397 (± .028)	.371
For the difference		$Q(1) = 10.80$, $p < .01$	$Q(1)=1.53$, *n.s.*

Preparation. Sometimes the need to lie appears without warning, and people are unprepared for the deceptions they attempt. On other occasions, the need has been anticipated, and a line has been prepared. In principle, the opportunity to prepare might influence a liar's success.

Table 4

Prepared and Unprepared Deceptions Within and Between Studies

Within Studies

Comparison	*k*	Weighted mean accuracy *d* (95% CI)	
Prepared vs. Unprepared	24	-.144 (± .063)	Unprepared is more accurate

----

Between Studies

Total Truth classifications

	k	Raw M *(95% CI)*	Adjusted M
No preparation	118	56.33% (± .28)	57.18%
Preparation	99	55.49% (± .30)	55.15%
For the difference		$t'(1130) = 1.96$, $p < .05$	

Correct L/T classifications

	k	*Raw M (95% CI)*	*Adjusted M*
No preparation	177	53.18% (± .21)	53.13%
Preparation	130	53.70% (± .26)	53.75%
For the difference		$t'(506) = 1.13$	

Accuracy *d*

	k	*Raw M (95% CI)*	*Adjusted M*
No preparation	217	.439 (± .029)	.403
Preparation	184	.365 (± .028)	.361
For the difference		$Q(1)=12.37, p < .001$	$Q(1)=4.10, p < .05$

To examine this possibility, we identified fifteen studies that experimentally manipulated a sender's time to prepare lies. These studies reported 24 experimental effects of sender preparation on the accuracy of lie/truth judgments and 10 experimental effects on the sender's general tendency to appear truthful. A fixed-effects standardized meta-analysis shows that receivers achieve higher lie/truth detection accuracy when judging unplanned, rather than planned messages (weighted mean $d = -.144$, $Z = 4.49$, $p < .01$), and that planned messages appear more truthful than messages which were unplanned (weighted mean $d = .133$, $Z = 2.35$, $p < .05$).

Relevant between-study evidence is displayed in Table 4. Although the results there for judgment accuracy are mixed, they suggest that it may be harder to discriminate deceptive from truthful messages when the messages are planned. Unlike the within-study evidence, between-study comparisons suggest that planned messages appear slightly *less* honest than spontaneous messages.

Baseline exposure to sender.   The current meta-analysis focuses on judgments of deception among strangers. Even so, we included in the analysis 38 samples in which perceivers were exposed to a target before making judgments of that target. We also included 28 samples in which perceivers judged a given target eight or more times and four samples in which perceivers made a forced choice between a target's lie and that same target's truth. For purposes of the analyses below, all of these receivers were deemed to have received a baseline exposure to the target.

For a controlled analysis, we identified 21 experimental comparisons of the detection of a target's messages by judges who had (vs. judges who had not) been previous exposed to that target. All of these comparisons were made on percentage correct lie/truth judgments. Results indicate that baseline exposure improves lie/truth discrimination: receivers achieve a mean of 55.91% accuracy when given a baseline exposure vs. 52.26% accuracy in the absence of any exposure, $t'(364) = 6.37$, $p < .01$.

Between-study evidence on the impact of baseline exposure is displayed in Table 5. Results there suggest that baseline exposure may improve judgmental accuracy. At the same time, senders who are familiar to the receiver are likely to be given the benefit of the doubt, as results on the percentage of truth judgments indicates. Consistent with our double-standard framework, people are reluctant to imply that someone familiar to them is a *liar*.

Table 5

Baseline Exposure to Sender Within and Between Studies

Within Studies

Comparison	k	Weighted mean accuracy d (95% CI)[1]
Exposure vs. No exposure	21	.239 (± .091) Exposure is more accurate

----

Between Studies

Total Truth classifications

	k	Raw M (95% CI)	Adjusted M
No exposure	187	56.11% (± .23)	55.31%
Exposure	31	58.37% (± .46)	61.92%
For the difference		t'(452) = 3.47, p < .01	

Correct L/T classifications

	k	Raw M (95% CI)	Adjusted M
No exposure	250	53.35% (± .18)	53.06%
Exposure	61	54.22% (± .33)	54.55%
For the difference		t'(294) = 2.09, p < .05	

Accuracy d

	k	Raw M (95% CI)	Adjusted M
No exposure	331	.400 (± .022)	.356
Exposure	72	.443 (± .051)	.499
For the difference		Q(1) = 2.25	Q(1)=32.12, p < .001

Interaction. In many studies, people lie while alone or in the presence of a passive experimenter. In other studies, people are involved in social interactions when lying. Sometimes, the interaction partner is attempting to judge the liar's veracity; and on other occasions, a third party may be making this judgment. The latter occurs, for example, when the interaction partner is the experimenter and the third party is the receiver making judgments from a videotape. In principle, interaction might influence one's success at lying. Interaction might, for example, impose cognitive demands on the liar (Buller & Burgoon, 1996).

We found eleven studies that experimentally manipulated whether senders were interacting with the receiver or with a third party. Results indicate no significant difference in lie/truth discrimination by interaction partners (vs. third-party observers), weighted mean ds = .286 vs. .209, Z = 1.41, *n.s.* We also tabulated evidence within five studies of receivers' general tendency to perceive senders as truthful. Results show that individuals are judged to be more truthful by their interaction partners than by third-party observers; for this comparison, weighted mean d = .26, Z = 4.10, p < .0001.

Table 6

Sender Interaction Within and Between Studies

Within Studies

Comparison	k	Weighted mean accuracy d (95% CI)[1]
Interaction with receiver vs. third party	10	.081 (± .094)

Between Studies

Total Truth classification

	k	Raw M (95% CI)	Adjusted M
No interaction	66	54.51% (± .34)	57.58%
Interaction with receiver	13	65.32% (± 2.05)	61.60%
Interaction with third party	128	55.51% (± .28)	56.27%
For the differences		$F_w(2,1403) = 58.15$, p < .001	

Correct L/T classifications

	k	Raw M (95% CI)	Adjusted M
No interaction	85	52.56% (± .27)	52.60%
Interaction with receiver	18	52.27% (±1.68)	52.75%
Interaction with third party	189	54.06% (± .20)	53.97%
For the differences		$F_w(2,2051) = 37.67, p < .001$	

Accuracy d

	k	Raw M (95% CI)	Adjusted M
No interaction	127	.375 (± .036)	.302
Interaction with receiver	33	.234 (± .076)	.316
Interaction with third party	224	.416 (± .027)	.471
For the differences		$Q(2) = 20.24, p < .01$	$Q(2)=57.14, p < .001$

For between-study evidence on the impact of interaction, see Table 6. There it is again clear that receivers are inclined to judge their interaction partners as truthful. Overall patterns in the literature suggest that third-party observers are better than interaction partners at discriminating lies from truths. In our view, the reluctance to attribute deception to interaction partners results from an unwanted dispositional implication – of insinuating that the partner is a *liar*.

Receiver expertise. In most research, college students function as the judges of deception. Perhaps people who had more experience would be better at judging deceit. To assess this possibility, we identified studies of deception experts. These are individuals whose occupations expose them to lies. They include law enforcement personnel, judges, psychiatrists, job interviewers, and auditors – anyone whom deception researchers regard as experts.

In 19 studies, expert and non-expert receivers judged the veracity of the same set of messages. From these studies, we extracted 20 independent expert/non-expert comparisons, and expressed each as a standardized mean difference. This cumulation yields no evidence that experts are superior to non-experts in discriminating lies from truths; weighted mean $d = -.025$, 95% confidence interval = $-.105$ to $+.055$. Indeed, the direction of the within-study difference favors higher non-expert accuracy, though this difference is not statistically significant, $Z = -.61$, *n.s.* Within-study comparisons also reveal no statistically significant difference between experts and non-experts in the tendency to perceive others as truthful; weighted mean percentage truth judgments = 54.09% and 55.74% for experts and non-experts, respectively; $t'(246)=1.41$.

For a broader assessment of experts' deception judgments, see Table 7. From the between-study evidence, it would appear that experts are more skeptical than non-experts, being less inclined to believe that people are truthful. Having been targets of deceit in their professional roles, experts may have surmounted the usual reluctance to imply that people are *liars*.   If raw between-study comparisons suggest that experts may be better than non-experts at discriminating lies from truths, it is clear that experts are not good lie detectors. On the average, they achieve less than 55% lie/truth discrimination accuracy. In any case, experts' apparent superiority in lie/truth discrimination disappears when means are statistically adjusted.

Publication Status. Lie detection results might influence the likelihood of a research project being published. To assess this possibility, we did a few other analyses. These reveal no statistically significant differences between published and unpublished studies in lie/truth discrimination performances. For example, the weighted mean percentage correct lie/truth classifications is 53.19% in published studies and 53.75% in unpublished studies, $t'(872)=1.49$, *n.s.* Truthfulness biases were, however, stronger in unpublished research; weighted mean percentage truth classifications = 56.75% vs. 54.27% in unpublished vs. published research, $t'(498)=4.75, p <$ .001.

Table 7

Receiver Expertise Within and Between Studies

Within Studies

Comparison	k	Weighted mean accuracy d (95% CI)[1]
Expert vs. Non-expert	20	-.025 (± .080)

Between Studies

Total Truth classifications

	k	Raw M (95% CI)	Adjusted M
Non-expert	177	55.69% (± .20)	55.84%
Expert	30	52.28% (± .58)	52.02%
For the difference		$t'(361) = 4.95$, $p < .001$	

Correct L/T classifications

	k	Raw M (95% CI)	Adjusted M
Non-expert	250	53.31% (± .17)	53.29%
Expert	42	54.51% (± .47)	53.81%
For the difference		$t'(556) = 2.37, p < .05$	

Accuracy d

	k	Raw M (95% CI)	Adjusted M
Non-expert	338	.380 (± .022)	.387
Expert	46	.488 (± .064)	.388
For the difference		$Q(1) = 9.77, p < .01$	$Q(1)=.01$

Note: Expert receivers have a background researchers deem relevant to detecting deception. They include police officers, detectives, judges, interrogators, criminals, customs officials, mental health professionals, polygraph examiners, job interviewers, federal agents, and auditors.

DISCUSSION

Having captivated human imagination for millenia, deception was destined to attract psychological investigators. Our goal has been to synthesize their research – more specifically, to quantify people's ability to detect deceit from behavior. Here we summarize the findings of our meta-analysis, discuss the literature in light of a double-standard framework, and note limitations in the existing evidence.

Meta-analytic Findings

How successful are people at duping others? How often do people detect others' deception attempts? To address these questions, psychologists arrange for people to make truthful and deceptive statements and for others to classify these statements as truths or lies. Across hundreds of experiments, typical rates of lie/truth discrimination are slightly above 50%. For the grand mean, 54% is a reasonable estimate.

Having noted that the average person discriminates lies from truths at a level slightly better than s/he could achieve by flipping a coin, let us also note this ability corresponds to a nontrivial standardized effect size. In producing a mean difference of approximately .40 standard deviations in judgments of lies vs. truths, typical detection abilities are larger than 60% of the research phenomena studied by social psychologists (Richard, Bond, & Stokes-Zoota, 2003).

Our finding of a 54% lie/truth discrimination rate represents an average of correct judgments to deceptive messages and truthful messages. It is clear that truthful messages are more often judged correctly than deceptive messages; hence the percentage of correct judgments to messages encountered in any real-world setting may depend on the base rate of deception there. In a setting where virtually no lies were told, the research literature would suggest a detection rate of roughly 60%; while in a situation where virtually every statement was a lie, a detection rate of, say, 48% might be expected (cf. Levine, Park, & McCornack, 1999). These estimates assume that there is no cross-situational correlation between observers' tendency to infer deception in a setting and the actual rate of lying there. More likely, deception base rates enter into a tactical calculus. As observers have intuitions about the frequency of deception in different situations, liars have intuitions too. If the latter can choose *where* to attempt their deceptions, they should opt for settings in which targets are most trusting.

Like earlier reviewers, we find that people are more inclined to judge deceptive messages as truthful than truthful messages as deceptive. No doubt, receivers contribute to this truth bias, but senders' contributions should also be acknowledged. When people try to appear truthful, their efforts are rewarded – the accumulated literature shows. The relative impact of senders and receivers on the truth bias remains to be determined. In the meantime, the present contribution is to document the magnitude of this effect. Across 206 studies, people render a mean of some 56% truth judgments. However, this figure may understate the presumption of truth telling in real life. If in their daily interactions people accept without reflection much of what they hear, in the laboratory they are forced to make veracity judgments. Thus, researchers circumvent some of the usual impediments to inferring deceit – social norms that discourage skepticism, liars' tactics for pre-empting suspicion, and a cognitive inertia that would be disrupted by critical inquiry (Levine, Park, & McCornack, 1999).

We see a pattern in this research literature. In their reading of the literature, scholars find an unwanted implication -- that people can barely discriminate lies from truths. Heirs to the moralistic tradition, scholars resist this implication by identifying a feature of researchers' methods that could in principle explain low lie/truth discrimination rates. They label the feature an *artifact*, *correct* the *error*, run a study, and announce that their findings are uniquely valid. Sometimes, the methodological *correction* yields a higher than average detection rate, and sometimes it does not. Never, however, has this quest for accuracy yielded levels of lie detection that would be of much practical use. Occasionally, a researcher finds a detection rate of 70% (or so) and proclaims a momentous discovery. However, those rates occur on tests that include only a small number of messages and are attained by only a subset of the receivers (or on a subset of the tests) studied. From a meta-analytic perspective, random variation is the most plausible explanation for the occasionally high detection rate, as the funnel pattern in Figure 2 suggests.

Rather than marveling at the outliers in this literature, we are more impressed by the regularity of the results obtained. Despite decades of research effort to maximize the accuracy of deception judgments, detection rates rarely budge. Professionals' judgments, interactants' judgments, judgments of high-stakes lies, judgments of unsanctioned lies, judgments made by long-term acquaintances – all reveal detection rates within a few points of 50%. We wonder if it is premature to abort the quest for 90% lie detection and accept the conclusion implied by the first 384 research samples – that to people who must judge deception in real time with no special aids, many lies are undetectable.

Although rates of lie detection vary within a narrow range, the variation is not random. Some factors facilitate lie/truth discrimination, and others impede it – our meta-analytic results confirm. The medium in which deception is attempted affects its likelihood of detection – lies being more detectable when they can be heard. By contrast, facial behaviors provide no indication of a speaker's veracity, corroborating the theory that the face is well controlled (Ekman & Friesen, 1969). Ekman and Friesen also suggested that bodily behaviors go uncontrolled, hence should be indicative of deceit. Unfortunately, the latter hypothesis has so rarely been tested that its validity remains unknown.

A more recent perspective (Buller & Burgoon, 1996) emphasizes the role of social interaction in deception judgments. The accumulated research suggests that lies told in the midst of social interaction are spotted by on-lookers, while they are fooling the liar's interaction partner. However, controlled experiments show no difference in lie detection by interaction partners, as opposed to on-lookers. As common sense might have predicted, judges achieve better lie/truth discrimination if they have a baseline exposure to the sender and if the sender is unprepared. The accumulated evidence suggests that people who are motivated to be believed look deceptive, whether or not they are lying. Expert judges may be slightly more skeptical than novices. Relative to novices, experts may (or may not) be better at lie/truth discrimination; in any case, they make many mistakes.

The Double Standard

Having reviewed the research literature on deception judgments and cataloged some factors that influence detection accuracy, let us note the relevance of our favored framework for understanding this subject – our assumption that people judge others' deceptions more harshly than their own.

We do not regard the current meta-analysis as a test of the notion of a double standard. In our view, no test for so obvious an idea is needed – though relevant evidence can be found in primary research (Gordon & Miller, 2000). Instead, we begin with the premise that people construe others' lies more critically than their own and explore the implications of this premise for understanding research findings.

Indignant at the prospect of being duped, people project onto the deceptive a host of morally fueled emotions – anxiety, shame, and guilt. Drawing on this stereotype to assess others' veracity, people find that the stereotype seldom fits. In underestimating the liar's capacity for self-rationalization, judges' moralistic stereotype has the unintended effect of enabling successful deceit. Because deceptive torment resides primarily in the judge's imagination, many lies are mistaken for truths. When torment is perceived, it is often not a consequence of deception but of a speaker's motivation to be believed. High stakes rarely make people feel guilty about lying; more often, they allow deceit to be easily rationalized. When motivation has an impact, it is on the speaker's fear of being disbelieved; and it matters little whether or not the highly motivated are lying. The impact of motivation is most evident when judges can see the speaker's resemblance to a visual stereotype of the *liar*.

People are critical of lies, unless the lies are their own. To maintain an exception for themselves, judges may sometimes need to excuse lying by others. As the research literature shows, people avoid attributing deception to others with whom they are familiar – whether from a live interaction, or a long-term relationship (Anderson, Ansfield, & DePaulo, 1999). Judges may also be loath to perceive as *liars* people who resemble the judge. Perhaps the truth bias we observe in this literature represents an extension of the self bias to others who are reminiscent of the self. In this view, the bias reflects the similarity of the deceivers in this research literature to their judges – often, the two are students at the same University. Maybe there would be less bias in judgments made of dissimilar others. As we have noted, deception researchers find that expert judges are willing to imply that others are *liars*. What we have not noted is a procedural detail -- that these experts are rarely sitting in judgment of their peers; instead, they are judging members of other groups. Self biases do not extend to outsiders.

The judges in this research literature are given the goal of achieving 100% accuracy, and their failure to attain this objective has been widely lamented. The senders in this research literature are also given a goal: to convey an impression of honesty 100% of the time. Results show that research participants disbelieve nearly 50% of senders' deception attempts and nearly 40% of their attempts at truth telling. Although in the rough actuarial aggregate of deception research liars fail as often as detectors, deception failures have rarely been discussed. Let us comment on these failures from a double standard perspective.

Liars who are often judged deceptive should come to learn that their stratagems have been penetrated. Thus, it may seem paradoxical that the average person lies several times a day (DePaulo, Kashy, Kirkendohl, Wyer, & Epstein, 1996). Evidently, most lies are little, and the consequences of detection benign. In the interest of interacting smoothly, the liar and judge conspire to preserve a fiction (DePaulo *et al*, 2003).

A few lies involve high stakes: large benefits to the liar and large costs to the dupe. Moralists focus on these big bad lies. The research literature has explored judgments made at the time deception is attempted, judgments that could pre-empt the payoffs liars pursue. However, research reveals that many people avoid being caught in the act of lying; hence, it is important to explore the likely course of subsequent events.

High-stakes deceptions are motivated by non-correspondent outcomes, one person seeking advantage at another's expense. There are costs of being duped, and these should impose limits on the dupe's naiveté. Some lies are discovered well after they have been told (Park, Levine, McCornack, Morrison, & Ferrara, 2002). Then the dupes become indignant. They retaliate by shunning their exploiter and publicizing the liar's duplicity. As a consequence, people who are most successful in the short-term perpetration of lies have trouble maintaining relationships. Moralists have opined that skilled liars are worse relationship partners than highly honest folk. Let us suggest that skilled liars may also be worse partners than people whose lies are transparent (Andrews, 2002). Inept liars pose no threat to their partners insofar as their deception attempts fail before any damage is done. This line of reasoning suggests that skill at high-stakes deception may be an interpersonal liability and that so-called deception *failures* are in the long run adaptive.

Maybe the craftiest can benefit from lying. Cognizant of the dispositional nature of moral attributions (Reeder, 1993), they cultivate reputations for honesty by telling the truth on trivial matters, while noting advantages that fibbing might have conferred. Then when deceit promises the largest reward, others will have been lulled into an unwarranted trust (Sternglanz, 2003). Having laid the tactical groundwork, liars must nonetheless recognize that deceptions may ultimately be exposed. In the moment of lying, the shrewdest affect a distancing from their falsehoods, so that they can later disavow the lies. For deception to show long-term profitability, reputational damage must be contained.

Limitations in the Evidence

Commentators have criticized research on deception judgments, pointing to ways in which the lies studied in the research literature differ from the lies of most interest to the critic. Those who are interested in high-stakes lies (Ekman, 2001) note that many experimental deceptions are trivial. Those who are interested in deceptive interactions (Burgoon & Buller, 1996) denounce experimentally constrained lies. Legal scholars (*e.g.,* Fisher, 1997) note aspects of the forensic world that are not reproduced in research contexts.

Deception researchers have tried to accommodate critics' reservations. They have studied murderers' lies and lies that could harm children (Lusby, 1999; Vrij & Mann, 2001a), lies to lovers and deceit during criminal interrogations (Anderson, Ansfield, & **DePaulo**, 1999; Davis,

Markus, Walters, Vorus, & Conners, In press). Researchers have studied naturalistic deceptive interactions and jurors' credibility judgments (Frank, 1989; Park, Levine, Harms, & Ferrara, 2002). In light of these efforts, we find no merit in blanket dismissals of this research literature as trivial, asocial, and irrelevant.

We ourselves have reservations about the literature on deception judgments, concerns that have not (we think) been addressed. To illuminate lie detection from language and behavior, psychologists have excluded from their research other potential cues to deception. They have restricted the time span over which issues of deception can be pondered, blinded judges to the motivational contingencies surrounding deceit, and neutralized naturally occurring correlates of the propensity to lie.

In experiments, judges encounter a message and must judge the veracity of that message on the spot with no time to gather additional information. Outside the laboratory, additional information is important. When asked to describe their discovery of a lie, people rarely state that the discovery was prompted by behaviors displayed at the time of the attempted deception. Rather, they say that lie detection took days, weeks, or even months, and involved physical evidence or third parties (Park, Levine, McCornack, Morrison, & Ferrara, 2002). Surely, motivational information conditions real-world deception judgments – when, for instance, jurors discount expert testimony after learning that the expert received a fee (Hilton, Fein, & Miller, 1993). In venues of frequent deception, people may base their veracity judgments more strongly on perceived incentives than any behavioral information. People differ widely in the propensity to lie (Kashy & DePaulo, 1996), and this individual difference may be discernable (Bond, Berry, & Omar, 1994). Researchers bypass naturally occurring correlates of deceptiveness by compelling lies from every experimental participant – even those who are loath to lie. Future studies will be needed to explore the impact on lie detection of these and other forms of extra-behavioral information. Perhaps the 90% lie detection barrier will someday be broken.

In the meantime, we have accumulated knowledge about judgments of deception from speech content and behavior. Yes, people often fail in their efforts to divine deception, and this raises questions about the American legal system, where jurors are responsible for detecting lies. It is important also to note that research participants often fail when trying to dupe others. Perhaps it would be unsurprising if liars and would-be detectors had arrived at an equilibrium. If liars were much better, truth telling would be less common; if detectors were much better, few lies would be attempted.

Authors' Note:

We are grateful to Harris Cooper, Laura Muhlenbruck, Bob Rosenthal, and Jenny Tornqvist for help with this project. We also thank the many deception researchers who answered questions about their work.

REFERENCES

Anderson, D. E., Ansfield, M.E., & DePaulo, B. M. (1999). Love's best habit: Deception in the context of relationships. In Philippot, P., & Feldman, R.S. (Eds.) *Social context of nonverbal behavior* (pp. 372-409). New York: Cambridge University Press.

Anderson, N.H. (1968). Likeableness ratings of 555 personality-trait words. *Journal of Personality and Social Psychology, 9,* 272-279.

Andrews, P.W. (2002). The influence of postreliance detection on the deceptive efficacy of dishonest signals of intent: Understanding facial clues to deceit as the outcome of signaling tradeoffs. *Evolution and Human Behavior, 23,* 103-121.

Bok, S. (1989). *Lying: Moral choice in public and private life.* New York: Vintage Books.

Bond, C. F., Jr., Berry, D. S., and Omar, A. (1994). The kernel of truth in judgments of deceptiveness. *Basic and Applied Social Psychology, 15,* 523-534.

Bond, C.F., Jr., & Robinson, M. (1988). The evolution of deception. *Journal of Nonverbal Behavior, 12,* 295-307.

Bond, C.F., Jr., Wiitala, W., & Richard, F.D. (2003). Meta-analysis of raw mean differences. *Psychological Methods, 8,* 406-418.

Buller, D.B., & Burgoon, J.K. (1996). Interpersonal deception theory. *Communication theory, 6,* 203-242.

Davis, M., Markus, K.A., Walters, S.B., Vorus, N., & Connors, B. (In press). Behavioral cues to deception vs. topic incriminating potential in criminal confessions. *Law and Human Behavior.*

DePaulo, B.M., Ansfield, M.E., & Bell, K.L. (1996). Theories about deception and paradigms for studying it: A critical appraisal of Buller and Burgoon's interpersonal deception theory and research. *Communication Theory, 3,* 297-310.

DePaulo, B.M., Kashy, D.A., Kirkendol, S.E., Wyer, M.M., & Epstein, J.A. (1996). Lying in everyday life. *Journal of Personality and Social Psychology, 70,* 979-995.

DePaulo, B.M., Lindsay, J.J., Malone, B.E., Muhlenbruck, L., Charlton, K., & Cooper, H. (2003). Cues to deception. *Psychological Bulletin, 129,* 74-118.

DePaulo, B.M., Stone, J.L., & Lassiter, G.D. (1985). Deceiving and detecting deceit. In B.R. Schenkler (Ed.), *The self and social life* (pp. 323-370). New York: McGraw-Hill.

DePaulo, B.M., Zuckerman, M., & Rosenthal, R. (1980). Humans as lie detectors. *Journal of Communication, 30,* 129-139.

Ekman, P. (2001). *Telling lies: Clues to deceit in the marketplace, politics, and marriage* (Third edition). New York: Norton.

Ekman, P., & Friesen, W.V. (1969). Nonverbal leakage and clues to deception. *Psychiatry, 32,* 88-105.

Fisher, G. (1997). The rise of the jury as lie detector. *Yale Law Journal, 103,* 575-713.

Fleiss, J.L. (1994). Measures of effect size for categorical data. In H. Cooper and L. Hedges (Eds) *The handbook of research synthesis* (pp. 245-260). New York: Russell Sage.

Global Deception Research Team (In press). A world of lies. *Journal of Cross Cultural Psychology.*

Gordon, A.K., & Miller, A.G. (2000). Perspective differences in the construal of lies: Is deception in the eye of the beholder? *Personality and Social Psychology Bulletin, 26,* 46-55.

Hedges, L.V., & Vevea, J.L. (1998). Fixed- and random-effects models in meta-analysis. *Psychological Methods, 3,* 486-504.

Hilton, J.L., Fein, S., & Miller, D.T. (1993). Suspicion and dispositional inference. *Personality and Social Psychology Bulletin, 19,* 501-512.

Hubbell, A.P., Mitchell, M.M., & Gee, J.C. (2001). The relative effects of timing of suspicion and outcome involvement on biased message processing. *Communication Monographs, 68,* 115-132.

Judicial Committee on Modern Jury Instructions for the Eighth Circuit (2002). *Manual of modern criminal jury instructions.* Published on-line at www.are.uscourts.gov/jury/crjury2002.pdf.

Kalbfleisch, P.J. (1990). Listening for deception: The effects of medium on accuracy of detection. In R.N. Bostrom (Ed.) *Listening behavior: Measurement and application* (pp. 155-176). New York: Guilford Press.

Kashy, D.A., & DePaulo, B.M. (1996). Who lies? *Journal of Personality and Social Psychology, 70,* 1037-1051.

Kraut, R. (1980). Humans as lie detectors: Some second thoughts. *Journal of Communication, 30,* 209-216.

Levine, T.R., Park, H.S., & McCornack, S.A. (1999). Accuracy in detecting truths and lies: Documenting the "veracity effect". *Communication Monographs, 66,* 125-144.

Light, R.J., Singer, J.D., & Willett, J.B. (1994). The visual presentation and interpretation of meta-analyses. In H. Cooper and L.V. Hedges (Eds.) *The handbook of research synthesis* (pp. 439-453). New York: Russell Sage.

Lusby, David J. (1999). Effects of motivation to lie and sanctioned deception of the accuracy of observers' veracity judgments. Unpublished M.A. thesis, SUNY-Buffalo.

Mattson, M., Ryan, D.J., Allen, M., & Miller, V. (2000). Considering organizations as a unique interpersonal context for deception detection: A meta-analytic review. *Communication Research Reports, 17,* 148-160.

Miller, G.R., & Stiff, J.B. (1993). *Deceptive communication.* Newbury Park, CA: Sage.

O'Sullivan, M. (2003). The fundamental attribution error in detecting deception: The boy-who-cried-wolf effect. *Personality and Social Psychology Bulletin, 29,* 1316-1327.

Park, H.S., & Levine, T.R. (2001). A probability model of accuracy in deception detection experiments. *Communication Monographs, 68,* 201-210.

Park, H.S., Levine, T.R., McCornack, S.A., Morrison, K., & Ferrara, S. (2002). How people really detect lies. *Communication Monographs, 69,* 144-157.

Reeder, G.D. (1993). Trait-behavior relations and dispositional inference. *Personality and Social Psychology Bulletin, 19,* 586-593.

Richard, F.D., Bond, C.F., Jr., & Stokes-Zoota, J.J. (2003). One hundred years of social psychology quantitatively described. *Review of General Psychology, 7,* 331-363.

Saxe, L. (1991). Lying: Thoughts of an applied social psychologist. *American Psychologist, 46,* 409-415.

Sternglanz, R. W. (2003). Exoneration of serious wrongdoing via confession to a lesser defense. Unpublished Ph..D. dissertation, University of Virginia, Charlottesville, VA.

Swets, J.A. (1996). *Signal detection theory and ROC analysis in psychology and diagnostics.* Mahwah, NJ: Erlbaum.

Trovillo, P.V. (1939). A history of lie detection. *Journal of Criminal Law and Criminology, 29,* 848-881.

Vrij, A. (2000). *Detecting lies and deceit: The psychology of lying and the implications for professional practice.* New York: John Wiley.

Vrij, A., Edward, K., Roberts, K., & Bull, R. (2000). Detecting deceit via analysis of verbal and nonverbal behavior. *Journal of Nonverbal Behavior*, *24*, 239-263.

Vrij, A., & Mann, S. (2001a). Telling and detecting lies in a high-stake situation: The case of a convicted murderer. *Applied Cognitive Psychology*, *15*, 187-203.

Vrij, A., & Mann, S. (2001b). Who killed my relative? Police officers' ability to detect real-life high-stake lies. Psychology, Crime, & Law, 7, 119-132.

Walter, S.D. (2002). Properties of the summary receiver operating characteristic (SROC) curve for diagnostic test data. Statistics in Medicine, 21, 1237-1256.

Zuckerman, M., DePaulo, B.M., & Rosenthal, R. (1981). Verbal and nonverbal communication of deception. In L. Berkowitz (Ed.) *Advances in experimental social psychology* (Volume 14, pp. 1-60). New York: Academic Press.

Appendix A

Studies Included in the Meta-analysis

1. Al-Simadi, F.A. (2000). Detection of deceptive behavior: A cross-cultural test. *Social Behavior & Personality, 28,* 455-461.

2. Anderson, D.E. (1999). Cognitive and motivational processes underlying truth bias. Unpublished Ph.D. dissertation, University of Virginia.

3. Anderson, D.E., DePaulo, B.M., & Ansfield, M.E. (2002). The development of deception detection skill: A longitudinal study of same-sex friends. *Personality and Social Psychology Bulletin, 28,* 536-543.

4. Ask, K., & Granhag, P.A. (2003). Individual determinants of deception detection performance: need for closure, attributional complexity, and absorption. *Goteborg Psychological Reports, 33,* 1-13.

5. Atmiyanandana, V. (1976). An experimental study of the detection of deception in cross- cultural communication. Unpublished doctoral dissertation, Florida State University.

6. Bailey, J.T. (2002). Detecting deception when motivated: The effects of accountability and training on veracity judgments. Unpublished M.S. thesis, Ohio University.

7. Bauchner, J.E., Kaplan, E.A., & Miller, G.R. (1980). Detecting deception: The relationship of available information to judgmental accuracy in initial encounters. *Human Communication Research, 6,* 253-264.

8. Berger, R.E. (1977). Machiavellianism and detecting deception in facial nonverbal communication. *Towson State University Journal of Psychology, 1,* 25-31.

9. Billings, F.J. (2004). Psychopathy and the ability to deceive. Unpublished Ph.D. dissertation, University of Texas at El Paso.

10. Blair, J.P., & McCamey, W.P. (2002). Detection of deception: An analysis of the behavioral analysis interview technique. *Illinois Law Enforcement Executive Forum, 2,* 165-169.

11. Bond, C.F., Jr., & Atoum, A.O. (2000). International deception. *Personality and Social Psychology Bulletin, 26,* 385-395.

12. Bond, C.F., Jr., & Fahey, W.E. (1987). False suspicion and the misperception of deceit. *British Journal of Social Psychology, 26,* 41-46.

13. Bond, C.F., Jr., Kahler, K.N., & Paolicelli, L.M. (1985). The miscommunication of deception: An adaptive perspective. *Journal of Experimental Social Psychology, 21,* 331-345.

14. Bond, C.F. Jr., Lashley, B.R., & Kirk, C.T. (2002). Responding to deception. Unpublished manuscript, Texas Christian University.

15. Bond, C.F., Jr., Omar, A., Mahmoud, A., & Bonser, R.N. (1990). Lie detection across cultures. *Journal of Nonverbal Behavior, 14,* 189-204.

16. Bond, C.F., Jr., Omar, A., Pitre, U., Lashley, B.R., Skaggs, L.M., & Kirk, C.T. (1992). Fishy-looking liars: Deception judgment from expectancy violation. *Journal of Personality and Social Psychology, 63,* 969-977.

17. Bond, C.F., Jr., Paulson, R.M., & Thomas, B.J. (2003). Multiple-audience messages. Unpublished data, Texas Christian University.

18. Bond, C.F., Jr., & Prestwood, D. (2004). Investigating deceptive claims. Unpublished manuscript, Texas Christian University.

19. Bond, C.F., Jr., Thomas, B.J., & Paulsen, R.M. (2004). Maintaining lies: The multiple-audience problem. *Journal of Experimental Social Psychology, 40,* 29-40.

20. Bond, G.D., Malloy, D.M., Arias, E.A., Nunn, S.N., & Thompson, L.A. (2005). Lie-biased decision making in prison. *Communication Reports, 18,* 1-11.

21. Bond, G.D., Malloy, D.M., Thompson, L.A., Arias, E.A., & Nunn, S.N. (2004). Post-probe decision making in a prison context. *Communication Monographs, 71,* 269-283.

22. Bond, G.D., Thompson, L.A., & Malloy, D.M. (2005). Vulnerability of older adults to deception. *Psychology and Aging, 20,* 60-70.

23. Boone, R.T., Blumenthal, J.A., Simon, T., Cunningham, J.G., & Tucker, J.S. (1998). Discriminating the truth: The effect of presentation, order, and gender on the detection of deception in an adversarial dispute. Unpublished manuscript, Brandeis University.

24. Brand, R.J, Hodges, S.D, & Williams, J.L. (2003). Sex differences in encoding sexual attraction. Paper presented at the annual meeting of the American Psychological Society.

25. Brandt, D.R., Miller, G.R., & Hocking, J.E. (1980a). Effects of self-monitoring and familiarity on deception detection. *Communication Quarterly, 28,* 3-10.

26. Brandt, D.R., Miller, G.R., & Hocking, J.E. (1980b). The truth-deception attribution: Effects of familiarity on the ability of observers to detect deception. *Human Communication Research, 6,* 99-110.

27. Brandt, D.R., Miller, G.R., & Hocking, J.E. (1982). Familiarity and lie detection: A replication and extension. *Western Journal of Speech Communication, 46,* 276-290.

28. Briggs, J.R. (1992). Counselor assessments of honest and deceptive clients (honest clients). Unpublished Ph.D. dissertation, Ball State University.

29. Buchanan, J.N. (1998). UJOS as lie detectors: Exploring University Judicial Officers' judgments of deception. Unpublished Ph.D. dissertation, Florida State University.

30. Buller, D.B., & Hunsaker, F.G. (1995). Interpersonal deception: XIII. Suspicion and the truth-bias of conversational participants. In J. Aitken (Ed.) *Interpersonal communication processes reader* (pp. 237-257). Westland, MI: McNeil.

31. Buller, D.B., Strzyzewski, K.D., & Hunsaker, F.G. (1991). Interpersonal deception: II. The inferiority of conversational participants as deception detectors. *Communication Monographs, 58,* 25-40.

32. Burgoon, J.K., Blair, J.P., & Strom, R.E. (2005). Heuristics and modalities in determining truth versus deception. Paper presented at the 38th Hawaii International conference on system sciences.

33. Burgoon, J.K., Buller, D.B., Dillman, L., & Walther, J.B. (1995). Interpersonal deception: IV. Effects of suspicion on perceived communication and nonverbal behavior dynamics. *Human Communication Research, 22,* 163-196.

34. Burgoon, J.K., Buller, D.B., Ebesu, A.S., & Rockwell, P. (1994). Interpersonal deception: V. Accuracy in deception detection. *Communication Monographs, 61,* 303-325.

35. Burgoon, J.K., Buller, D.B., & Floyd, K. (2001). Does participation affect deception success? A test of the interactivity principle. *Human Communication Research, 27,* 503-533.

36. Burgoon, J. K., Buller, D. B., Floyd, K., & Grandpre, J. (1996). Deceptive realities: Sender, receiver, and observer perspectives in deceptive conversations. *Communication Research, 23,* 724-748.

37. Burgoon, J.K., Buller, D.B., Guerrero, L.K., Afifi, W.A., & Feldman, C.M. (1996). Interpersonal deception: XII. Information management dimensions underlying deceptive and truthful messages. *Communication Monographs, 63,* 50-69.

38. Burgoon, J.K., Buller, D.B., White, C.H., Afifi, W., & Buslig, A.L.S. (1999). The role of conversational involvement in deceptive interpersonal interactions. *Personality and Social Psychology Bulletin, 25,* 669-685.

39. Burgoon, J.K., Stoner, G.M., Bonito, J.A., & Dunbar, N.E. (2003). Trust and deception in mediated communication. Paper presented at the 36th Hawaii conference on system sciences.

40. Cardena, E. (1983). The face of deception: Perception of lying and facial expression. Unpublished M.A. thesis, York University.

41. Cheng, H.C. (1996). A study of baseline familiarity on deception detection: Effects of rehearsal and consequences for lying. Unpublished MA thesis, SUNY-Buffalo Dept. of Communication.

42. Childers, C.D. (1980). An exploration of multiple channel evaulations in attributions of deception. Unpublished M.A. thesis, University of Mississippi.

43. Christensen, D. (1980). Decoding of intended versus unintended nonverbal messages as a function of social skill and anxiety. Unpublished doctoral dissertation, University of Connecticut.

44. Clark, L.M. (1983). Training humans to become better decoders of deception. Unpublished M.A. thesis, University of Georgia.

45. Cogburn, R.K. (1993). A study of psychopathy and its relation to success in interpersonal deception. Unpublished doctoral dissertation, University of Oregon.

46. Dawes, D. H. (1988). Preconscious processing and the detection of deception, Unpublished Ph.D. dissertation, University of Texas.

47. DePaulo, B.M., Blank, A.L., Swain, G.W., & Hairfield, J.G. (1992). Expressiveness and expressive control. *Personality and Social Psychology Bulletin, 18*, 276-285.

48. DePaulo, B. M., Jordan, A., Irvine, A., & Laser, P. S. (1982). Age changes in the detection of deception. *Child Development, 53*, 701-709.

49. DePaulo, B.M., Kirkendol, S.E., Tang, J., & O'Brien, T.P. (1988). The motivational impairment effect in the communication of deception: Replications and extensions. *Journal of Nonverbal Behavior, 12,* 177-202.

50. DePaulo, B. M., Lanier, K., & Davis, T. (1983). Detecting the deceit of the motivated liar. *Journal of Personality and Social Psychology, 45*, 1096-1103.

51. DePaulo, B. M., Lassiter, G. D., & Stone, J. I. (1982). Attentional determinants of success at detecting deception and truth. *Personality and Social Psychology Bulletin, 8*, 273-279.

52. DePaulo, B.M., LeMay, C.S., & Epstein, J.A. (1991). Effects of importance of success and expectations for success on effectiveness at deceiving. *Personality and Social Psychology Bulletin, 17*, 14-24.

53. DePaulo, B.M., & Pfeifer, R.L. (1986). On-the-job experience and skill at detecting deception. *Journal of Applied Social Psychology, 16*, 249-267.

54. DePaulo, B. M., & Rosenthal, R. (1979). Telling lies. *Journal of Personality and Social Psychology, 37*, 1713-1722.

55. DePaulo, B.M., Rosenthal, R., Green, C. R., & Rosenkrantz, J. (1982). Diagnosing deceptive and mixed messages from verbal and nonverbal cues. *Journal of Experimental Social Psychology, 18*, 433-446.

56. DePaulo, B.M., Stone, J.I., & Lassiter, G.D. (1985). Telling ingratiating lies: Effects of target sex and target attractiveness on verbal and nonverbal deceptive success. *Journal of Personality and Social Psychology, 48*, 1191-1203.

57. DePaulo, B.M., & Tang, J. (1994). Social anxiety and social judgment: The example of detecting deception. *Journal of Research in Personality, 28*, 142-153.

58. DePaulo, B.M., Tang, J., & Stone, J.I. (1987). Physical attractiveness and skill at detecting deception. *Personality and Social Psychology Bulletin, 13*, 177-187.

59. DePaulo, P.J., & DePaulo, B.M. (1989). Can deception by salespersons and customers be detected through nonverbal behavioral cues? *Journal of Applied Social Psychology, 19*, 1552-1577.

60. deTurck, M.A. (1991). Training observers to detect spontaneous deception. Effects of gender. *Communication Reports, 4*, 81-89.

61. deTurck, M.A., Feeley, T.H., & Anastasiou, L. (1997). Effects of motivation to deceive and rehearsal on deception detection. Unpublished manuscript.

62. deTurck, M.A., Feeley, T.H., & Roman, L.A. (1997). Vocal and visual cue training in behavioral lie detection. *Communication Research Reports, 14*, 249-259.

63. deTurck, M.A., Harszlak, J.J., Bodhorn, D.J., & Texter, L.A. (1990). The effects of training social perceivers to detect deception from behavioral cues. *Communication Quarterly, 38*, 189-199.

64. deTurck, M.A., & Miller, G.R. (1990). Training observers to detect deception: Effects of self-monitoring and rehearsal. *Human Communication Research, 16*, 603-620.

65. Ekman, P., Frank, M., & O'Sullivan, M. (1994). Detecting deceit from demeanor. Unpublished manuscript. University of California at San Francisco.

66. Ekman, P., & Friesen, W.V. (1974). Detecting deception from the body or face. *Journal of Personality and Social Psychology, 29*, 288-298.

67. Ekman, P., Friesen, W.V., & Simons, R.C. (1985). Is the startle reaction an emotion? *Journal of Personality and Social Psychology, 49*, 1416-1426.

68. Ekman, P., & O'Sullivan, M. (1991). Who can catch a liar? *American Psychologist, 46*, 913-920.

69. Ekman, P., O'Sullivan, M., & Frank, M.G. (1999). A few can catch a liar. *Psychological Science, 10*, 263-266.

70. Elaad, E. (2003). Effects of feedback on the overestimated capacity to detect lies and the underestimated ability to tell lies. *Applied Cognitive Psychology, 17*, 249-263.

71. Elliott, G.L. (1979). Some effects of deception and level of self-monitoring on planning and reacting to a self-presentation. *Journal of Personality and Social Psychology, 37*, 1282-1292.

72. Etcoff, N.L., Ekman, P., Magee, J.J., & Frank, M.G. (2000). Lie detection and language comprehension. *Nature, 405*, 139.

73. Fan, R.M., Wagner, H.L., & Manstead, A.S.R. (1995). Anchoring, familiarity, and confidence in the detection of deception. *Basic and Applied Social Psychology, 17*, 83-96.

74. Fay, P.J., & Middleton, W.C. (1941). The ability to judge truth-telling, or lying, from the voice as transmitted over a public address system. *Journal of Genetic Psychology, 24,* 211-215.

75. Feeley, T.H. (1996). Conversational competence and perceptions of honesty in interpersonal deception. Paper presented at the annual meeting of the Speech Communication Association, San Diego, CA.

76. Feeley, T.H., & deTurck, M.A. (1995). Global cue usage in behavioral lie detection. *Communication Quarterly, 43,* 420-430.

77. Feeley, T.H., & deTurck, M.A. (1997a). Case-relevant vs case-irrelevant questioning in experimental lie detection. *Communication Reports, 10,* 35-45.

78. Feeley, T.H., deTurck, M.A. (1997b). Perceptions of communication as seen by the actor and as seen by the observer: The case of lie detection. Paper presented at the International Communication Association, Montreal, Canada.

79. Feeley, T.H., deTurck, M.A., & Young, M.J. (1995). Baseline familiarity in lie detection. *Communication Research Reports, 12,* 160-169.

80. Ferran-Urdaneta, C., & Storck, J. (1997) Truth or deception: The impact of videoconferencing for job interviews. *Proceedings of the 18th International Conference on Information Systems.* Atlanta, GA.

81. Fiedler, K., Schmid, J., Kurzenhauser, S., & Schroter, V. (1997). Lie detection as an attribution process: The anchoring effect revisited. Unpublished manuscript.

82. Fiedler, K., & Walka, I. (1993). Training lie detectors to use nonverbal cues instead of global heuristics. *Human Communication Research, 20,* 199-223.

83. Fontenot, K.A. (1993). The relationship of conversational sensitivity and employment interview experience to deception detection in employment interviews. Unpublished doctoral dissertation, Louisiana State University.

84. Forrest, J.A. (2001). A social cognitive model of detecting deception. Unpublished Ph.D. dissertation. University of Massachusetts.

85. Forrest, J.A., & Feldman, R.S. (2000). Detecting deception and judge's involvement: Lower task involvement leads to better lie detection. *Personality and Social Psychology Bulletin, 26,* 118-125.

86. Fraidin, S.N., Hollingshead, A.B., & Kruger, J. (2002). Effects of suspicion on perceptions, judgments, and truth bias in lie detection. Paper presented at the annual meeting of the Midwestern Psychological Association, Chicago.

87. Frank, M.G. (1989). Human lie detection ability as a function of the liar's motivation. Unpublished doctoral dissertation, Cornell University.

88. Frank, M.G., & Ekman, P. (1997). The ability to detect deceit generalizes across different types of high-stakes lies. *Journal of Personality and Social Psychology, 72,* 1429-1439.

89. Frank, M.G., Paolantonio, N., Feeley, T.H., & Servoss, T.J. (2004). Individual and small group accuracy in judging truthful and deceptive communication. *Group Decision and Negotiation, 13,* 45-59.

90. Fugita, S.S., Hogrebe, M.C., & Wexley, K.N. (1980). Perceived expertise in detecting deception, successfulness of deception and nonverbal cues. *Personality and Social Psychology Bulletin, 6,* 637-643.

91. Galarza, L. (1996). On the accuracy of detecting deception in selection interviews: The effects of applicant rehearsal, applicant job interest, and self-monitoring. Unpublished M.A. thesis, Rice University.

92. Garrido, E., & Masip J. (2001). Previous exposure to the sender's behavior and accuracy at judging credibility. In R. Roesch, R.R. Corrado, & Dempster, R. (Eds.) *Psychology in the courts* (pp. 271-287). London: Routledge.

93. Geis, F.L., & Moon, T.H. (1981). Machiavellianism and deception. *Journal of Personality and Social Psychology, 41,* 766-775.

94. Geizer, R.S., Rarick, D.L., & Soldow, G.F. (1977). Deception and judgment accuracy: A study in person perception. *Personality and Social Psychology Bulletin, 3,* 446-449.

95. George, J.F., Marett, K., Burgoon, J.K., Crews, J., Cao, J., Lin, M., & Biros, D.P. (2004). Training to detect deception: An experimental investigation. *Proceedings of the 37th Hawaii International Conference on System Sciences.* Big Island, HI.

96. Gilovich, T., Savitsky, K., & Medvec, V.H. (1998). The illusion of transparency: Biased assessments of others' ability to read one's emotional states. *Journal of Personality and Social Psychology, 75,* 332-346.

97. Goldenberg, E.I. (1996). Emotion and perceived transparency in the context of lying versus honesty. Unpublished honours thesis, University of Manitoba.

98. Granhag, P.A., & Strömwall, L.A. (2001). Deception detection based on repeated interrogations. *Legal & Criminological Psychology, 6,* 85-101.

99. Hall, S. (1989). The generalizability of learning to detect deception in effective and ineffective deceivers. Unpublished Ph.D. thesis, Auburn University.

100. Harrison, A.A., Hwalek, M., Raney, D., & Fritz, J.G. (1978). Cues to deception in an interview situation. *Social Psychology, 41,* 156-161.

101. Hartwig, M., Granhag, P.A., Stromwall, L.A., & Andersson, L.O. (2002). Suspicious minds: Criminals' ability to detect deception. Paper presented at 12th European Conference on Psychology and Law: Leuven, Belgium: September 2002.

102. Hartwig, M., Granhag, P.A., Strömwall, L.A., & Vrij, A. (2002). Deception detection: Effects of conversational involvement and probing. *Göteborg Psychological Reports, 32,* 1-12.

103. Hartwig, M., Granhag, P.A., Strömwall, L.A., & Vrij, A. (2004). Police officers' lie detection accuracy: Interrogating freely versus observing video. *Police Quarterly, 7,* 429-456.

104. Heinrich, C.U., & Borkenau, P. (1998). Deception and deception detection: The role of cross-modal inconsistency. *Journal of Personality, 66,* 687-711.

105. Hemsley, G.D. (1977). Experimental studies in the behavioral indicants of deception. Unpublished doctoral dissertation, University of Toronto.

106. Hendershot, J. (1981). Detection of deception in low and high socialization subjects with trained and untrained judges. Unpublished M.S. thesis, Auburn University.

107. Hess, U., & Kleck, R.E. (1994). The cues decoders use in attempting to differentiate emotion-elicited and posed facial expressions. *European Journal of Social Psychology, 24,* 367-381.

108. Hocking, J.E., Bauchner, J., Kaminski, E.P., & Miller, G.R. (1979). Detecting deceptive communication from verbal, visual, and paralinguistic cues. *Human Communication Research, 6,* 33-46.

109. Horn, D.B. (2001). Seeing is believing: Video quality and lie detection. Unpublished Ph.D. dissertation, University of Michigan.

110. Hubbell, A.P., Mitchell, M.M., & Gee, J.C. (2001). The relative effects of timing of suspicion and outcome involvement on biased message processing. *Communication Monographs, 68,* 115-132.

111. Hughes, S.D. (1997). The truth 'bias' in judging acquaintances. Unpublished M.S. thesis, Texas Christian University.

112. Hurd, K., & Noller, P. (1988). Decoding deception: A look at the process. *Journal of Nonverbal Behavior, 12,* 217-233.

113. Johnson, A.K, et al (2005). Me, myself, and lie: The role of self-awareness in deception. *Personality and Individual Differences, 38,* 1847-1853.

114. Kassin, S.M., & Fong, C.T. (1999). "I'm innocent!": Effects of training on judgments of truth and deception in the interrogation room. *Law & Human Behavior, 23,* 499-516.

115. Kassin, S.A., Meissner, C.A., & Norwick, R.J. (2002). "I'd know a false confession if I saw one": A comparative study of college students and police investigators. *Law and Human Behavior, 29,* 211-227.

116. Kirk, C.T. (1993). A nonspecific factor in deception judgments. Unpublished M.S. thesis, Texas Christian University.

117. Koehnken, G. (1987). Training police officers to detect deceptive eyewitness statements: Does it work? *Social Behaviour, 2,* 1-17.

118. Kraut, R.E. (1978). Verbal and nonverbal cues in the perception of lying. *Journal of Personality and Social Psychology, 36,* 380-391.

119. Kraut, R.E., & Poe, D. (1980). Behavioral roots of person perception: The deception judgments of customs inspectors and laymen. *Journal of Personality and Social Psychology, 39,* 784-798.

120. Kurasawa, T. (1988). Effects of contextual expectancies on deception-detection. *Japanese Psychological Research, 30,* 114-121.

121. Landry, K.L., & Brigham, J.C. (1992). The effect of training in Criteria-Based Content Analysis on the ability to detect deception in adults. *Law and Human Behavior, 16,* 663-676.

122. Lane, J.D., & DePaulo, B.M. (1999). Completing Coyne's cycle: Dysphorics' ability to detect deception. *Journal of Research in Personality, 33,* 311-329.

123. Lashley, B.R. (1993). Anxiety cues versus verbal-nonverbal inconsistency: Two factors in deception judgments. Unpublished M.S. thesis, Texas Christian University.

124. Lavrakas, P.J., & Maier, R.A. (1979). Differences in human ability to judge veracity from the audio medium. *Journal of Research in Personality, 13,* 139-153.

125. Lee, C.C. (2000). The effect of levels of probing on the detection of deception in audit oral evidence. Unpublished doctoral dissertation, Southern Illinois University.

126. Lee, C.C. & Welker, R.B. (2002). Professional skepticism and the detection of intentional oral misrepresentation. Working paper, Florida International University.

127. Levine, T.R., Anders, L.N., et al (2000). Norms, expectations, and deception: A norm violation model of veracity judgments. *Communication Monographs, 67,* 123-137.

128. Levine, T.R., & McCornack, S.A. (2001). Behavioral adaptation, confidence, and heuristic-based explanations of the probing effect. *Human Communication Research, 27,* 471-502.

129. Levine, T.R., Park, H.S., & McCornack, S.A. (1999). Accuracy in detecting truths and lies: Documenting the "veracity effect". *Communication Monographs, 66,* 125-144.

130. Lin , Y.C. (1999). A study of training on deception detection: The effects of the specific six cues versus heuristics on deception detection accuracy. Unpublished M.A. thesis, SUNY-Buffalo.

131. Littlepage, G.E., McKinnie, R., & Pineault, M.A. (1983). Relationship between nonverbal sensitivities and detection of deception. *Perceptual and Motor Skills, 57,* 651-657.

132. Littlepage, G.E., Maddox, J., & Pineault, M.A. (1985). Recognition of discrepant nonverbal messages and detection of deception. *Perceptual and Motor Skills, 60,* 119-124.

133. Littlepage, G.E., & Pineault, M.A. (1979). Detection of deceptive factual statements from the body and the face. *Personality and Social Psychology Bulletin, 5,* 325-328.

134. Littlepage, G.E., & Pineault, M.A. (1981). Detection of truthful and deceptive interpersonal communications across information transmission modes. *Journal of Social Psychology, 114,* 57-68.

135. Littlepage, G.E., & Pineault, M.A. (1985). Detection of deception of planned versus spontaneous communications. *Journal of Social Psychology, 125,* 195-201.

136. Littlepage, G.E., & Pineault, T. (1978). Verbal, facial, and paralinguistic cues to the detection of truth and lying. *Personality and Social Psychology Bulletin, 4,* 461-464.

137. Littlepage, G.E., Tang, D.W., & Pineault, M.A. (1986). Nonverbal and content factors in the detection of deception in planned and spontaneous communications. *Journal of Social Behavior and Personality, 1,* 439-450.

138. Lusby, D. J. (1999). Effects of motivation to lie and sanctioned deception of the accuracy of observers' veracity judgments. Unpublished M.A. thesis, SUNY-Buffalo.

139. Malcolm, S.R., & Keenan, J.P. (2005). Hemispheric asymmetry and deception detection. *Laterality, 10,* 103-110.

140. Mann, S., Vrij, A., & Bull, R. (2004). Detecting true lies: Police officers' ability to detect suspects' lies. *Journal of Applied Psychology, 89*, 137-149.

141. Manstead, A.S., Wagner, H.L., & MacDonald, C.J. (1984). Face, body, and speech as channels of communication in the detection of deception. *Basic and Applied Social Psychology, 5*, 317-332.

142. Manstead, A.S.R., Wagner, H.L., & MacDonald, C.J. (1986). Deceptive and nondeceptive communications: Sending experience, modality, and individual abilities. *Journal of Nonverbal Behavior, 10*, 147-167.

143. Masip, J. (2002). Credibility assessment of the testimony on the basis of behavioral indicators in criminal justice settings. Unpublished doctoral dissertation, University of Salamanca.

144. Masip, J., Garrido, E., & Herrero, C. (In press). Observers' decision moment in deception detection experiments: Its impact on judgment, accuracy and confidence. *International Journal of Psychology.*

145. Masip, J., Garrido, E., & Herrero, C. (2003). Statement length and credibility judgments: Questioning the truth bias. Paper presented at the Psychology and Law International Interdisciplinary Conference, Edinburgh.

146. Meissner, C.A., & Kassin, S.M. (2002). "He's guilty:" Investigator bias and judgments of truth and deception. *Law and Human Behavior, 26*, 469-480.

147. Millar, M., & Millar, K. (1995). Detection of deception in familiar and unfamiliar persons: The effects of information restriction. *Journal of Nonverbal Behavior, 19*, 69-84.

148. Millar, M.G., & Millar, K. (1997a). Effects of situational variables on judgments about deception and detection accuracy. *Basic and Applied Social Psychology, 19*, 401-410.

149. Millar, M.G., & Millar, K.U. (1997b). The effects of cognitive capacity and suspicion on truth bias. *Communication Research, 24*, 556-570.

150. Miller, G.R., & Fontes, N.E. (1979). *Videotape on trial: A view from the jury box.* Beverly Hills, CA: Sage.

151. Miller, G.R., deTurk, M.A., & Kalbfleisch, P.J. (1983). Self-monitoring, rehearsal, and deceptive communication. *Human Communication Research, 10*, 97-117.

152. Morris, K.A. (2003). Teaching students about classic findings on the detection of deception. *Teaching of Psychology, 30,* 111-113.

153. Motley, M.T. (1974). Acoustic correlates of lies. *Western Speech, 38*, 81-87.

154. Murray, J. (1983). The detection of interviewees' verbal deceptions from their accompanying overt nonverbal behavior. Unpublished doctoral dissertation, Florida State University.

155. Nance, C.H. (1993). The effect of specificity of experience on the ability to detect deception in same- and other-race target persons. Unpublished M.S. thesis, Florida State University.

156. Nance, C.H. (1995). The effects of high versus low context congruity on accuracy in detecting deception. Unpublished Ph.D. dissertation, Florida State University.

157. Oberleitner, D., McLarney-Vesotski, A., Bernieri, F., & Okdie, B. (2004). Musical mood induction and its effects on lie detection accuracy. Paper presented at the annual meeting of the Society for Personality and Social Psychology, Austin, TX.

158. Oldfield, S.E. (1999). The influence of self-monitoring on the detection of deception. Unpublished MA thesis, Radford University.

159. O'Sullivan, M. (2003). The fundamental attribution error in detecting deception: The boy-who-cried-wolf effect. *Personality and Social Psychology Bulletin, 29,* 1316-1327.

160. O'Sullivan, M., Ekman, P., & Friesen, W.V. (1988). The effect of comparisons on detecting deceit. *Journal of Nonverbal Behavior, 12,* 203-215.

161. Park, E.S., Levine, T.R., Harms, C.M., & Ferrara, M.H. (2002). Group and individual accuracy in deception detection. *Communication Research Reports, 19,* 99-106.

162. Parker, R.J. (1978). Age, sex, and the detection of deception through nonverbal cues. Unpublished doctoral dissertation, California School of Professional Psychology.

163. Pietras, K.R., & Bond, C.F., Jr. (1985). The reliability of lie detection judgments. Paper presented at the annual meeting of the Eastern Psychological Association, Boston, MA.

164. Porter, S., Campbell, M.A., Stapleton, J., & Birt, A.R. (2002). The influence of judge, target, and stimulus characteristics on the accuracy of detecting deceit. *Canadian Journal of Behavioural Science, 34,* 172-185.

165. Porter, S., Woodworth, M., & Birt, A.R. (2000). Truth, lies, and videotape: An investigation of the ability of federal parole officers to detect deception. *Law & Human Behavior, 24,* 643-658.

166. Potamkin, G.G. (1982). Heroin addicts and nonaddicts: The use and detection of nonverbal deception cues. Unpublished doctoral dissertation, California School of Professional Psychology.

167. Raichle, W. (1990). The roles of verbal and nonverbal behavior in impression formation during an employment interview. Unpublished doctoral dissertation, New York University.

168. Riggio, R.E., & Friedman, H.S. (1983). Individual differences and cues to deception. *Journal of Personality and Social Psychology, 45,* 899-915.

169. Riggio, R.E., Tucker, J., & Throckmorton, B. (1987). Social skills and deception ability. *Personality and Social Psychology Bulletin, 13,* 568-577.

170. Rockwell, P. (1996). Hemispheric differences in detection of deception with content-filtered speech. *Perceptual and Motor Skills, 82,* 1241-1242.

171. Rotkin, H.G. (1980). Information used in detecting deception. Unpublished doctoral dissertation, New York University.

172. Rudin, J.P. (1999). Effect of reward size in performance of a deception detection task. Proceedings of the annual meeting of the Southwest Academy of Management (pp. 182-184). Houston.

173. Rudin, J.P., & Wazeter, D. (1998). Employment interviewers as lie detectors: More harm than good? *Central Business Review, 17*, 32-36.

174. Russo-Devosa, Y.M. (1999). The credibility of adult and child witnesses: Implications for detecting deception in child sexual abuse cases. Unpublished MS thesis, Pennsylvania State University.

175. Sahlman, J.M., & Koper, R.J. (1992). Do you hear what I hear? Deception detection by the blind. Paper presented at the annual meeting of the International Communication Association, Miami: May 1992.

176. Sakai, D.J. (1981). Nonverbal communication in the detection of deception among women and men. Unpublished doctoral dissertation, University of California, Davis.

177. Schoephoerster, B.T. (1996). Deception detection accuracy: The effects of suspicion and antisocial personality traits. Unpublished MA thesis, University of Nevada at Las Vegas.

178. Seager, P.B. (2001). Improving the ability of people to detect lies. Unpublished doctoral dissertation, University of Hertfordshire.

179. Seiter, J. S. (1997). Honest or deceitful? A study of persons' mental models for judging veracity. *Human Communication Research, 24,* 216-259.

180. Skaggs, L.M. (1993). The effects of behavior coordination on judgments of deception. Unpublished M.S. thesis, Texas Christian University.

181. Steinberg, J.R., & Bernieri, F. (2001). How locus of control affects accuracy of detecting deception. Paper presented at the annual meeting of the American Psychological Society, Toronto, CA.

182. Stiff, J.B., & Miller, G.R. (1986). "Come to think of it...": Interrogative probes, deceptive communication, and deception detection. *Human Communication Research, 12,* 339-357.

183. Streeter, L.A., Krauss, R.M., Geller, V., Olsen, C., & Apple, W. (1977). Pitch changes during attempted deception. *Journal of Personality and Social Psychology, 35,* 345-350.

184. Strömwall, L.A., Granhag, P.A., & Jonsson, A.C. (2003). Deception among pairs: "Let's say we had lunch and hope they will swallow it!" *Psychology, Crime, and Law, 9,* 109-124.

185. Swann, W.B., Jr., Silvera, D.H., & Proske, C.U. (1995). On "knowing your partner": Dangerous illusions in the age of AIDS? *Personal Relationships, 2,* 173-186.

186. Swinkels, A.H. (1989). The effects of cognitive busyness on human lie detection ability. Unpublished Ph.D. dissertation, University of Texas at Austin.

187. Taylor, R. (1999) Relationships between accuracy of detecting deception and beliefs about the cues involved. Paper presented at the Division of Forensic Psychology Annual Conference. Cambridge.

188. Toris, C., & DePaulo, B.M. (1984). Effects of actual deception and suspiciousness of deception on interpersonal perceptions. *Journal of Personality and Social Psychology, 47*, 1063-1073.

189. Tornqvist, J.S. (2002) The detectability and believability of lies and truths in the e-mail medium. Unpublished Ph.D. dissertation, University of Virginia.

190. Vrij, A. (1993). Credibility judgments of detectives: The impact of nonverbal behavior, social skills, and physical characteristics on impression formation. *Journal of Social Psychology, 133,* 601-610.

191. Vrij, A. (1994). The impact of information and setting on detection of deception by police detectives. *Journal of Nonverbal Behavior, 18,* 117-136.

192. Vrij, A., & Baxter, M. (1999). Accuracy and confidence in detecting truths and lies in elaborations and denials: Truth bias, lie bias and individual differences. *Expert Evidence, 7,* 25-36.

193. Vrij, A., Edward, K., & Bull, R. (2001). Police officers' ability to detect deceit: The benefit of indirect deception detection measures. *Legal & Criminological Psychology, 6,* 185-196.

194. Vrij, A., & Graham, S. (1997). Individual differences between liars and the ability to detect lies. *Expert Evidence, 5,* 144-148.

195. Vrij, A., Harden, F., Terry, J., Edward, K., & Bull, R. (2001). The influence of personal characteristics, stakes and lie complexity on the accuracy and confidence to detect deceit. In R. Roesch, R.R. Corrado, and R. Dempster (Eds.) *Psychology in the courts* (pp. 289-302). London: Routledge.

196. Wetzel, C., Addison, S., & Mueller, J. (2005). Detecting imposters: To tell the truth, we don't do it well. Unpublished manuscript, Rhodes College.

197. Williams, D. (1989). Effects of familiarity and communication mode on the detection of deception. Unpublished M.A. thesis, University of West Florida.

198. Wilson, S.J. (1975). Channel differences in the detection of deception. Unpublished doctoral dissertation, Florida State University.

199. Yang, C.C. (1996). The effects of training, rehearsal, and consequences for lying on deception detection accuracy. Unpublished M.A. thesis, SUNY-Buffalo.

200. Zuckerman, M., Amidon, M.D., Bishop, S.E., & Pomerantz, S.D. (1982). Face and tone of voice in the communication of deception. *Journal of Personality and Social Psychology, 43,* 347-357.

201. Zuckerman, M., DeFrank, R.S., Hall, J.A., Larrance, D.T., & Rosenthal, R. (1979). Facial and vocal cues of deception and honesty. *Journal of Experimental Social Psychology, 15,* 378-396.

202. Zuckerman, M., Driver, R., & Guadagno, N.S. (1985). Effects of segmentation patterns on the perception of deception. *Journal of Nonverbal Behavior, 9,* 160-168.

203. Zuckerman, M., Fischer, S.A., Osmun, R.W., Winkler, B.A., & Wolfson, L.R. (1987). Anchoring in lie detection revisited. *Journal of Nonverbal Behavior, 11,* 4-12.

204. Zuckerman, M., Koestner, R., & Alton, A.O. (1984). Learning to detect deception. *Journal of Personality and Social Psychology, 46,* 519-528.

205. Zuckerman, M., Koestner, R., & Colella, M.J. (1985). Learning to detect deception from three communication channels. *Journal of Nonverbal Behavior, 9*, 188-194.

206. Zuckerman, M., Koestner, R., Colella, M.J., & Alton, A.O. (1984). Anchoring in the detection of deception and leakage. *Journal of Personality and Social Psychology, 47*, 301-311.

Appendix B

Coding of the 206 Documents

Doc#	Send#	Rec#	Truth%	Acc%	d	Med	Mot	Prep	Base	Inter	Exp
1	72	72		52.31		2	0	0	0	0	0
1	72	72		48.88		1	0	0	0	0	0
1	72	72		54.22		3	0	0	0	0	0
2	200	200	51.50	58.50		3	0	0	0	0	0
3	52	8		50.60	0.414	3	0	0	0	2	0
4	8	69	50.70	60.50		3	1	1	0	2	0
5	8	24	47.96	53.62		1	0	1	0	2	0
6	30	25	58.94	59.07		3	0	1	0	2	0
6	30	25	56.18	58.33		3	0	1	0	2	0
7	12	60		45.48		4	1	0	0	2	0
8	8	30		52.81		1	0	0	0	2	0
9	60	150		56.83	0.602	3	1	1	0	0	0
10	10	25		67.50		3	1	0	1	2	0
11	32	20	48.60	52.76		2	0	0	0	0	0
11	32	20	52.17	51.02		3	0	0	0	0	0
11	32	20	49.53	51.51		1	0	0	0	0	0
11	32	40	60.31	57.27		2	0	0	0	0	0
11	32	40	60.14	53.60		3	0	0	0	0	0
11	32	40	51.85	48.92		1	0	0	0	0	0
11	32	40	56.54	51.08		1	2	0	0	0	0
11	32	40	57.02	49.53		2	2	0	0	0	0
11	32	40	57.49	54.35		3	2	0	0	0	0
12	32	2	53.00	56.00		3	0	0	0	0	0
12	32	45	49.63	49.79		3	0	0	0	0	0
13	32	34	49.26	63.46		3	1	0	0	2	0
14	48	40	57.39	53.54		3	0	0	0	0	0
15	24	48	57.17	51.97		1	0	0	0	0	0
15	24	48	54.92	54.80		1	0	0	0	0	0
16	48	40	67.42	55.15		3	0	0	0	0	0
16	48	192	56.08	50.12		1	0	0	0	0	0
17	48	67	57.40	47.70		5	0	0	0	0	0
18	16	15	57.62	60.42		3	1	0	0	0	0
19	48	40	52.58	46.85		1	0	0	0	0	0
19	48	50	52.93	48.60		2	0	0	0	0	0
19	48	40	55.00	48.13		3	0	0	0	0	0
19	48	196	55.64	48.57		3	0	0	0	0	0
19	32	14	54.69	51.56		3	0	0	0	0	0
20	12	12	45.85	48.63		3	0	1	0	1	1
20	15	15	42.20	58.90		3	0	1	0	1	1

20	15	15	76.65	53.35		3	0	1	0	1	0
21	36	36	35.44	49.98		3	0	0	0	1	1
21	36	36	61.48	58.68		3	0	0	0	1	0
22	56	56	53.00	60.00		3	0	0	0	1	1
22	56	56	74.75	51.50		3	0	0	0	1	0
23	48	31	46.64	53.00		3	1	1	0	0	0
23	48	31		49.98		3	1	1	0	0	0
23	48	33	46.72	50.59		3	1	1	0	2	0
23	48	31		50.13		3	1	1	0	2	0
24	15	48	52.26	53.46		3	0	0	0	0	0
25	4	50		42.00		3	1	0	0	2	0
26	16	50		44.50		3	1	0	0	2	0
27	16	66		41.65	-0.379	3	1	0	0	2	0
28	40	20			1.410	3	0	0	0	1	1
29	8	124	59.59	57.09		3	0	1	0	2	1
30	2	92	52.00	60.00		3	0	0	0	2	0
31	2	50	76.00	55.00		3	0	0	0	2	0
31	2	150	60.00	59.00		3	0	0	0	2	0
32	17	17	82.35	45.14	-0.471	3	1	0	0	2	0
32	17	17	70.59	57.64	0.876	2	1	0	0	2	0
32	17	17	47.06	35.42	0.013	5	1	0	0	2	0
33	60	60			0.365	3	0	0	1	1	0
34	18	18			0.646	3	0	1	0	1	0
34	19	19			0.399	3	0	1	0	1	1
35	16	16			0.278	3	0	0	1	1	0
36	13	13			0.620	3	0	0	0	1	0
36	10	10			0.000	3	0	0	0	2	0
37	106	2			1.195	3	0	4	0	2	0
38	61	61			0.498	3	0	1	0	1	0
39	16	16			0.099	3	0	0	0	1	0
39	16	16			0.796	3	0	0	0	2	0
39	16	16			0.695	2	0	0	0	2	0
39	16	16			-0.453	5	0	0	0	2	0
40	10	36	52.04	52.58		1	0	0	0	2	0
41	12	100		54.00		3	2	4	2	2	0
42	5	16	52.49	71.27		3	0	0	0	2	1
42	5	122	54.98	60.24		3	0	0	0	2	0
42	5	151	54.62	71.00		3	0	0	0	2	0
43	12	38	59.48	59.42		3	0	0	0	2	0
43	12	46	57.82	58.83		3	0	0	0	2	0
43	12	19	70.91	48.24		3	0	0	0	2	0
44	20	46	54.89	67.49		3	0	0	1	2	0
45	52	9			0.120	3	1	0	0	2	0
46	8	20	67.88	56.63		3	0	0	0	0	0
47	32	115			-0.060	1	1	1	0	0	0
47	32	115			0.110	5	1	1	0	0	0
47	32	115			0.230	2	1	1	0	0	0
47	32	115			0.240	3	1	1	0	0	0
48	8	43			0.311	3	0	1	0	0	0
49	131	74			0.361	3	1	1	0	0	0
50	32	24			0.620	3	1	4	0	1	0
50	32	64			0.583	1	1	4	0	2	0
51	12	11			-0.258	3	0	1	0	0	0
52	96	3			0.307	3	1	1	0	1	0
52	96	816			0.375	5	1	1	0	2	0

53	16	114	60.20	52.30		2	1	4	0	2	1
53	16	144	61.00	52.90		2	1	4	0	2	1
53	16	161	62.00	54.30		2	1	4	0	2	0
54	40	40			0.810	3	0	1	0	0	0
55	40	16			0.040	1	0	1	0	0	0
55	40	16			-0.130	2	0	1	0	0	0
55	40	16			0.270	5	0	1	0	0	0
55	40	16			0.310	3	0	1	0	0	0
55	40	16			0.570	2	0	1	0	0	0
56	64	271			0.164	3	1	1	0	0	0
57	64	102			0.360	3	1	1	0	0	0
58	64	102			0.340	3	1	1	0	0	0
59	14	107			0.001	3	1	1	0	0	0
60	16	91		58.97		3	1	0	0	2	0
61	12	198		52.17		3	1	4	0	2	0
62	8	41	48.50	57.50		3	1	0	1	2	0
63	8	94		54.00		3	1	0	1	2	0
64	32	195		50.00		3	1	4	0	2	0
65	20	43	39.05	62.80		3	2	1	0	2	1
65	30	23	43.05	61.60		3	2	1	0	2	1
66	16	113	46.63	46.16		1	1	0	0	2	0
66	16	120	45.21	52.27		1	1	0	0	2	0
67	14	98		60.00		1	0	4	0	2	0
68	10	39		52.82		3	1	0	0	2	0
68	10	34		64.12		3	1	0	0	2	1
68	10	73		55.34		3	1	0	0	2	1
68	10	67		57.61		3	1	0	0	2	1
68	10	60		55.67		3	1	0	0	2	1
68	10	110		56.73		3	1	0	0	2	1
68	10	126		55.79		3	1	0	0	2	1
69	10	36	53.05	50.80		3	2	1	0	2	1
69	10	84	51.10	62.00		3	2	1	0	2	1
69	10	125	50.70	57.70		3	2	1	0	2	0
69	10	107	46.45	67.50		3	2	1	0	2	1
69	10	209	47.75	62.10		3	2	1	0	2	1
70	8	60	49.60	45.60		3	1	1	0	0	1
71	64	6			0.000	3	1	1	0	1	0
72	10	10		47.00		3	1	0	0	2	0
72	10	48		46.00		3	1	0	0	2	0
73	14	56	55.50	58.00		3	1	0	0	2	0
74	6	47	44.53	55.75		2	0	0	0	2	0
75	95	95	82.25	50.75		3	0	0	1	1	0
76	12	50	59.00	63.00		3	0	0	1	2	0
77	4	30		65.00		3	0	0	1	2	0
78	95	95	74.25	55.75		3	0	0	0	2	0
79	4	52	59.05	59.50		3	0	0	2	2	0
80	30	28	86.36	58.39		4	1	0	0	1	0
81	12	32			0.800	3	0	1	0	2	0
82	10	24	52.50	53.00	0.613	3	0	1	0	2	0
83	2	80	60.04	54.97		3	1	4	0	2	1
83	2	150	53.24	57.57		3	1	4	0	2	0
84	16	68	60.85	55.33	0.513	3	0	1	0	0	0
84	30	40			0.355	3	1	0	0	2	0
85	16	60			0.493	3	1	1	0	0	0
86	24	46			0.030	3	1	1	0	0	0

86	24	55	57.05	55.85		3	1	1	0	0	0
87	5	45	50.80	47.00		3	1	0	0	2	0
87	5	44	50.80	50.00		3	1	0	0	2	0
87	5	38		51.00		3	1	0	0	2	0
87	5	38		48.00		2	1	0	0	2	0
87	5	38		46.80		3	1	0	0	2	0
87	5	40		47.00		1	1	0	0	2	0
87	5	40		45.00		1	0	0	0	2	0
87	32	37		55.50		3	1	1	0	0	0
87	32	37		55.50		3	1	1	0	0	0
88	20	30		59.50		3	2	1	0	2	0
88	20	48		58.50		3	2	1	0	2	0
89	10	54	52.80	56.10		3	2	1	0	2	0
89	10	165	49.45	59.60		3	2	1	0	2	0
90	40	2	52.81	60.88		3	0	0	0	1	0
91	56	108	67.75	53.75		3	1	4	0	2	0
92	1	121	29.00	47.50		3	1	1	0	0	1
92	1	146	42.50	58.50		3	1	1	0	0	0
93	64	64			0.839	3	1	0	0	2	0
94	12	50			0.180	3	1	1	0	2	0
95	36	86		59.50		5	0	0	0	2	0
95	6	85		51.83		5	0	0	0	2	0
95	36	29		58.11		5	0	0	0	2	0
96	4	5		54.36		3	0	0	0	1	0
97	56	56			0.300	3	0	0	0	1	0
98	24	22	78.33	61.67		3	0	1	0	2	0
98	24	144	54.88	59.70		3	0	1	0	2	0
99	14	81	53.07	53.36		3	1	0	0	0	0
99	8	281		58.00		3	1	0	0	0	0
99	46	90	52.00	57.50		3	1	0	0	0	0
100	72	72	63.72	61.28		3	0	0	0	2	0
101	20	52	42.30	57.70		3	0	1	0	2	0
101	20	52	26.90	65.40		3	0	1	0	2	1
102	40	40	45.00	50.00		3	1	1	0	2	0
102	40	40	57.50	47.50		3	1	1	0	2	0
102	40	40	57.50	62.50		3	1	1	0	2	0
103	30	30	50.00	56.67		3	1	1	0	2	1
104	40	8			0.947	3	0	1	0	0	0
104	40	4			0.093	1	0	1	0	0	0
104	40	4			1.250	2	0	1	0	0	0
105	20	1		60.75		3	0	1	0	1	0
105	20	20	70.85	51.88		3	0	1	0	2	0
105	20	1		57.25		3	0	1	0	1	0
106	16	14	44.75	49.75		3	0	1	0	2	0
106	16	14	48.65	47.35		3	0	1	0	2	1
107	35	40	56.25	58.25	1.610	1	0	4	0	0	0
108	16	40	47.21	54.30		2	1	1	0	2	0
108	16	47	47.21	57.40		5	1	1	0	2	0
108	16	96	44.30	48.40		1	1	1	0	2	0
108	16	103	47.21	54.40		3	1	1	0	2	0
108	16	107	43.32	46.80		1	1	1	0	2	0
108	16	108	47.21	55.60		3	1	1	0	2	0
108	16	109	47.21	53.20		3	1	1	0	2	0
108	16	109	47.21	48.60		1	1	1	0	2	0
109	6	42			0.717	4	1	0	1	2	0

109	6	113			0.794	4	1	0	1	2	0
110	1	249	62.00	46.50		3	0	0	0	0	0
111	29	29			0.665	3	0	0	0	0	0
112	8	19	55.78	50.78		3	0	1	0	0	0
113	12	42		55.15		3	0	1	0	0	0
114	16	18	43.75	55.63		3	1	1	0	2	0
114	16	1		37.50		3	1	1	0	2	0
1156	10	48	58.65	45.35		3	0	0	0	2	1
1156	10	50	51.45	53.60		3	0	0	0	2	0
1156	10	29	65.50	54.50		2	0	0	0	2	1
1156	10	32	56.00	64.00		2	0	0	0	2	0
116	48	24	57.46	54.51		3	0	0	0	0	0
117	4	20	65.50	47.00		3	1	1	1	0	1
118	5	41			0.960	3	1	0	1	2	0
119	62	49			-0.510	3	1	0	0	2	0
119	62	39			-0.280	3	1	0	0	2	1
120	8	20			0.671	3	0	0	0	0	0
121	12	24	65.45	51.90		3	0	1	0	0	0
121	12	26	60.51	47.22		5	0	1	0	0	0
122	4	39	83.02	58.00		2	1	1	0	2	0
123	48	40	58.10	56.30		3	0	0	0	0	0
123	48	40	51.39	48.58		1	0	0	0	0	0
124	20	100		54.45		2	0	4	0	0	0
125	20	120	57.35	55.65		3	1	1	0	2	0
126	22	66	50.00	58.00		3	1	1	0	2	1
126	22	110	31.00	51.00		3	1	1	0	2	0
127	4	128			0.114	3	0	1	0	1	0
128	8	337	72.00	52.75		3	0	1	0	2	0
128	2	71	64.25	52.25		3	0	1	0	2	0
128	2	136	68.77	57.99		3	0	1	0	2	0
129	2	58	68.00	50.64		3	0	1	0	2	0
129	2	60	70.00	51.88		3	0	1	0	2	0
129	2	59	65.00	46.44		3	0	1	0	2	0
130	96	100		51.00		3	2	0	1	2	0
131	4	61	58.16	57.70		3	0	0	0	2	0
132	4	60	58.30	58.90		3	0	0	0	2	0
133	2	32	53.88	64.20		4	0	0	0	2	0
134	4	20	58.00	56.10		5	0	0	0	2	0
134	4	20	53.00	62.50		2	0	0	0	2	0
134	4	21	59.00	49.40		1	0	0	0	2	0
134	4	22	54.00	58.80		5	0	0	0	2	0
134	4	26	56.00	63.50		3	0	0	0	2	0
135	12	32	75.30	55.68		3	0	4	0	2	0
136	6	25			0.682	2	1	0	0	2	0
136	6	23			0.696	3	1	0	0	2	0
136	6	17			0.398	5	1	0	0	2	0
136	6	16			-0.213	1	1	0	0	2	0
137	4	26	74.28	51.70		2	0	4	0	2	0
137	4	36	80.21	51.40		5	0	4	0	2	0
137	4	36	60.94	52.92		1	0	4	0	2	0
138	24	24		31.00		3	1	0	1	2	0
138	24	72		53.67		3	0	0	1	2	0
139	2	32	64.62	58.87		2	0	1	0	0	0
140	14	99	46.54	64.89		3	1	3	0	2	1
141	4	43			0.314	3	0	1	0	0	0

141	2	43			-0.501	3	0	1	0	0	0
141	2	16			-0.484	3	0	1	0	0	0
141	2	16			0.693	3	0	1	0	0	0
141	4	15			-0.589	1	0	1	0	0	0
141	2	15			-1.033	1	0	1	0	0	0
142	36	36			0.315	4	0	1	0	0	0
143	24	54	54.63	54.32		3	1	1	0	0	0
144	1	224	27.48	51.48		2	1	1	0	0	1
145	24	52	52.57	55.13		3	1	1	0	0	0
146	16	44	35.50	47.50		3	1	1	0	2	1
147	31	53		50.00		4	0	1	0	0	0
147	27	58		54.50		4	0	1	0	0	0
148	8	242	70.00	49.00		3	1	0	0	2	0
149	12	107	86.00	49.00		3	1	0	0	0	0
150	16	94		53.23		3	1	1	0	2	0
150	16	99		53.43		3	1	1	0	2	0
151	32	151		51.00		3	1	4	1	2	0
152	82	82		44.84		3	0	1	0	1	0
153	17	10		48.79		2	0	0	0	2	0
154	16	48	48.39	59.04		1	0	0	0	2	0
155	16	189		50.25	0.630	3	0	1	0	0	0
156	8	150	62.00	47.00	0.032	3	1	1	0	2	0
156	8	147	55.50	39.50	-0.159	3	1	1	0	2	0
157	20	105		53.60		3	0	0	0	0	0
158	16	116	46.48	49.23		3	0	0	0	0	0
159	10	34	53.90	59.70		3	1	0	0	2	0
159	10	55	59.10	50.90		3	1	0	0	2	0
160	31	35		53.80		3	1	0	0	2	0
160	31	109		51.00		3	1	0	0	2	0
161	2	47	65.05	51.55		3	0	1	0	2	0
162	12	35	58.43	47.71		1	0	0	1	2	0
163	32	56	61.61	52.90		3	1	0	0	2	0
164	8	310	46.65	57.65		4	1	1	0	0	0
165	6	32	30.00	40.40		3	1	1	0	0	1
165	6	32	50.00	42.20		3	1	1	0	0	0
166	6	20	57.50	62.50		1	1	1	0	2	0
167	4	30	68.00	67.00		2	1	1	0	2	0
167	4	30	68.00	40.00		5	1	1	0	2	0
167	4	30	68.00	73.00		3	1	1	0	2	0
167	4	30	68.00	57.00		1	1	1	0	2	0
168	63	44			0.098	3	0	1	0	0	0
168	63	44			0.117	1	0	1	0	0	0
168	63	44			0.258	1	0	1	0	0	0
168	63	14			0.320	5	0	1	0	0	0
168	63	44			0.380	3	0	1	0	0	0
169	38	34			0.692	3	0	1	0	0	0
170	15	139		47.11		2	0	1	0	2	0
171	8	20			0.063	1	1	0	0	2	0
171	8	20			0.091	1	1	0	0	2	1
171	8	20			0.283	1	1	0	0	2	0
171	8	20			0.860	3	1	0	0	2	0
171	8	20			0.930	3	1	0	0	2	0
171	8	20			0.934	3	1	0	0	2	0
171	8	20			0.969	3	1	0	0	2	0
171	8	20			1.443	2	1	0	0	2	0

172	5	188		51.11		3	0	4	0	2	0
173	5	47		50.05		3	0	4	0	2	1
174	4	200	79.69	50.81	0.819	3	1	2	0	2	0
175	8	71		66.38		2	0	0	0	2	0
176	2	180		55.77		4	0	0	0	2	0
177	8	133	81.68	54.00		3	0	0	0	2	0
178	11	18	61.62	59.60		3	1	0	0	2	0
178	10	125	60.24	56.48		3	1	0	0	2	0
178	5	77			0.058	5	1	0	0	2	0
178	5	27			-0.392	2	0	0	0	2	0
178	5	25	54.00	39.20	-0.462	3	0	0	0	2	0
178	5	62	57.99	59.47		2	0	0	0	2	0
178	5	69	55.35	61.49		3	0	0	0	2	0
178	5	87	53.03	59.90		5	0	0	0	2	0
178	5	19	53.68	61.58		2	0	0	0	2	0
178	5	277	53.32	62.85		3	0	0	0	2	0
179	2	120	58.50	41.50		3	0	1	0	2	0
180	16	48	63.37	49.83		3	0	0	0	2	0
181	46	47	49.44	52.69		3	0	2	0	0	0
181	46	47	53.46	49.59		2	0	2	0	0	0
182	40	139	63.12	54.06		3	1	0	0	2	0
183	32	15			0.236	2	1	0	0	2	0
183	32	15			0.291	2	1	0	0	2	0
184	40	120	58.75	58.75		3	0	1	0	2	0
185	6	103	68.20	51.90		3	0	1	0	1	0
186	20	110	54.39	54.86		3	0	0	0	0	0
187	19	58	53.68	55.57		3	1	0	0	2	0
187	19	58	51.27	57.93		3	1	0	0	2	1
188	72	72			0.264	3	0	1	0	1	0
189	8	19	67.82	60.50		2	0	1	0	0	0
189	8	19	71.50	66.00		5	0	1	0	0	0
189	8	19	81.55	54.00		5	0	1	0	0	0
189	8	19	69.76	54.50		5	0	1	0	0	0
190	20	91	52.50	49.00		3	0	0	0	2	1
191	20	36		47.00		3	0	0	0	2	1
191	20	36		50.00		3	0	0	0	2	1
191	20	36		51.00		3	0	0	0	2	1
191	20	36		44.00		1	0	0	0	2	1
192	20	50	48.75	53.00		3	2	0	0	2	0
193	28	21			0.587	3	1	1	0	2	1
194	10	15		54.00		3	0	0	0	2	1
194	10	20		42.00		3	0	0	0	2	0
195	30	61	50.33	55.00		3	0	1	0	2	0
195	30	60	47.67	54.00		3	1	4	0	2	0
196	1	137			-0.216	3	1	1	0	1	0
196	1	548			0.189	3	1	1	0	1	0
197	2	40	86.21	51.59		3	1	0	2	0	0
197	2	40	90.00	52.50		2	1	0	2	0	0
198	10	36		62.00		1	0	0	0	2	0
198	10	36		60.50		1	0	0	0	2	0
198	10	36		57.20		3	0	0	0	2	0
198	10	36		53.20		2	0	0	0	2	0
198	10	36		48.70		1	0	0	0	2	0
199	4	22		56.50		3	0	2	1	2	0
199	4	44		53.50		3	1	3	1	2	0

130

Doc#	Send#	Rec#	Truth%	Acc%	d	Med	Mot	Prep	Base	Inter	Exp
200	60	9			0.639	4	0	0	0	0	0
201	60	77	54.20	51.80	0.200	2	0	1	0	0	0
201	60	60	46.70	52.70		1	0	1	0	0	0
202	24	68			0.186	1	0	1	0	0	0
202	24	68			0.299	3	0	1	0	0	0
203	8	201			1.250	3	0	1	0	0	0
204	8	19		55.00		3	0	1	0	0	0
204	8	43		58.00		3	0	1	0	0	0
205	8	17		53.00		1	0	1	0	0	0
205	8	23		61.00		2	0	1	0	0	0
205	8	23		59.00		3	0	1	0	0	0
206	8	46			1.184	3	0	1	0	0	0
206	24	32	55.50	50.00		3	0	1	0	0	0
206	24	32	59.50	50.50		3	0	1	0	0	0
206	24	32	53.50	50.50		1	0	1	0	0	0

Note: Doc# = Document # (as listed in Appendix A), Send# = Number of Senders, Rec# = Number of Receivers, Truth% = Percent Truth Classifications, Acc% = Percent Correct Lie/Truth Classifications, d = Rating Scale Standardized Mean difference, Med = Deception Medium (1=Video, 2=Audio, 3=Audiovisual, 4=Within-Receiver Manipulation, 5=Other), Mot = Sender motivation (0=None, 1=Some, 2=Within-Receiver Manipulation), Prep = Preparation Time (0=None, 1=Some, 2=Within-Receiver Manipulation), Base = Baseline Exposure to Sender (0=No, 1=Yes, 2=Within-Receiver Manipulation), Inter = Interaction (0=Sender is Not Interacting, 1=Sender is Interacting with Receiver, 2=Sender is Interacting with Someone Else), Exp = Expert Receiver (0=No, 1=Yes).

Psychological Bulletin. 2008, Vol.134 , No. 4, pp. 477-492.

Individual Differences in Judging Deception : Accuracy and Bias

Charles F. Bond Jr.
Department of Psychology, Texas Christian University

Bella M. DePaulo
Department of Psychology, University of California at Santa Barbara

The authors report a meta-analysis of individual differences in detecting deception, confining attention to occasions when people judge strangers' veracity in real-time with no special aids. The authors have developed a statistical technique to correct nominal individual differences for differences introduced by random measurement error. Although researchers have suggested that people differ in the ability to detect lies, psychometric analyses of 247 samples reveal that these ability differences are minute. In terms of the percentage of lies detected, measurement-corrected standard deviations in judge ability are less than 1%. In accuracy, judges range no more widely than would be expected by chance, and the best judges are no more accurate than a stochastic mechanism would produce. When judging deception, people differ less in ability than in the inclination to regard others' statements as truthful. People also differ from one another as lie- and truth-tellers. They vary in the detectability of their lies. Moreover, some people are more credible than others whether lying or truth-telling. Results reveal that the outcome of a deception judgment depends more on the liar's credibility than any other individual difference.

It has been widely believed (indeed, "virtually axiomatic"; Hubbell, Mitchell, & Gee, 2001, p. 115) that people are not very accurate at detecting deception. This is the consensus among psychologists who arrange for people to judge lies and truths and to assess the percentage of those lies and truths they correctly detect. In a large research literature, overall rates of lie/truth discrimination average less than 55%, when 50% would be expected by chance (Aamodt & Mitchell, 2006). Moreover accuracy rates vary little across studies (C. F. Bond & DePaulo, 2006).

In fact, though, what is known concerns the *average* lie detection abilities of groups of people. Although much has been said about the *mean* accuracy of these groups, there has been less evidence on individuals' abilities.

Researchers have assumed that people vary in the ability to detect lies. Buller and Burgoon (1996) posited that lie detection accuracy depends, in part, on the receiver's decoding skill; Malone and DePaulo (2001) discussed individual differences in sensitivity to deception; and O'Sullivan (2007) based some recent work on the assumption that "lie detection is an ability that can be measured" (p. 118). Presupposing that this ability exists, researchers have attempted to discover the characteristics of people who have unusual lie detection skills. No such characteristics have been uncovered. Of course, in this literature of over 200 articles, one can find a study (or two) in which a given characteristic covaries with lie detection performance. Yet across the research literature as a whole, no individual difference has been found that is consistently correlated with the detection of deceit.

In an early meta-analysis, Zuckerman, DePaulo, and Rosenthal (1981) found no reliable effects of a judge's Machiavellianism, self-monitoring, or sex on the judge's accuracy at detecting lies. In a recent quantitative review, Aamodt and Mitchell (2006) sought to relate individual differences in lie/truth discrimination accuracy to a large number of variables—including the judge's age, education, expertise, confidence, and sex. Aamodt and Mitchell found no variables that were significantly related to lie detection.

It has been supposed that people differ from one another in lie detection ability. However, this supposition may be false. Under an alternative hypothesis, differences observed in detection performances reflect nothing more than chance variation. Kraut (1980) argued that people vary little in their lie detection skills. Consistent with this view, C. F. Bond, Kahler, and Paolicelli (1985) reported negligible differences from judge-to-judge in lie/truth discrimination performances; Kraut (1978) found no relationship between a perceiver's accuracy in judging one person and that same perceiver's accuracy in judging a second person; DePaulo and Rosenthal (1979) reported that a person's success at spotting men's lies is independent of his (or her) success at spotting women's lies; and Levine, Park, and McCornack (1999) found no positive relationship between a person's accuracy in identifying lies and that same person's accuracy in identifying truths. Unfortunately, only a handful of investigators have studied individual differences in lie detection ability, and there has never been a large-scale analysis of ability differences.

Although it may seem obvious that people differ in the ability to detect lies, psychometric theory encourages us to entertain the possibility that they do not. The theory provides a framework for understanding variation in test performances. Here, each test consists of a series of truthful and deceptive statements. To each statement, each judge gives a dichotomous response by indicating whether the statement is a lie or the truth. Each response is either correct or incorrect, and our interest is in the variation across judges in the percentage of correct responses. Under traditional psychometric theory (Lord & Novick, 1968), this variation includes two components: real variance and error variance. Real variance consists of the variance across test-takers that would be observed in a hypothetical test much longer than the test at hand—consisting of all possible test items from a universe. Here the putative universe would include all truthful and deceptive statements analogous to the ones being judged. Under psychometric theory, the *observed* variance across judges in percentage correct is larger than the *real* variance because judges see only a sample of statements. Observed variance is artifactually inflated to a degree that depends on the brevity of the test—with the briefest tests showing the highest variance.

Theoretically, it is possible for all of the variance in a set of test performances to be error variance. In such cases, we would say that the test was completely unreliable or (equivalently) that performances do not generalize over test items. For explanations of test theory, see Nunnally and Bernstein (1994); Ghiselli, Campbell, and Zedeck (1981); or Lord and Novick (1968).

Here, we offer the first large-scale analysis of individual differences in detecting deception. There has been related work. In a discussion of various measures of interpersonal sensitivity, J. A. Hall (2001) concluded that tests of accuracy for judgments of emotion show reasonable levels of internal consistency, whereas those that tap judgment accuracy across a variety of interpersonal domains do not. As part of a large-scale meta-analysis of mean lie detection accuracy, C. F. Bond and DePaulo (2006) noted that standard deviations in accuracy seem to be small. However, the meta-analysts did not test for the possibility that individual differences in accuracy are artifactual, nor did they try to estimate the magnitude of ability differences.

Individual Differences in Judging Deception

Our goal is to determine the magnitude of individual differences in deception judgments. We are primarily interested in differences across judges in percentage of correct lie/truth discrimination. With a statistical technique, we correct apparent judge-to-judge differences in accuracy for the differences that would be expected by chance. If psychometric theory is correct, chance variation should be greatest among individuals who judge only a small number of lies and truths. Perhaps our analyses will reveal that there are no real differences in the ability to detect lies. If so, this would explain why meta-analysts have found no individual- difference characteristics that are consistently related to lie detection performances. In the absence of differences in lie detection ability, it is unlikely that any nonchance correlates of lie detection performances will ever be found.

Although psychometric techniques can be used to assess abilities, they can also be used for a second purpose—to analyze test-taking biases. On personality inventories, for example, respondents differ in their inclination to agree with a statement, regardless of the statement's content (Paulhus, 1991). In a similar way, people who are judging the veracity of a series of statements might vary in their tendency to label statements as *truths*. While probing for differences among judges in accuracy at discriminating lies from truths, we also test for judge-to-judge differences in *credulity*—that is, in the general predisposition to regard others' statements as truthful.

Deception judgments have consequences (Granhag & Strömwall, 2004). Often the consequences do not depend on whether a deception judgment is correct. Some murder suspects are freed, and others are sentenced to die because of jurors' *judgments* of the suspects' truthfulness. Some international negotiations succeed, and others fail because of the negotiators' *judgments* of one another's honesty (C. F. Bond et al., 1992). Thus, it is important to understand any biases people may have toward viewing others as deceptive (or truthful).

Many have noted that the average judge labels more than 50% of the statements s/he hears as truthful, when 50% are in fact truthful (Levine et al., 1999). However, less has been said about individual differences in this tendency. People vary in chronic levels of trust (Levine & McCornack, 1991). Perhaps this influences deception judgments, such that some people are more likely than others to accept statements as truthful. If so, our psychometric analyses should reveal the magnitude of this individual difference—disentangling real variance in judge credulity from artifactual variance.

Deception involves two people—the liar as well as the judge. While gauging differences among individuals as judges of deceit, we also assess differences among them as liars. In the current article, we refer to people who lie as *senders*—recognizing that they do not invariably lie. Often, they tell the truth.

C. F. Bond et al. (1985) maintained that the outcome of a deception judgment depends more on the liar than the lie detector. Consistent with this view, the researchers found larger individual differences among people as lie- and truth-tellers than as judges. Kraut (1980) found that people who are judged to be honest by one person are judged to be honest by another. C. F. Bond and Atoum (2000) discovered that groups of people who are making judgments independently of one another reach consensus. They agree that certain individuals are lying and that others are telling the truth. People reach this consensus even when they are wrong. Judges seem to base their inferences about a person's truthfulness on the person's demeanor, in that the people who appear most honest when lying are the people who appear most honest when telling the truth (DePaulo & Rosenthal, 1979).

Although these earlier studies suggest that individuals differ as lie- and truth-tellers, no large-scale analysis of this putative difference has been reported. Here, we assess differences among senders along two dimensions: detectability and credibility. By our definition, a sender is perfectly *detectable* if that sender is always judged to be lying when s/he is telling a lie and always judged to be telling the truth when s/he is telling the truth. A sender is perfectly *credible* if that sender is invariably perceived to be truthful—whether lying or telling the truth. Perhaps our analysis of sender detectability will reveal that the veracity of some individuals is obvious and that the veracity of others is inscrutable. Maybe our analysis of sender credibility will indicate that some people are invariably believed and others invariably disbelieved, whether lying or telling the truth.

Before drawing any conclusions about differences among people who are lying and telling the truth, it will again be important to distinguish real individual differences from artifactual differences. When telling lies and truths, senders are judged for their veracity, and random error is introduced because the judgments of each sender are only a sample of all possible judgments that might have been made. Under psychometric theory, the smaller the number of times each sender is judged, the greater should be the artifactual variance in senders' detectability and credibility. We report analyses designed to separate artifactual differences in these variables from real differences. If any real sender differences are found, their magnitude will be of interest, and we will want to compare real differences among senders with real differences among judges.

In sum, our psychometric investigation may reveal that all variation in deception judgments is illusory and reflects nothing more than chance. If there is nonrandom variation in deception judgments, our analysis should allow a partitioning of that variation between liars and lie detectors. It should reveal the extent to which a deception judgment depends on the judge's detection ability, the judge's credulity, the sender's detectability, and the sender's credibility.

Our database consists of all relevant studies of deception detection we could find. An analysis of hundreds of studies will let us draw generalizations that a handful of studies would not permit.

This meta-analytic investigation will also allow us to examine conditions that may moderate the size of individual differences in judging deception. In some of the studies in this research literature, liars have no particular motivation to succeed; in others, they are motivated. Perhaps judge-to-judge differences in lie detection ability are large when liars have motivation to succeed and small when liars lack motivation. With statistical analyses, we assess this and a number of related possibilities.

Having gauged individual differences in detection ability, credulity, detectability, and credibility in the deception judgment research literature as a whole, we assess the magnitude of those differences in various subsets of this literature—for instance, in studies in which lies are significantly discriminated from truths and in studies in which they are not.

Statistically, we measure individual differences in judging deception with standard deviations. We analyze standard deviations across judges, as well as standard deviations across senders. In supplementary analyses, we examine the range in these variables. O'Sullivan (2007) has claimed that a few people have extraordinary lie detection ability. We assess this hypothesis by comparing the top lie detection performances reported in the deception detection research literature with the top performances that would be expected by chance. More generally, we supplement our analyses of standard deviations in judge ability, judge credulity, sender detectability, and sender credibility with analyses of a second measure of the dispersion in each individual difference variable: the range.

Method
Literature Search Procedures

We used standard methods to locate relevant research. We conducted computer-based searches of Psychological Abstracts, PsycInfo, PsycLit, Communication Abstracts, Dissertation Abstracts International, WorldCat, and Yahoo through December 2006, using the phrases "deception judgment," "deception detection," and "lie detection." We searched the Social Sciences Citation Index for articles that cited key references, examined reference lists from previous reviews, and reviewed the references cited in every document that we found. Through e-mail, we requested articles from over 25 scholars who had published relevant articles.

Criteria for Inclusion and Exclusion of Studies

Our goal was to summarize all relevant English-language reports of original research on the accuracy of judgments of lies and truths available to us prior to January 2007. To be included in this review, a document had to report (or allow computation of) a measure of individual differences in accuracy at discriminating lies from truths. The measure had to be based on dichotomous judgments of statements as lies or truths by individuals who had made more than one such judgment.

Given our interest in lie/truth discrimination, we excluded studies in which individuals judged only lies and studies in which individuals judged only truths. To avoid the influence of varying degrees and types of acquaintanceship on lie detection, we excluded investigations in which judges and senders knew one another prior to participating in the study. Hoping to understand deception judgments as they are made in everyday life, we also excluded studies in which judges could draw on aids to lie detection (e.g., polygraph records or behavior codings). We excluded judgments made by people who were less than 17 years of age, leaving to child psychologists questions about the early acquisition of lie detection skills. To confine attention to statements that could properly be considered lies, we excluded reports in which senders role-played an imagined person in an imagined situation. We excluded studies in which deception judgments were made on multipoint rating scales because we could not determine from most rating-scale results a quantitative index of individual differences that would be expected by chance. We excluded studies in which each judge made only a single lie/truth judgment. In such studies, the variability among judges is completely determined by their mean judgment.

Defining Samples

Research studies in this literature exhibit two forms of interdependence: sender interdependence and judge interdependence. Senders are interdependent when the lies and truths told by a given sample of people are shown to multiple samples of judges. Judges are interdependent when researchers report multiple measures of lie/truth accuracy for a given sample of judges.

Below, we report analyses of judge differences and analyses of sender differences. For our overall analyses of judge differences, we extract one standard deviation from each independent sample of judges. For our overall analyses of sender differences, we extract one estimate from each independent sample of lie- and truth-tellers. For analyzing the moderation of individual differences, we extract multiple estimates from a sample if those estimates reflect different levels of the moderator variable that we are analyzing. [1]

Coding Individual Differences

We coded individual differences in judge ability, judge credulity, sender detectability, and sender credibility. To understand these variables, readers may find it helpful to think of the results of a deception detection study as a rectangular matrix of 0 s and 1 s (see Figure 1). Each row of the matrix represents the responses on a lie/truth discrimination test given by a particular judge. Each column represents the judgments made in response to a particular sender. A judge's response to a sender is dichotomous and can be scored for either of two characteristics: accuracy or bias. A 1 in the cell (i, j) of the *accuracy matrix* implies that judge i correctly detected sender j's lie or truth. A 0 in the cell (i, j) implies that judge i was incorrect in assessing sender j's truthfulness. In this matrix, judge i's accuracy in discriminating lies from truths is reflected in the marginal mean of row i, whereas the detectability of sender j's lies and truths is reflected in the marginal mean of column j.

From each document that reported it, we coded the standard deviation across judges in the percentage of correct lie-or-truth judgments—that is, the standard deviation across the row marginal means of the 0–1 accuracy matrix, multiplied by 100. Whenever possible, we also coded the standard deviation across senders in the percentage of times each sender's truthfulness was judged correctly. This is the standard deviation across the column marginal means of the accuracy matrix, multiplied by 100.

Each judgment in the deception detection literature can be scored not only for accuracy but also for bias. A 1 appears in the cell (i, j) of the *bias matrix* if judge i believed that sender j was telling the truth; a 0 appears if judge i believed that sender j was lying. Judge i's tendency to regard statements as truthful is reflected in the marginal mean for row i of the bias matrix, whereas sender j's tendency to be believed is reflected in the marginal mean for column j.

From each document that reported it, we coded the standard deviation across judges in the percentage of messages judged to be truths—that is, the standard deviation across the row marginal means for the bias matrix, multiplied by 100. Whenever possible, we also coded the standard deviation across senders in the percentage of times each sender was judged to be telling the truth. This is the standard deviation across the column marginal means of the bias matrix, multiplied by 100.

We also sought to code the extremes on our four individual difference variables. When possible, we coded the maximum percentage of messages that any judge detected, as well as the minimum that any judge detected. We also coded the maximum and minimum for the following: percentage of messages any judge believed to be true, percentage of accuracy in judgments made of any sender, and percentage of times any sender was judged to be telling the truth.

The *number of judges* and *number of senders* were coded from each document. So was the number of lie/truth judgments made by each judge, as well as the number of lie/truth judgments made of each sender. We coded the mean percentage of correct lie/truth judgments and the mean percentage of truth judgments when available.

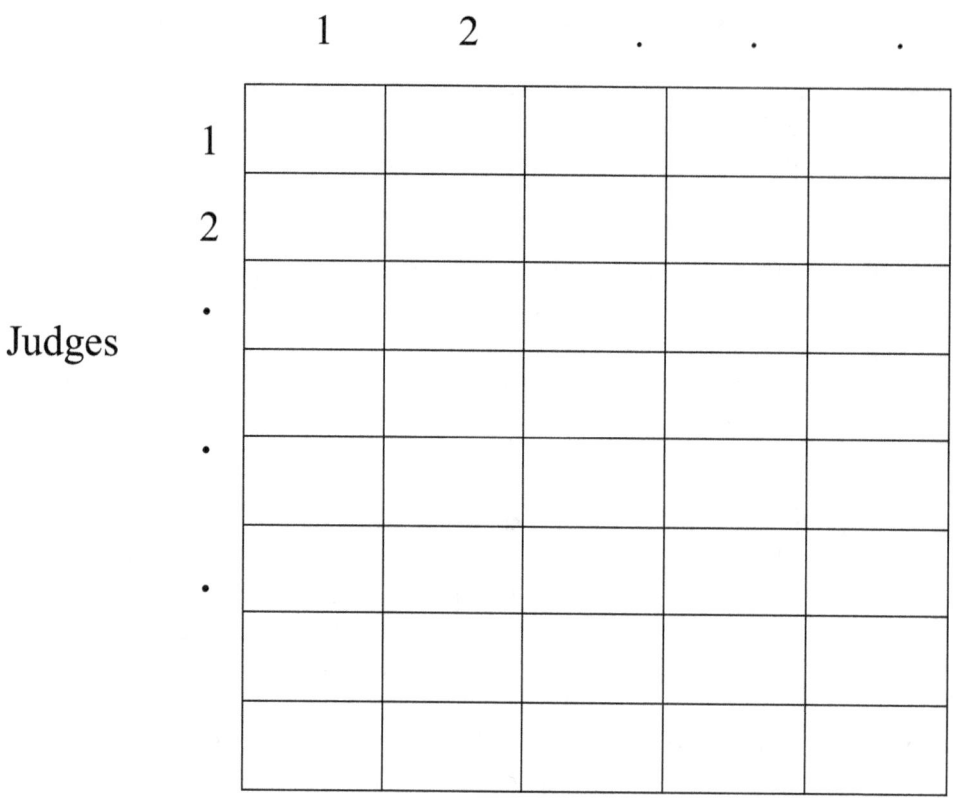

Figure 1. Results of a deception detection study.

Other Variables

The other variables of interest to us are categorical. People perpetrate lies over various media. Here we coded *deception medium* by noting whether receivers were trying to detect lies over a video medium, an audio medium, or an audiovisual medium. We coded *liar motivation* by noting whether participants had any special motivation to dupe others. We coded *lie preparation* by noting whether participants had any time to prepare their remarks.

In some studies, senders are interacting with others as they lie and tell the truth; in other studies, they are not. For purposes of coding *liar interaction*, we regarded senders as not interacting if when lying they were alone or in the presence of a passive observer. We deemed them to be interacting if they lied in the presence of a person who was not passive. Most of the judges in this literature are college students. Others are people whose occupations are thought to provide them with special experience in detecting lies, such as mental health professionals or law enforcement agents. We noted this variable of *judge experience*. In many studies, research participants must judge whether a sender is lying or telling the truth without any baseline information about how that sender acts when being truthful; in other studies, judges get a baseline exposure of each sender's truthful behavior. We noted this variable of *baseline exposure*. We also distinguished standard deviations reported in unpublished documents from those reported in published documents. Finally, we noted whether (in each study) mean lie/truth discrimination significantly exceeded 50% by a one-tailed test with $p < .05$.

For their meta-analysis of mean lie detection accuracy, C. F. Bond and DePaulo (2006) applied the current coding scheme to 123 of the 142 documents in the current compilation. They established the interrater reliability of the codes we are using here. For details, see C. F. Bond and DePaulo (2006, p. 219). As noted there, the two authors of the earlier article reached a mean of 92.2% agreement coding deception medium, liar motivation, lie preparation, liar interaction, judge experience, and baseline exposure in 24 documents randomly chosen from C. F. Bond and DePaulo's corpus. Nineteen of the documents in the current compilation did not appear in the earlier meta-analysis. C. F. Bond coded these latter documents.

Results

Our literature search uncovered 142 relevant documents. Of the documents, 89 were published, and 53 were unpublished. These documents, designated by asterisks in our References list, chronicle the efforts of 19,801 judges to assess the veracity of 2,945 senders. For a listing of study-by-study results, see Appendix A, which is available online as supplemental material. Averaging across all of the studies in this database, judges achieved a mean accuracy of 54.05% in discriminating lies from truths while rendering a mean of 55.50% truth judgments. These results are consistent with those reported in our earlier meta-analysis.

We analyzed individual differences in judge ability, judge credulity, sender detectability, and sender credibility. We measured the dispersion in each of these individual differences with two statistics: the standard deviation and the range.

Judge Ability

Standard deviation

We evaluated differences from judge to judge in the ability to discriminate lies from truths, measuring these differences with standard deviations. We chose to work with standard deviations, rather than variances, because standard deviations are in the familiar metric of percentage correct, whereas variances would assess ability differences as percentages squared (Howell, 2006). For comparison, it may be useful to note that the maximum possible standard deviation in a distribution of percentages is 50. This would occur if half of the percentages were equal to 0, and the other half were equal to 100. More generally, it is easy to determine the standard deviation in a distribution that consists of two equally likely percentages: a lower percentage (L) and a higher percentage (H). That standard deviation is $(H - L)/2$.

For analyzing standard deviations, we draw on traditional psychometric theory (Lord & Novick, 1968). We distinguish a perceiver's *observed accuracy* on a lie/truth detection test from the perceiver's *real accuracy*—defining the latter as the percentage of messages the perceiver would judge correctly on a test that included an *infinite* number of lies and truths. From standard deviations in observed accuracy, our methods will allow an inference about the standard deviation in real accuracy. Theoretically, this *real standard deviation* in lie detection abilities must be smaller than the observed standard deviation, and the difference between observed and real standard deviation should (under psychometric theory) depend on the length of the lie/truth test: the smaller the number of messages on a test, the greater should be the artifactual inflation of observed individual differences (Lord & Novick, 1968). [2]

To study individual differences in detection abilities, we began by determining the judge-to-judge standard deviation in percentage of correct lie/truth judgments from as many samples as possible. We managed to compute the value of this statistic from 247 independent samples of judges. In these samples, we find that the observed standard deviation in lie detection ability has an average value of 12.78.

According to psychometric theory, there should be an inverse relationship between the standard deviation among a set of lie detection performances, and the number of judgments each performance entails. To assess this prediction, we examined the relationship between number of judgments and observed standard deviation across our 247 samples. Results appear in Figure 2. As shown there, accuracy differences are much smaller among judges who make a large number of lie/truth judgments than judges who make only a few. This pattern of results corroborates the psychometric expectation and suggests that detection performance differences are inflated by the brevity of researchers' lie/truth tests.

142

Given our interest in *real* ability differences, we focused on people who make a large number of judgments. Those data appear to the right of Figure 2. There we see a depiction of results for the longest test to date (Parker, 1978): one that required each judge to classify 120 statements as lies or truths. It is noteworthy that the standard deviation in accuracy across judges on Parker's lie/truth test is the lowest of the 247 standard deviations reported to date: 3.09%. In our view, 3.09% provides a preliminary upper bound to *real* individual differences in detection ability. However, we sought a more precise estimate. We wished to infer the magnitude of differences from judge-to-judge in percentage correct that would be obtained on a lie/truth test much longer than 120 items – a test of *infinite* length.

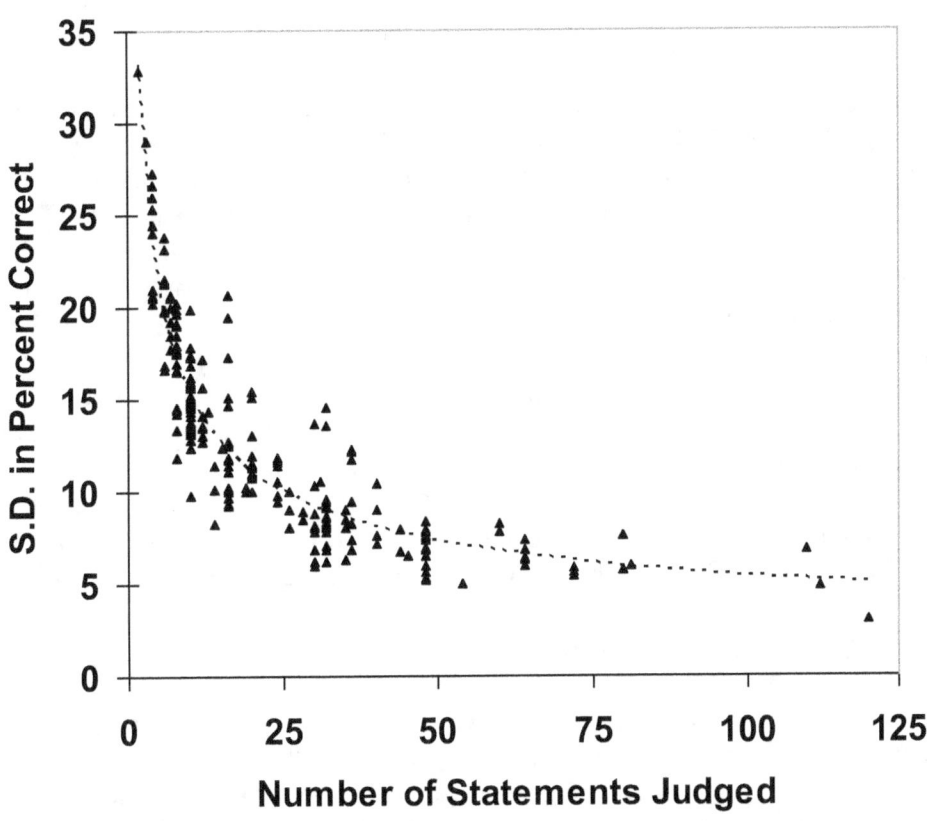

Figure 2. Standard deviation in percentage of statements judged correctly by number of statements judged.

Before describing our method for estimating this *real* standard deviation, let us note that in each study included in Figure 2, judges classified messages into one of two categories—indicating that the message was either a lie or the truth. For purposes of analysis, let us suppose that each judge in a given sample has a certain probability of classifying a given message correctly and that this probability is the same for all messages. Then we could use the binomial distribution to model the percentage of correct judgments in the sample. Under this model, the standard deviation across perceivers in percentage correct would be inversely proportional to the square root of the number of lie/truth judgments each judge made. For details, see Lord and Novick (1968, Chapter 23). We exploited this fact to estimate the standard deviation that one would expect in a sample that made an infinite number of judgments. To do so, we fit to the data in Figure 2 the regression equation

$$s_i = a + b \left(\frac{1}{\sqrt{n_i}} \right)$$

1) where s_i is

the observed standard deviation in sample i among judges in the percentage of lies and truths that they correctly detected, and n_i is the number of lie/truth judgments made by each judge in that sample.

Let us explain the logic of this equation. Note that b is the regression coefficient in the equation. A positive value for b would allow us to accommodate the pattern of results in Figure 2—the inverse relationship between the standard deviation in lie/truth accuracy across judges in a sample and the number of lie/truth judgments that each judge rendered. We use the equation to predict the standard deviation in a hypothetical sample in which each judge made an infinite number of lie/truth judgments. Given an infinitely large value of n_i, the term inside the parentheses to the right of Equation 1 becomes 0, and the predicted standard deviation across perceivers for that sample would be a—the intercept of Equation 1. This intercept provides a model-based estimate of *real standard deviation*, the standard deviation across judges in lie/truth discrimination ability that would be observed on a test of infinite length. Here, we call this estimate the *measurement-corrected standard deviation*.

Fitting Equation 1 to the data in Figure 2, we found $a = 0.80$, $b = 45.75$. This model fits the data very well. Across the 247 samples depicted in Figure 2, the predicted standard deviations correlate .92 with the actual standard deviations. We have inserted the standard deviations predicted by Equation 1 into Figure 2 as a dashed line.

A conventional hypothesis test suggests that there are real individual differences in lie detection ability—for comparison of the intercept with 0, $t(244) = 2.33$, $p < .05$. However, these ability differences are small. On a test of infinite length, the standard deviation across judges in percentage correct would be less than 1%. It would be 0.80%. The 95% confidence interval for this measurement-corrected standard deviation is 0.12%–1.47%. [3]

O'Sullivan (2007) hypothesized that differences in lie detection ability are normally distributed. In light of that conjecture, let us remind the reader that roughly 95% of the observations in a normal distribution are within two standard deviations of the mean. Let us also note that in such a distribution less than 1 observation in 2 million is more than five standard deviations above the mean.

If we make O'Sullivan's (2007) distributional assumption and further assume that the mean percentage correct lie/truth judgments is 54% (C. F. Bond & DePaulo, 2006), our current results allow a complete specification of the distribution of lie detection abilities. On a test of infinite length taken under the typical conditions of deception detection research, 95% of judges would achieve between 52.4% and 55.6% correct lie/truth discrimination (that is, the mean plus and minus two measurement-corrected standard deviations). If 2 million judges took a test of infinite length under the usual conditions, we would expect less than 1 to achieve more than 58% correct (that is, five real standard deviations above the mean).

Perhaps people differ widely in the ability to spot deception cues but not in the ability to identify truths as truths. To assess this possibility, we found 115 samples in which it was possible to code separately the standard deviation across judges in accuracy for deceptive messages and accuracy for truthful messages. Averaging across studies, there are no differences in these standard deviations, $M = 17.97$ for the standard deviation in detecting lies versus 18.29 for the standard deviation in detecting truths, $t(114) = -0.76$, ns.

Under the hypothesis of ability differences in lie/truth discrimination, one might suppose that individuals who were good at spotting lies would also be good at spotting truths. To assess this possibility, we determined in 154 samples the correlation between a judge's accuracy at detecting lies and that same judge's accuracy at detecting truths. In fact, the relevant correlation is negative in 97 of the 154 samples (that is, 63% of the time). For the relationship between accuracy at judging lies and accuracy at judging truths, standard meta-analytic methods yield a weighted mean r-to-Z-to-r = $-.09$ (95% confidence interval = $-.11$ to $-.07$). The most accurate judges of lies tend to be the least accurate judges of truths.

Range

We also had an interest in the range in judges' lie detection performances. In 88 independent samples of judges, we were able to determine the highest and lowest percentage accuracy achieved by any individual. We coded these statistics.

In Appendix B (which is available online as supplemental material), we derive an equation for the maximum and minimum percentage of correct lie-or-truth judgments that would be expected in a sample—if there were no ability differences among the judges in that sample (see David & Nagaraja, 2003). In applying this equation to the research literature, we assume that the probability of a lie/truth judgment being correct in a sample is the proportion of correct judgments observed in that sample.

We used this technique to analyze each of the 88 samples, for which we knew the range across judges in percentage correct. Results show that there is a very strong correlation between the observed range in detection accuracy in a sample and the range that would be expected if there were no ability differences ($r = .88$, $p < .0001$). Averaging across the 88 samples, the mean observed range in percentage correct is 44.38%; the mean range that would be expected given no ability differences from judge to judge is 44.18%. The observed range is less than 1% wider than the expected range. In fact, it is 0.20% wider. This difference is not statistically significant, $t(87) = 0.21$, *ns*. For the mean observed and expected range in judge ability across our 88 samples, see the two bars that appear in the left side of Figure 3. Each bar extends from the minimum percentage correct to the maximum percentage correct, the dark bar representing percentages observed and the light bar representing percentages expected by chance.

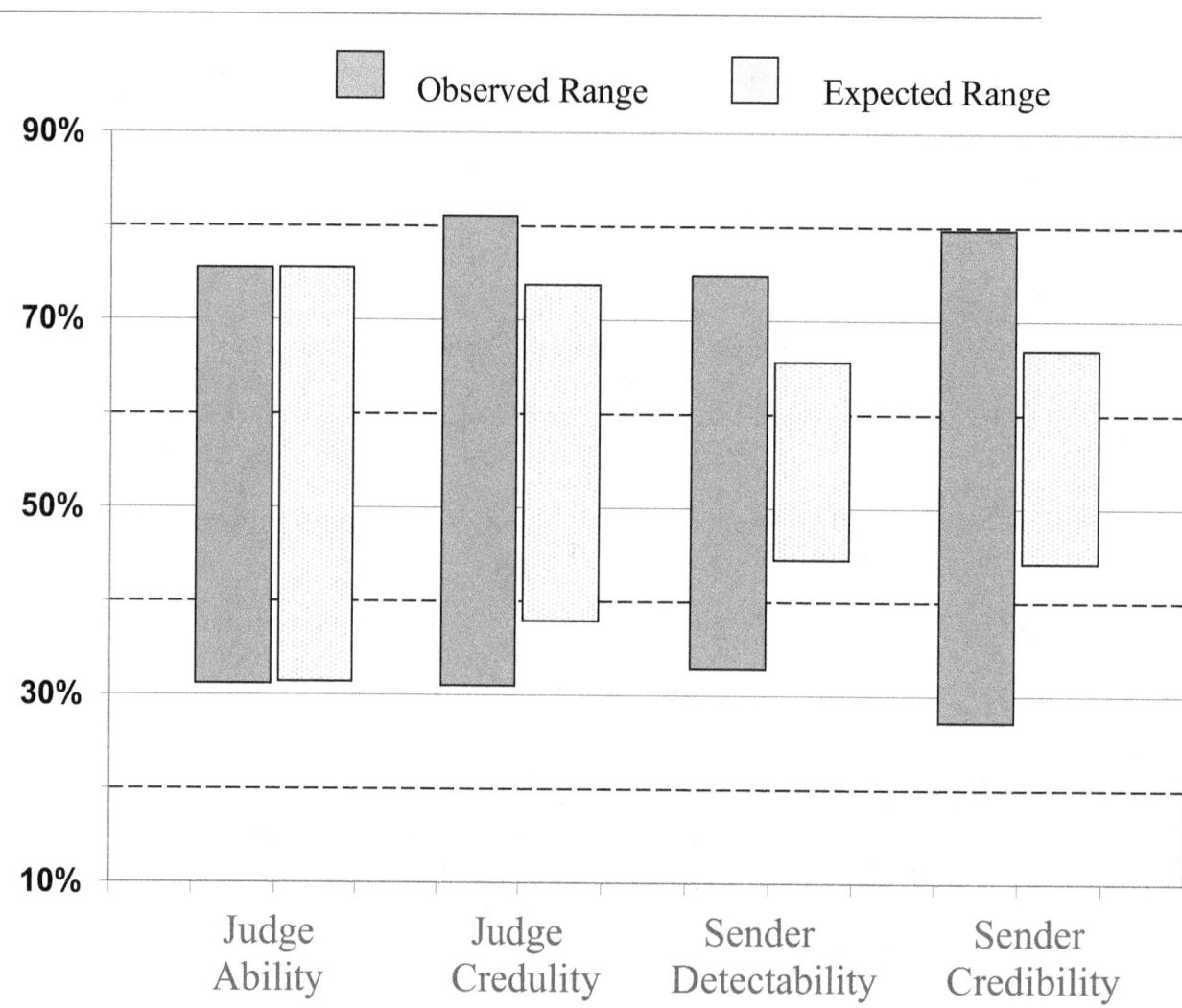

Figure 3. Observed and expected range in four individual differences.

O'Sullivan (2007) has maintained that a few people have extraordinary skill at detecting deceit. To assess this claim, we analyzed the maximum percentage correct achieved in 93 samples of judges (the 88 in which a minimum accuracy was reported and 5 others). Averaging across all 93 samples, the observed maximum percentage correct is 75.70%; the maximum that would be expected if judges did not differ in ability is 76.44%. Observed and expected maximum performances are highly correlated ($r = .81$) and do not differ significantly from one another, $t(92) = -1.07$, ns. These data provide no evidence that the best lie detection performances in this research literature reflect any extraordinary ability. The highest detection rates are no higher than chance would produce.

Judge Credulity

Next, we analyzed differences from judge to judge in the tendency to regard others as truthful.

Standard deviation

In 162 samples, it was possible to determine the standard deviation from judge to judge in the percentage of statements classified as truthful. The mean standard deviation observed in these samples was 13.55. We hoped to partition the differences researchers observed in credulity into real differences and artifactual differences.

To do so, we fit Equation 1 to the 162 standard deviations. The equation fit the data well, for the relationship between predicted and observed standard deviations ($r = .77$, $p < .0001$). Again, our interest is in the real standard deviation, the standard deviation across judges in the percentage of messages they would classify as truths on a test of infinite length. Again, the intercept of Equation 1 provides our meta-analytic estimate of this quantity and indicates that perceivers do differ from one another in credulity (for this measurement-corrected standard deviation, $a = 5.13\%$; 95% confidence interval = 3.94%–6.32%), $t(160) = 8.52$, $p < .0001$.

Although our psychometric analyses suggest that judges differ more in credulity than ability, one wonders whether similar results would be apparent in a more controlled comparison. They are. In 152 samples, we were able to determine both the standard deviation among a set of judges in percentage correct lie/truth judgments as well as the standard deviation among those same judges in percentage truth judgments. These judges vary more in credulity than in accuracy; mean observed standard deviations = 13.18 versus 12.25, respectively; for the difference, $t(151) = 3.15$, $p < .01$.

Range

It was possible in 32 samples to determine the largest and smallest percentage of statements classified as truthful by any judge. To analyze these statistics, we adapted the methods of Appendix B. These allow us to determine the range in the percentage of truth judgments judges rendered that we would observe in a sample of judges who were equal in credulity. Averaging across the 32 samples, the mean observed range in truth judgments was 50.06%; a mean of

35.86% would be expected if there were no real differences in credulity. Judges range more widely in credulity than would be expected by chance—for comparison of the means in observed and expected range, $t(31) = 6.25$, $p < .0001$. In fact, the observed range is 40% wider than what would be expected by chance. For these results, see the third and fourth bars of Figure 3.

Sender Detectability

Having found that judges show negligible differences in lie detection ability and nonnegligible differences in credulity, we turn our attention to the targets of judges' detection efforts: people who lie and tell the truth. Some researchers have claimed that people differ more as liars than as lie detectors (C. F. Bond et al., 1985).

People might differ in the transparency of their veracity. If so, it would be easy to spot some individuals' lies and truths, and it would be impossible to determine whether others were lying.

Standard deviation

We noted (in 54 samples in which data were available) the standard deviation from sender to sender in the percentage of times that judges correctly detected the sender's lies and truths. These observed standard deviations had a mean of 11.83.

We are interested in the real standard deviation in sender detectability, the standard deviation that would be observed if each sender was judged an infinite number of times. To estimate that hypothetical quantity, we used a variant of Equation 1. We predicted the standard deviation in a sample of senders from the reciprocal of the square root of the number of judgments made of each sender in that sample. Theoretically, differences among senders should be smaller, the larger is the number of judgments made of each sender. Our analysis confirms this theoretical prediction, and the relevant regression equation fits the data well—for the correlation between observed and predicted standard deviations in 54 samples ($r = .74$, $p < .001$). From the equation, we estimate that if an infinite number of lie and truth judgments were made of each sender, some would be more detectable than others. The measurement-corrected standard deviation in detectability is 5.49% (95% confidence interval = 3.51%–7.46%), $t(52) = 5.57$, $p < .0001$.

Range

In 37 samples, we could determine the largest and smallest percentage of correct lie/truth judgments made of any sender's statements. Averaging across these samples, the mean observed range in accurate judgments received was 41.93%. The methods of Appendix B reveal that a mean range of 21.13% would be expected if there were no real differences in sender detectability. People range more widely in detectability than would be expected by chance—for comparison of mean observed with mean expected range, $t(36) = 8.19$, $p < .0001$. The observed range is 1.98 times as wide as the expected range (see the fifth and sixth bars in Figure 3).

148

Sender Credibility

When telling lies and truths, some people are more detectable than others—as we have discovered. In principle, people may also differ in credibility. Some may appear honest and others dishonest, regardless of their veracity.

Standard deviation

In 45 samples, we could determine a standard deviation from sender to sender in the percentage of times their statements were judged as truthful. These standard deviations show a mean value of 14.77.

To estimate the real standard deviation in sender credibility, we again used Equation 1 to predict the standard deviation in a sample of senders, substituting for ni the number of judgments made of each sender in that sample. The equation fit moderately well—predicted standard deviations in sender credibility yielding an r of .49 with observed standard deviations ($p < .005$). From the fitted intercept of our regression equation, we infer that if people made an infinite number of judgments of senders, the senders would differ from another in credibility (measurement-corrected standard deviation = 11.58%; 95% confidence interval = 9.36%–13.80%), $t(43) = 10.52, p < .0001$.

From our analyses, it would appear that people vary more from one another in credibility than detectability. This difference also emerged in a controlled comparison. In 38 samples, we were able to code the standard deviation in the detectability and credibility of the same senders, on the basis of the same lie/truth judgments. The senders vary more from one another in credibility than detectability (mean observed standard deviations = 15.06% vs. 12.70%), $t(37) = 2.77, p < .01$.

Perhaps people vary more widely in credibility when lying than when telling the truth. To assess this possibility, we found 33 studies in which it was possible to code separately standard deviations in the percentage of truth judgments senders received when lying and in the percentage of truth judgments they received when telling the truth. Results show that, in fact, credibility differences are greater when people are lying rather than telling the truth (observed SDs = 17.98 and 15.95 for percentage of truth judgments to lies vs. truths, respectively), $t(32) = 2.59, p < .05$.

DePaulo and Rosenthal (1979) reported evidence of a demeanor bias—that the individuals who appear most honest when lying are the ones who appear most honest when telling the truth. In 35 samples, it was possible to determine the correlation between the percentage of truth judgments to a person's lie and that same person's truth. These data corroborate DePaulo and Rosenthal's evidence of demeanor bias—the correlation is positive in 29 of 35 samples. By standard meta-analytic methods, the relationship between percentage of truth judgments to an individual's truth and that same individual's lie yields a weighted r-to-Z-to-r = .39, $p < .01$ (95% confidence interval = .34–.44).

Range

It was possible in 31 independent samples to determine the largest and smallest percentage of truth judgments made about any sender's statements. Averaging across these samples, the mean observed range in truth judgments received was 52.51%; by the methods of Appendix B, a mean of 22.73% would be expected if senders did not differ in credibility. Senders range more widely in credibility than would be expected by chance—for comparison of mean observed with mean expected range, $t(30) = 12.54$, $p < .0001$. For the observed and expected range in sender credibility, see the right-most two bars in Figure 3. The observed range is 2.43 times as wide as the expected range.

Comparing Differences

In contrast to small differences in judge lie detection ability, there are substantial individual differences in the senders' apparent honesty. In terms of percentages, measurement-corrected differences in sender credibility are roughly 14 times the size of the corresponding differences in judge ability (11.58% vs. 0.80%). Differences in sender detectability and judge credulity are roughly equal to one another (5.49% and 5.13%), and each is roughly half as large as sender credibility differences (see Figure 4).

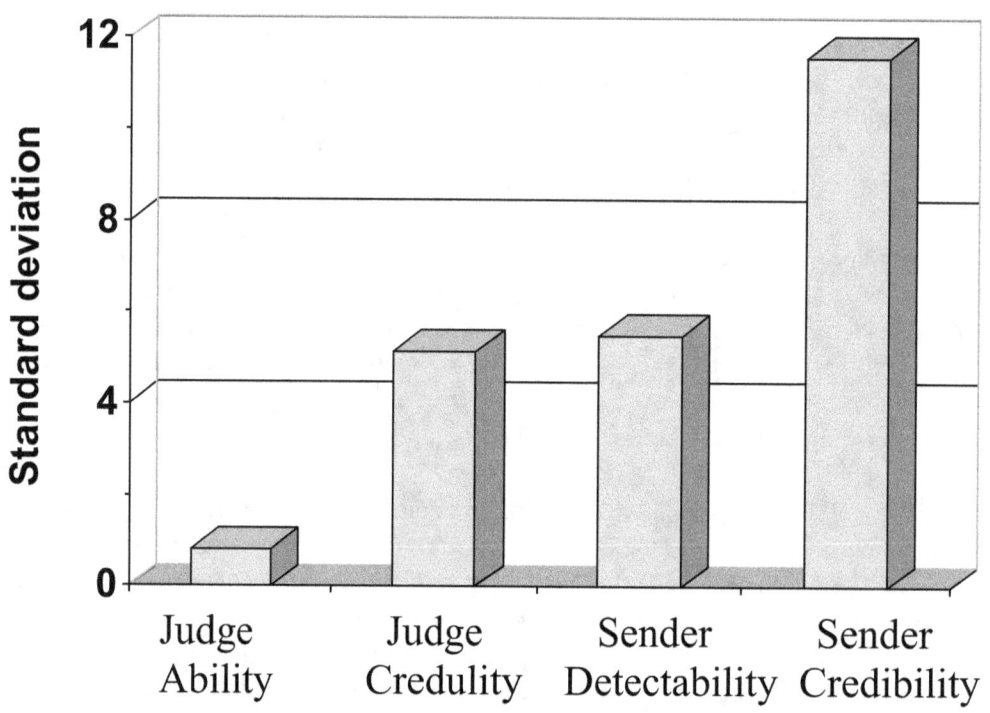

Figure 4. Measurement-corrected standard deviation in four individual differences

It is possible to compare the impact of these individual differences on deception judgments with the impact of situational factors—for example, the sender's veracity. Sometimes people are lying; sometimes they are telling the truth. An earlier meta-analysis revealed that on average 61.34% of truths and 52.45% of lies are judged to be truths (C. F. Bond & DePaulo, 2006). This implies that sender veracity introduces a standard deviation in percentage truth judgments of 4.44% (half of 61.34 – 52.45). In percentage terms, a person's credibility has more than twice the impact of the person's veracity in determining whether s/he will be judged truthful.

Although for ease of interpretability we have assessed individual differences as standard deviations, it is conventional to express them as variances. In the latter metric, the comparisons we have been making are more striking. Correcting for sampling error, the variance in sender credibility is over 200 times as large as the corresponding variance in judge ability. Relatively speaking, ability variance is trivial.

Psychologists are interested in the reliability of individual difference measures. Under traditional theory, the reliability coefficient for a measure is the ratio of the real variance in that measure to the observed variance. We estimated reliability coefficients for judge ability, judge credulity, sender detectability, and sender credibility by forming the ratio of our model-based measurement-corrected variance in each of those measures to the mean of the observed variances in each measure that have been reported in the research literature. This method yields the following reliability coefficients: judge ability = .07, judge credulity = .30, sender detectability = .58, and sender credibility = .91. In this metric, differences in detectability from sender to sender are more reliable than differences in credulity from judge to judge. Judges show no reliable differences in ability, whereas sender differences in credibility are highly reliable.

We also assessed individual differences by analyzing another statistic—the range. These analyses corroborate our conclusions. Here, a useful metric is the ratio of the mean of the observed ranges to the mean of the ranges expected by chance. Our results reveal that this ratio is 1.00 for judge ability, 1.40 for judge credulity, 1.98 for sender detectability, and 2.43 for sender credibility.

Moderator Analyses
Individual differences in judging deception could be influenced by many factors. Individual differences might, for example, be larger when deception must be inferred from audio than from video. They might be unusually large when liars are motivated not to get caught.

To assess the moderation of individual differences in judging deception, we conducted a number of analyses. Each analysis yielded a measurement-corrected standard deviation in 1 of 17 subsets of the research literature. These subsets of the literature were defined by eight variables: deception medium (audio-only, video-only, or audiovisual), liar motivation (high or low), liar interaction (some or none), lie preparation (some or none), judge experience (some or none), baseline exposure (some of none), document status (published or unpublished), and lie/truth discrimination (mean percentage correct is or is not significantly greater than 50% at one-tailed $p < .05$). With the regression-based procedure outlined in Equation 1 above, we computed measurement-corrected standard deviations within each of these subsets of the literature on our four individual-difference variables: judge ability, judge credulity, sender detectability, and sender credibility.

	Judge Ability	Judge Credulity	Sender Detectability	Sender Crediblity
Audio only	.44	8.47	5.92	8.85
Video only	1.47	4.40	2.75	6.80
Audiovisual	.71	4.86	5.15	7.97
Unmotivated liar	1.21	5.40	5.57	11.76
Motivated liar	.32	4.39	3.85	7.41
No Interaction	.98	5.02	4.31	12.74
Interaction	.93	4.67	5.56	7.47
Unprepared liar	.89	6.50	4.91	12.50
Prepared liar	.63	4.93	7.46	9.26
Inexperienced judge	.84	4.91	5.18	11.23
Experienced judge	-.19	6.58	16.35	18.58
No Baseline Exposure	.78	5.04	5.42	11.58
Baseline Exposure	1.10	5.32	8.13	----[a]
Unpublished document	.06	5.27	4.68	7.59
Published document	1.30	5.06	5.25	11.87
No significant Mean Detection	.41	5.24	6.84	12.24
Significant Mean Detection	1.44	5.88	4.84	7.93

[a] Note: No standard deviations in sender credibility could be computed in this subset of the research literature.

Table 1. Measurement-Corrected Standard Deviations in Subsets of the Research Literature

Let us briefly describe the pattern of results produced by our analyses: Differences in judge ability are consistently small, and differences in sender credibility are consistently large. Across 17 subsets of this research literature, measurement-corrected standard deviations in judge ability range from −0.19% (among experienced judges) to 1.47% (for video lies). [4] Measurement-corrected standard deviations in judge credulity range from 4.39% (for motivated liars) to 8.47% (for audio lies). Measurement-corrected standard deviations in sender detectability range from 2.75% (for video lies) to 16.35% (when the judged are experienced). Measurement-corrected standard deviations in sender credibility range from 6.80% (for video lies) to 18.59% (when judges are experienced). For relevant results, see Table 1.

Above, we noted that the largest of four individual differences in judging deception is sender credibility, and the smallest is judge ability. As Table 1 reveals, this pattern holds true in each of 17 subsets of the research literature. In studies in which liars are motivated, in studies of interactive deception, in studies in which judges discriminate lies from truths, and in studies that are published (as well as those that are unpublished), measurement-corrected standard deviations are highest for sender credibility, lowest for judge ability, and intermediate for judge credulity and sender detectability.

The small size of individual differences in judge ability should be apparent from an inspection of Table 1. There it is noteworthy that the *highest* measurement-corrected standard deviation in judge ability for *any* subset of this literature (1.47%) is lower than the lowest measurement-corrected standard deviation in any of the other three individual differences in any subset of the literature (2.75%). Across 17 sets of studies, these distributions do not overlap. Thus, our conclusions about the relative size of individual differences in judging deception generalize across deception media, liar motivation, liar interaction, lie preparation, judge experience, baseline exposure, publication status, and lie/truth discrimination.

Discussion

Here, we have drawn conclusions about individual differences in judging deception. Our goal was to quantify such individual differences as would be apparent if researchers could measure the differences without error. Our database consists of all relevant studies that we could find, and to this database we applied a new meta-analytic technique. In this section, we discuss our individual difference findings, consider the applicability of these findings to lie detection in the real world, and comment on our method for meta analyzing individual differences.

Individual Differences in Accuracy

Although it has become virtually axiomatic that the *mean* lie detection performances of groups of people are barely above chance, the magnitude of individual differences in detection ability was not previously known. Now, several converging lines of evidence indicate that virtually all *individuals* are barely able to detect lies, and that real differences in detection ability are miniscule.

In demonstrating that people differ little from one another in the ability to detect lies, we build on earlier work. It showed that accuracy in judging the veracity of one person is independent of accuracy in judging the veracity of another (Kraut, 1978), that accuracy in judging lies is not positively correlated with accuracy in judging truths (Levine et al., 1999), and that no "wizardry" need be invoked to explain why a few people get high scores on lie detection tests (C. F. Bond & Uysal, 2007). Our contribution is to demonstrate the small size of lie detection ability differences not from a single study (as had earlier researchers) but from a meta-analysis of the research literature as a whole. A second contribution is to compare the magnitude of lie detection ability differences with the size of some related individual differences.

Our meta-analytic results clarify a phenomenon that would otherwise be curious. Many psychologists have attempted to uncover the traits of individuals who are particularly gifted in divining deceit—traits like the individual's education, sex, occupation, Machiavellianism, self-monitoring, and locus of control. Although each of these individual difference variables may be related to lie detection accuracy in a few studies, once a reasonable amount of evidence accumulates over a reasonable number of laboratories, these individual-difference relationships prove to be illusory (Aamodt & Mitchell, 2006; Zuckerman et al., 1981). Across the literature as a whole, there is no replicable predictor of lie detection accuracy. This is unsurprising. As currently measured, lie detection accuracy is not a reliable individual difference. Thus, nonchance correlates of current accuracy scores are unlikely to be found.

While yielding these null individual difference results, the small size of lie detection ability differences has made a positive contribution to experimental research. There, investigators test for the impact of situational factors on human lie detection, assessing these situational effects against an error term that consists of differences among judges' lie detection performances. Insofar as judges' performances show little variability, deception researchers have had high statistical power to uncover the effects that interest them. Small ability differences have also allowed many investigators to find that rates of lie/truth discrimination are statistically significant, even when the rates are only slightly above 50%. To accrue the benefits of high statistical power, those who conduct deception experiments should plan to give their research participants long lie detection tests. If the researcher's error term is to consist of the variability among judges' lie detection performances, this error term will be smaller the larger the number of lies and truths judged.

Although people hardly vary in the ability to detect deception, they differ in their detectability as liars. When lying, some people get caught, and others elude capture. Thus, in an individual-difference sense, the accuracy of a deception judgment depends more on the liar than the judge.

Having noted that on the whole lies can barely be distinguished from truths (C. F. Bond & DePaulo, 2006), let us mention a complicating factor. Some individuals tell lies and truths that are readily distinguishable, and their transparency merits discussion. Although we do not know why the veracity of certain individuals is obvious, perhaps these people have ethical compunctions against lying; perhaps they cannot regulate deception-related emotions; perhaps they are poor at masking those emotions; perhaps for them the truth is so cognitively prepotent that they have trouble concocting plausible tales. Future research will be needed to explain why (as lie- and truth-tellers) some people are highly transparent and others opaque. In the meantime, it is worth reiterating that there *is* an individual difference in detecting deception. Although differences from judge to judge in lie detection are small, differences from sender to sender in lie detectability are much larger.

Individual Differences in Bias

Deception judgments can have important consequences, and sometimes the consequences do not depend on whether the judgment is correct (C. F. Bond et al, 1992). Thus, we sought to understand individual differences that might bias one person to judge another as truthful (on the one hand) or deceptive (on the other).

On average, people show a bias toward judging others as truthful (Levine et al., 1999). However, individual differences in this judgmental bias have scarcely been discussed. Here, we found that people do, in fact, vary in the tendency to regard others as truthful. They vary from one another in ways that cannot be attributed to measurement error. This individual difference is related to a broader suspiciousness: People who are most leery of communications in general are the ones most likely to regard others as lying (Levine & McCornack, 1991). Perhaps these individuals have learned to be suspicious because they have often been the victims of deceit, or maybe those who are chronically suspicious of deception are themselves habitual liars. However they are explained, individual judge differences in the bias to perceive others as truthful are roughly equal in magnitude to individual sender differences in lie–truth detectability.

The largest determinant of a deception judgment is not, however, the judge's degree of truth bias or the sender's detectability. Instead, it is the credibility of the person being judged—some individuals appear substantially more truthful than others. In fact, a person's credibility has a bigger impact than the person's honesty on whether s/he will be seen to be telling the truth. High credibility liars are more likely to be believed than low credibility truth-tellers.

Let us try to explain why some people appear more truthful than others. In our view, differences in apparent honesty emerge soon after birth by virtue of facial anatomy. Some infants are anatomically gifted with an honest-looking face; others are facially disadvantaged. The gifted have baby faces, and the disadvantaged look mature (Masip, Garrido, & Herrero, 2004). Individual differences in facial honesty carry forward over the lifespan (Zebrowitz, Voinescu, & Collins, 1996) and help explain why some people are more likely than others to be seen as telling the truth.

Facial anatomy, however, is not sufficient to explain the accumulated research findings. As our meta-analytic results show, people differ more in credibility when lying than when telling the truth. Differential practice may account for this effect. As youngsters, all people have occasion to lie. Some children, the facially honest, will discover that they can avoid punishment by lying. This social reinforcement motivates them to continue lying, and with practice, they hone their deception skills. Others, children who have a dishonest face, learn that lying does them no good. Indeed, deceptive-looking youngsters may be punished for their failed attempts at deception. Thus, they learn to refrain from lying and never develop whatever behavioral potential for deception they might have had. So the deceptively rich get richer, and the poor stay the same. In this view (C. F. Bond & Robinson, 1988), social reinforcement contingencies augment anatomical differences to explain why some people appear more honest than others.

Real World Applicability

Having drawn conclusions about individual differences in judging deception from experimental studies, let us comment on the applicability of our findings to lie detection in the real world.

Critics characterize deception research as artificial. They argue that experimental deceptions are trivial and that research participants tell lies in an asocial context. They note that experimenters study lies between strangers and deprive would-be detectors of information about how liars appear when telling the truth. Perhaps in experimental research, liars act similarly to truth-tellers, and if judges do not differ from one another in detecting deceit, it is because they have no cues to detect.

Although these criticisms can be made of many studies of deception detection, they cannot be made of others. Researchers have studied high-stakes lies—lies told by murderers, for example (Vrij & Mann, 2001). Researchers have studied naturalistic deceptive interactions (Kassin & Fong, 1999) and have given judges baseline information about senders' truthful behaviors (Feeley, deTurck, & Young, 1995). Researchers have studied lies that *can* be discriminated from truths—with 72% accuracy, in one case (Vrij, Mann, Robbins, & Robinson, 2006).

Results show that our individual difference findings are not restricted to the most artificial of research studies; rather they are consistent across the deception detection research literature as a whole. Yes, people barely differ from one another in the ability to detect low-stakes lies told in noninteractive contexts when there is no evidence that the lies can be detected. Yet, there are also small differences in lie detection ability among individuals who judge motivated lies, among people who judge interactive lies, and among those who judge lies that have (in fact) been detected. Differences in judge ability are small whether judges receive baseline information about the way liars act when telling the truth.

As judge differences in detection ability are small in all parts of this research literature, sender differences in detectability are larger. In studies of low-stakes lies told in noninteractive contexts in which there is no evidence that the lies were discriminated from truths, people differ from one another in their detectability as lie- and truth-tellers. If artificial methodology masks individual differences in the ability to detect lies, it is peculiar that it leaves unmasked the corresponding differences in sender detectability.

Having noted that our meta-analytic findings are not specific to trivial lies, asocial lies, or undetectable lies, we do not mean to imply that this pattern of individual differences would emerge in every instance of lie detection in the real world. In our view, experimenters have not yet captured several features of real world lie detection. In the real world (but not the laboratory), lie detection requires unprompted suspicion, involves nonbehavioral evidence, and entails nonrandom liar–judge pairings

Experimenters forewarn the judges in their studies that they will be seeing deception and instruct them to consider whether each message they encounter is a lie. Under these conditions, people differ in the tendency to regard others as deceptive. Outside the laboratory, different conditions obtain. To detect a lie, one must first come to suspect deceit, and there may be individual differences in prerequisite suspicion. The possibility of deception may rarely occur to some people and be chronically salient to others. If so, individual differences in the tendency to regard others as deceptive may be larger outside the laboratory than the differences we have found here. It is also possible that people differ in responsiveness to real-world indications that suspicion is warranted. If this alertness is as much an acuity as a generalized distrust, there could be real-world individual differences in accuracy at detecting deception—differences that are obscured when experimenters prompt all judges to suspect deceit. These possibilities should be explored.

In experiments, judges must detect deception solely from the behavior and speech people display when lying. Outside the laboratory, people infer deception from other forms of evidence. They rely on motivational information, physical evidence, and information from third parties. Research indicates that in the real world people rarely detect deception at the time a lie is told. Rather, they infer deceit days, weeks, or months later (H. S. Park, Levine, McCornack, Morrison, & Ferrara, 2002). Perhaps there are individual differences in people's ability to use nonbehavioral cues to deceit, and people differ in sensitivity to evidence of lies they were told earlier. It is also possible that some people are better than others in spinning fabrications that will be immune to nonbehavioral evidence and resistant to delayed exposure. New research paradigms would be needed to uncover these skills.

In the natural ecology of deceit, individuals who have different traits may gravitate toward different interaction partners. It is conceivable, for instance, that certain kinds of individuals tend to interact with highly detectable liars, and others with people whose lies are opaque. If so, the former would achieve higher levels of real world lie detection than the latter. New naturalistic research would be required to explore this possibility.

Meta-Analytic Method

Finally, let us comment on our statistical method for assessing individual differences in judging deception. Our goal was to estimate a psychometric quantity: the standard deviation among a group of individuals in the percentage of lies and truths they would correctly detect, if each individual took a lie detection test of infinite length. We constructed a regression equation to estimate this quantity. In particular, our equation predicted the standard deviation in lie detection across the judges in a sample from the reciprocal of the square root of the number of lies and truths that each individual judged. Applying this equation to data from a large research literature, we found that it could accurately predict the standard deviations that investigators observed. We could then use the fitted equation to make predictions. For our hypothetical sample of individuals who made an infinite number of lie/truth judgments, the predictor variable in this equation would be 0 (i.e., one divided by infinity); hence, we would predict a standard deviation equal to the y-intercept of the equation. This was the psychometric quantity of interest—the real standard deviation, a standard deviation corrected for random error in the sampling of lies and truths.

Our regression-based method invites comparison with other methods. For estimating a real standard deviation in the ability of a single sample of judges, there are traditional procedures (Lord & Novick, 1968). Given access to raw data from a number of samples, one could estimate a real standard deviation within each sample and cumulate the estimates across samples. A cumulated within-study estimate of the real standard deviation might require fewer assumptions than the estimate we report here. However, within-study psychometric techniques are harder to understand than our regression-based approach. Also, the best within-study procedures require access to primary data that meta-analysts lack.

In its goal of correcting differences for statistical error, our regression-based procedure is reminiscent of random-effects meta-analysis (Hedges & Vevea, 1998). However, the similarity may be more apparent than real. Random-effects meta-analysis concerns the differences across *studies* in a summary statistic. It focuses on participant sampling error—random variability across the research findings in a literature that results from the fact that investigators study samples of research participants rather than populations. The smaller the number of research participants in a study, the greater is the participant sampling error introduced into the outcome of that study. Hunter and Schmidt (1990) developed procedures to estimate the participant sampling error that one would expect across the correlation coefficients in a research literature from the number of participants on which each correlation in the literature was based. These authors have advised meta-analysts to subtract this sampling error variance from the variance across the literature in the correlation coefficients observed and to regard the difference as a variance among population correlation coefficients. Applying this logic to research on deception detection, C. F. Bond and DePaulo (2006) used a random-effects meta-analysis to estimate that the standard deviation across studies in the percentage of lies and truths detected in this research literature would be 4.52% if an infinite number of individuals made judgments in each study.

The current regression-based procedure is, by contrast, not intended to assess differences across *studies* but rather differences across *individuals*. It estimates how much individuals would differ from one another as lie detectors on a test that was infinitely long and how much individuals would differ from one another as liars if each was subject to an infinite number of judgments. Thus, our analyses of judge differences correct for error in the sampling of lies and truths, whereas our analyses of sender differences correct for error in the sampling of judgments.

Like the methods outlined by C. F. Bond, Wiitala, and Richard (2003), our regression-based approach yields results that are in the raw metric used by researchers—percentage of correct lie/truth judgments, for instance. By contrast, most random-effects meta-analyses produce findings in a metric that has been subjected to statistical standardization, then squared—the variance among population standardized mean differences, for example (Hedges & Vevea, 1998). For advantages of retaining the raw metric, see C. F. Bond, Wiitala, and Richard (2003).

We invite colleagues to study other individual differences with our method. They might, for instance, use this technique to quantify individual differences among senders and receivers in the communication of emotion (J. A. Hall, 1984), empathic accuracy (Davis & Krauss, 1997), or meta-perception (Kenny, 1994). Here, we find that judges vary little in the ability to detect deception, whereas senders vary substantially in their tendency to appear deceptive. Perhaps this reflects a more general phenomenon—for social perception to depend more on the sender than on the receiver (Kenny & LaVoie, 1984). Further meta-analytic work will be needed to evaluate this possibility.

In the meantime, we have analyzed individual differences in a large research literature. Here, deception judgments depend more on the liar than the judge.

Note

Supplemental materials: http://dx.doi.org.ezproxy.lib.utexas.edu/10.1037/0033-2909.134.4.477.supp

Acknowledgement

We are grateful to David Kenny and Chris Wetzel for comments on a draft of this article.

Footnotes

[1] In defining samples, we tried to separate individual differences from experimental effects. Thus, from an experimental study of the impact of training on lie detection (Vrij, 2000, pp. 93–97), we would extract two standard deviations: one among the judges who received training and a second among the judges who did not. For analyses of the impact on deception judgments of experimental factors, see C. F. Bond and DePaulo (2006).

[2] The quantity of primary interest to us is the standard deviation among judges that would be observed if each judge responded to a lie/truth test of infinite length. In the text, we call this psychometric quantity the *real standard deviation*. Traditionally, it was called the*true standard deviation*—that is, the standard deviation among a set of true scores. As psychometricians know, these statistics are used to disattenuate correlation coefficients.

[3] In the text, we estimate real standard deviations by applying Equation 1 to the pattern of observed standard deviations across studies. We also estimated a real standard deviation within each study with traditional psychometric procedures (Lord & Novick, 1968). These within-study analyses yielded results similar to those we report in the text—extremely small measurement-corrected standard deviations in judge ability, larger measurement-corrected standard deviations in judge credulity and target transparency, and the largest measurement-corrected standard deviations in target credibility. Given the sample sizes in this literature, however, within-study estimates are unstable. For more information, contact Charles F. Bond Jr.

[4] Our model-based estimate for the real standard deviation among expert judges is −0.19%. Standard deviations cannot be negative; hence, our negative estimate would be anomalous if it differed significantly from zero. It does not; thus, we infer that expert judges do not differ from one another in the ability to detect lies.

References

References marked with an asterisk indicate studies included in the meta-analysis.

Aamodt, M. G., & Mitchell, H. (2006). Who can best catch a liar? A meta-analysis of individual differences in detecting deception. *Forensic Examiner*, *15*, 6–11.

*Al-Simadi, F. A. (2000). Detection of deceptive behavior: A cross-cultural test. *Social Behavior & Personality*, *28*, 455–461.

*Anderson, D. E., DePaulo, B. M., & Ansfield, M. E. (2002). The development of deception detection skill: A longitudinal study of same-sex friends. *Personality and Social Psychology Bulletin*, *28*, 536–543.

*Ask, K., & Granhag, P. A. (2003). Individual determinants of deception detection performance: Need for closure, attributional complexity, and absorption. *Goteborg Psychological Reports*, *33*, 1–13.

*Atmiyanandana, V. (1976). *An experimental study of the detection of deception in cross-cultural communication*. Unpublished doctoral dissertation, Florida State University, Tallahassee.

*Bailey, J. T. (2002). *Detecting deception when motivated: The effects of accountability and training on veracity judgments*. Unpublished mater's thesis, Ohio University, Athens.

*Bauchner, J. E., Kaplan, E. A., & Miller, G. R. (1980). Detecting deception: The relationship of available information to judgmental accuracy in initial encounters. *Human Communication Research*, *6*, 253–264.

*Berger, R. E. (1977). Machiavellianism and detecting deception in facial nonverbal communication. *Towson State University Journal of Psychology*, *1*, 25–31.

*Billings, F. J. (2004). *Psychopathy and the ability to deceive*. Unpublished doctoral dissertation, University of Texas at El Paso.

*Blair, J. P. (2006). *The impact of external information on deception detection*. Paper presented at the annual meeting of the National Communication Association, San Antonio, TX.

*Blair, J. P., & McCamey, W. P. (2002). Detection of deception: An analysis of the behavioral analysis interview technique. *Illinois Law Enforcement Executive Forum*, *2*, 165–169.

*Bond, C. F., Jr. (2006). *Accuracy in judging self-initiated lies*. Unpublished data, Texas Christian University, Fort Worth.

*Bond, C. F., Jr., & Atoum, A. O. (2000). International deception. *Personality and Social Psychology Bulletin, 26,* 385–395.

Bond, C. F., Jr., & DePaulo, B. M. (2006). Accuracy of deception judgments. *Personality and Social Psychology Review, 10,* 214–234.

*Bond, C. F., Jr., & Fahey, W. E. (1987). False suspicion and the misperception of deceit. *British Journal of Social Psychology, 26,* 41–46.

*Bond, C. F., Jr., & Gresky, D. P. (2006). *Investigations of deceit.* Paper presented at the annual meeting of the National Communication Association, San Antonio, TX.

*Bond, C. F., Jr., Howard, A. H., & Hutchison, J. (2006). *Overlooking the obvious: Incentives to lie.* Unpublished manuscript, Texas Christian University, Fort Worth.

*Bond, C. F., Jr., Kahler, K. N., & Paolicelli, L. M. (1985). The miscommunication of deception: An adaptive perspective. *Journal of Experimental Social Psychology, 21,* 331–345.

*Bond, C. F., Jr., Lashley, B. R., & Kirk, C. T. (2002). *Responding to deception.* Unpublished manuscript, Texas Christian University, Fort Worth.

*Bond, C. F., Jr., Omar, A., Mahmoud, A., & Bonser, R. N. (1990). Lie detection across cultures. *Journal of Nonverbal Behavior, 14,* 189–204.

*Bond, C. F., Jr., Omar, A., Pitre, U., Lashley, B. R., Skaggs, L. M., & Kirk, C. T. (1992). Fishy-looking liars: Deception judgment from expectancy violation. *Journal of Personality and Social Psychology, 63,* 969–977.

*Bond, C. F., Jr., Paulson, R. M., & Thomas, B. J. (2003). *Multiple-audience messages.* Unpublished data, Texas Christian University, Fort Worth.

Bond, C. F., Jr., & Robinson, M. (1988). The evolution of deception. *Journal of Nonverbal Behavior, 12,* 295–307.

*Bond, C. F., Jr., Thomas, B. J., & Paulsen, R. M. (2004). Maintaining lies: The multiple-audience problem. *Journal of Experimental Social Psychology, 40,* 29–40.

Bond, C. F., Jr., & Uysal, A. (2007). On lie detection "wizards."*Law and Human Behavior, 31,* 109–115.

Bond, C. F., Jr., Wiitala, W. L., & Richard, F. D. (2003). Meta-analysis of raw mean differences. *Psychological Methods, 8,* 406–418.

*Bond, G. D. (2006). *Deception detection expertise*. Unpublished manuscript, Winston-Salem State University, NC.

*Bond, G. D., Malloy, D. M., Arias, E. A., Nunn, S. N., & Thompson, L. A. (2005). Lie-biased decision making in prison. *Communication Reports*, *18*, 1–11.

*Bond, G. D., Malloy, D. M., Thompson, L. A., Arias, E. A., & Nunn, S. N. (2004). Post-probe decision making in a prison context. *Communication Monographs*, *71*, 269–283.

*Boone, R. T., Blumenthal, J. A., Simon, T., Cunningham, J. G., & Tucker, J. S. (1998). *Discriminating the truth: The effect of presentation, order, and gender on the detection of deception in an adversarial dispute*. Unpublished manuscript, Brandeis University, Waltham, MA.

*Brand, R. J., Hodges, S. D., & Williams, J. L. (2003). *Sex differences in encoding sexual attraction*. Paper presented at the annual meeting of the American Psychological Society, Atlanta, GA.

*Brandt, D. R., Miller, G. R., & Hocking, J. E. (1980b). Effects of self-monitoring and familiarity on deception detection. *Communication Quarterly*, *28*, 3–10.

*Buchanan, J. N. (1998). *UJOS as lie detectors: Exploring university judicial officers' judgments of deception*. Unpublished doctoral dissertation, Florida State University, Tallahassee.

Buller, D. B., & Burgoon, J. K. (1996). Interpersonal deception theory. *Communication Theory*, *6*, 203–242.

*Cardena, E. (1983). *The face of deception: Perception of lying and facial expression*. Unpublished master's thesis, York University, Toronto, Ontario, Canada.

*Chahal, K., & Cassidy, T. (1995). Deception and its detection in children: A study of adult accuracy. *Psychology, Crime, & Law*, *1*, 237–245.

*Cheng, H. C. (1996). *A study of baseline familiarity on deception detection: Effects of rehearsal and consequences for lying*. Unpublished master's thesis, State University of New York, Buffalo.

*Childers, C. D. (1980). *An exploration of multiple channel evaluations in attributions of deception*. Unpublished master's thesis, University of Mississippi, Oxford.

*Christensen, D. (1980). *Decoding of intended versus unintended nonverbal messages as a function of social skill and anxiety*. Unpublished doctoral dissertation, University of Connecticut, Storrs.

*Clark, L. M. (1983). *Training humans to become better decoders of deception.* Unpublished master's thesis, University of Georgia, Athens.

David, H. A., & Nagaraja, H. N. (2003). *Order statistics.* Hoboken, NJ: Wiley.

Davis, M. H., & Krauss, L. A. (1997). Personality and empathic accuracy. In W.Ickes (Ed.), *Empathic accuracy* (pp. 144–168). New York: Guilford Press.

*DePaulo, B. M., & Pfeifer, R. L. (1986). On-the-job experience and skill at detecting deception. *Journal of Applied Social Psychology, 16*, 249–267.

DePaulo, B. M., & Rosenthal, R. (1979). Telling lies. *Journal of Personality and Social Psychology, 37*, 1713–1722.

*deTurck, M. A. (1991). Training observers to detect spontaneous deception: Effects of gender. *Communication Reports, 4*, 81–89.

*deTurck, M. A., Feeley, T. H., & Anastasiou, L. (1997). *Effects of motivation to deceive and rehearsal on deception detection.* Unpublished manuscript.

*deTurck, M. A., Feeley, T. H., & Roman, L. A. (1997). Vocal and visual cue training in behavioral lie detection. *Communication Research Reports, 14*, 249–259.

*deTurck, M. A., & Miller, G. R. (1990). Training observers to detect deception: Effects of self-monitoring and rehearsal. *Human Communication Research, 16*, 603–620.

*Edelstein, R. S., Luten, T. L., Ekman, P., & Goodman, G. S. (2006). Detecting lies in children and adults. *Law and Human Behavior, 30*, 1–10.

*Ekman, P., & Friesen, W. V. (1974). Detecting deception from the body or face. *Journal of Personality and Social Psychology, 29*, 288–298.

*Ekman, P., & O'Sullivan, M. (1991). Who can catch a liar?*American Psychologist, 46*, 913–920.

*Ekman, P., O'Sullivan, M., & Frank, M. G. (1999). A few can catch a liar. *Psychological Science, 10*, 263–266.

*Elaad, E. (2003). Effects of feedback on the overestimated capacity to detect lies and the underestimated ability to tell lies. *Applied Cognitive Psychology, 17*, 249–263.

*Etcoff, N. L., Ekman, P., Magee, J. J., & Frank, M. G. (2000, May11). Lie detection and language comprehension. *Nature, 405*, 139.

*Fan, R. M., Wagner, H. L., & Manstead, A. S. R. (1995). Anchoring, familiarity, and confidence in the detection of deception. *Basic and Applied Social Psychology, 17*, 83–96.

*Fay, P. J., & Middleton, W. C. (1941). The ability to judge truth-telling, or lying, from the voice as transmitted over a public address system. *Journal of Genetic Psychology, 24*, 211–215.

*Feeley, T. H., & deTurck, M. A. (1997). Case-relevant vs. case-irrelevant questioning in experimental lie detection. *Communication Reports, 10*, 35–45.

*Feeley, T. H., deTurck, M. A., & Young, M. J. (1995). Baseline familiarity in lie detection. *Communication Research Reports, 12*, 160–169.

*Fiedler, K., & Walka, I. (1993). Training lie detectors to use nonverbal cues instead of global heuristics. *Human Communication Research, 20*, 199–223.

*Fontenot, K. A. (1993). *The relationship of conversational sensitivity and employment interview experience to deception detection in employment interviews*. Unpublished doctoral dissertation, Louisiana State University, Baton Rouge.

*Forrest, J. A. (2001). *A social cognitive model of detecting deception*. Unpublished doctoral dissertation, University of Massachusetts, Boston.

*Fraidin, S. N., Hollingshead, A. B., & Kruger, J. (2002). *Effects of suspicion on perceptions, judgments, and truth bias in lie detection*. Paper presented at the annual meeting of the Midwestern Psychological Association, Chicago.

*Frank, M. G. (1989). *Human lie detection ability as a function of the liar's motivation*. Unpublished doctoral dissertation, Cornell University, Ithaca, NY.

*Frank, M. G., & Ekman, P. (1997). The ability to detect deceit generalizes across different types of high-stakes lies. *Journal of Personality and Social Psychology, 72*, 1429–1439.

*Frank, M. G., & Ekman, P. (2005). Appearing truthful generalizes across different deception situations. *Journal of Personality and Social Psychology, 86*, 486–495.

*Frank, M. G., Paolantonio, N., Feeley, T. H., & Servoss, T. J. (2004). Individual and small group accuracy in judging truthful and deceptive communication. *Group Decision and Negotiation, 13*, 45–59.

*Galarza, L. (1996). *On the accuracy of detecting deception in selection interviews: The effects of applicant rehearsal, applicant job interest, and self-monitoring*. Unpublished master's thesis, Rice University, Houston, TX.

*George, J. F., Marett, K., Burgoon, J. K., Crews, J., Cao, J., Lin, M., & Biros, D. P. (2004). *Training to detect deception: An experimental investigation.* Proceedings of the 37th Hawaii International Conference on System Sciences, Big Island, HI.

Ghiselli, E. E., Campbell, J. P., & Zedeck, S. (1981). *Measurement theory for the behavioral sciences.* San Francisco: Freedman.

*Grandpre, J. R. (1993). *To catch a lie: An examination of the behavioral cues associated with deception detection.* Unpublished master's thesis, University of Wyoming, Laramie.

Granhag, P. A., & Strömwall, L. A. (2004). *The detection of deception in forensic contexts.* New York: Cambridge University Press.

Hall, J. A. (1984). *Nonverbal sex differences: Communication accuracy and expressive style.* Baltimore: Johns Hopkins.

Hall, J. A. (2001). The PONS test and the psychometric approach to measuring interpersonal sensitivity. In J. A.Hall & F. J.Bernieri (Eds.), *Interpersonal sensitivity: Theory and measurement* (pp. 143–182). Mahwah, NJ: Erlbaum.

*Hall, S. (1989). *The generalizability of learning to detect deception in effective and ineffective deceivers.* Unpublished doctoral thesis, Auburn University, AL.

*Harrison, A. A., Hwalek, M., Raney, D., & Fritz, J. G. (1978). Cues to deception in an interview situation. *Social Psychology, 41,* 156–161.

Hedges, L. V., & Vevea, J. L. (1998). Fixed- and random-effects models in meta-analysis. *Psychological Methods, 3,* 486–504.

*Hemsley, G. D. (1977). *Experimental studies in the behavioral indicants of deception.* Unpublished doctoral dissertation, University of Toronto, Ontario, Canada.

*Hendershot, J. (1981). *Detection of deception in low and high socialization subjects with trained and untrained judges.* Unpublished master's thesis, Auburn University, AL.

*Hocking, J. E., Bauchner, J., Kaminski, E. P., & Miller, G. R. (1979). Detecting deceptive communication from verbal, visual, and paralinguistic cues. *Human Communication Research, 6,* 33–46.

*Horn, D. B. (2001). *Seeing is believing: Video quality and lie detection.* Unpublished doctoral dissertation, University of Michigan, Ann Arbor.

Howell, D. C. (2006). *Statistical methods for psychology* (6th ed.). Belmont, CA: Wadsworth.

Hubbell, A. P., Mitchell, M. M., & Gee, J. C. (2001). The relative effects of timing of suspicion and outcome involvement on biased message processing. *Communication Monographs*, *68*, 115–132.

Hunter, J. E., & Schmidt, F. L. (1990). *Methods of meta-analysis: Correcting error and bias in research findings*. Beverly Hills, CA: Sage.

*Hurd, K., & Noller, P. (1988). Decoding deception: A look at the process. *Journal of Nonverbal Behavior*, *12*, 217–233.

*Johnson, A. K., Barnacz, A., Yokkaichi, T., Rubio, J., Racioppi, C., Shackelford, T. K., et al. (2005). Me, myself, and lie: The role of self-awareness in deception. *Personality and Individual Differences*, *38*, 1847–1853.

*Kassin, S. M., & Fong, C. T. (1999). "I'm innocent!": Effects of training on judgments of truth and deception in the interrogation room. *Law & Human Behavior*, *23*, 499–516.

*Kassin, S. M., Meissner, C. A., & Norwick, R. J. (2005). "I'd know a false confession if I saw one": A comparative study of college students and police investigators. *Law & Human Behavior*, *29*, 211–227.

*Keens, C. H. W., & Broadhurst, R. (2005). The detection of deception: The effects of first and second language on lie detection ability. *Psychiatry, Psychology, and Law*, *12*, 107–118.

Kenny, D. A. (1994). *Interpersonal perception: A social relations analysis*. New York: Guilford Press.

Kenny, D. A., & LaVoie, L. (1984). The social relations model. In L.Berkowitz (Ed.), *Advances in experimental social psychology* (*Vol. 18*, pp. 141–182). New York: Academic Press.

*Kirk, C. T. (1993). *A nonspecific factor in deception judgments*. Unpublished master's thesis, Texas Christian University, Fort Worth.

*Koehnken, G. (1987). Training police officers to detect deceptive eyewitness statements: Does it work?*Social Behavior*, *2*, 1–17.

Kraut, R. (1978). Verbal and nonverbal cues in the perception of lying. *Journal of Personality and Social Psychology*, *36*, 380–391.

Kraut, R. (1980). Humans as lie detectors: Some second thoughts. *Journal of Communication*, *30*, 209–216.

*Landry, K. L., & Brigham, J. C. (1992). The effect of training in criteria-based content analysis on the ability to detect deception in adults. *Law & Human Behavior*, *16*, 663–676.

*Lane, J. D., & DePaulo, B. M. (1999). Completing Coyne's cycle: Dysphorics' ability to detect deception. *Journal of Research in Personality*, *33*, 311–329.

*Lashley, B. R. (1993). *Anxiety cues versus verbal–nonverbal inconsistency: Two factors in deception judgments*. Unpublished master's thesis, Texas Christian University, Fort Worth.

*Lavrakas, P. J., & Maier, R. A. (1979). Differences in human ability to judge veracity from the audio medium. *Journal of Research in Personality*, *13*, 139–153.

*Leach, A., Talwar, V., Lee, K., Balan, N., & Lindsay, R. C. L. (2004). "Intuitive" lie detection of children's deception by law enforcement officials and university students. *Law & Human Behavior*, *28*, 661–685.

*Levine, T. R., Feeley, T. H., McCornack, S. A., Hughes, M., & Harms, C. M. (2005). Testing the effects of nonverbal behavior training on accuracy in deception detection with the inclusion of bogus training control group. *Western Journal of Communication*, *69*, 203–218.

*Levine, T. R., Kim, R. K., Park, H. S., & Hughes, M. (2006). Deception detection accuracy is a predictable linear function message veracity base-rate: A formal test of Park and Levine's probability model. *Communication Monographs*, *73*, 243–260.

Levine, T. R., & McCornack, S. A. (1991). The dark side of trust: Conceptualizing and measuring types of communication suspicion. *Communication Quarterly*, *39*, 325–340.

*Levine, T. R., & McCornack, S. A. (2001). Behavioral adaptation, confidence, and heuristic-based explanations of the probing effect. *Human Communication Research*, *27*, 471–502.

*Levine, T. R., Park, H. S., & McCornack, S. A. (1999). Accuracy in detecting truths and lies: Documenting the "veracity effect."*Communication Monographs*, *66*, 125–144.

*Lin, Y. C. (1999). *A study of training on deception detection: The effects of the specific six cues versus heuristics on deception detection accuracy*. Unpublished master's thesis, State University of New York, Buffalo.

*Littlepage, G. E., Maddox, J., & Pineault, M. A. (1985). Recognition of discrepant nonverbal messages and detection of deception. *Perceptual and Motor Skills*, *60*, 119–124.

*Littlepage, G. E., McKinnie, R., & Pineault, M. A. (1983). Relationship between nonverbal sensitivities and detection of deception. *Perceptual and Motor Skills*, *57*, 651–657.

*Littlepage, G. E., & Pineault, M. A. (1979). Detection of deceptive factual statements from the body and the face. *Personality and Social Psychology Bulletin*, *5*, 325–328.

*Littlepage, G. E., & Pineault, M. A. (1981). Detection of truthful and deceptive interpersonal communications across information transmission modes. *Journal of Social Psychology*, *114*, 57–68.

*Littlepage, G. E., & Pineault, M. A. (1985). Detection of deception of planned versus spontaneous communications. *Journal of Social Psychology*, *125*, 195–201.

*Littlepage, G. E., Tang, D. W., & Pineault, M. A. (1986). Nonverbal and content factors in the detection of deception in planned and spontaneous communications. *Journal of Social Behavior and Personality*, *1*, 439–450.

Lord, F. M., & Novick, M. R. (1968). *Statistical theories of mental test scores*. Reading, MA: Addison-Wesley.

*Lusby, D. J. (1999). *Effects of motivation to lie and sanctioned deception of the accuracy of observers' veracity judgments*. Unpublished master's thesis, State University of New York, Buffalo.

*Malcolm, S. R., & Keenan, J. P. (2005). Hemispheric asymmetry and deception detection. *Laterality*, *10*, 103–110.

Malone, B., & DePaulo, B. M. (2001). Measuring sensitivity to deception. In J. A.Hall & F. J.Bernieri (Eds.), *Interpersonal sensitivity: Theory and measurement* (pp. 103–124). Mahwah, NJ: Erlbaum.

*Mann, S., & Vrij, A. (2006). Police officers' judgments of veracity, tenseness, cognitive load, and attempted behavioural control in real-life police interviews. *Psychology, Crime, & Law*, *12*, 307–319.

*Mann, S., Vrij, A., & Bull, R. (2004). Detecting true lies: Police officers' ability to detect suspects' lies. *Journal of Applied Psychology*, *89*, 137–149.

*Marchioni, P. M. (1980). *The detection of deception in the body and the face*. Unpublished master's thesis, University of Texas at El Paso.

*Masip, J. (2002). *Credibility assessment of the testimony on the basis of behavioral indicators in criminal justice settings.* Unpublished doctoral dissertation, University of Salamanca, Madrid, Spain.

*Masip, J., Garrido, E., & Herrero, C. (2002). *When did you conclude she was lying? The impact of the moment the deception about the sender's veracity is made and the sender's facial appearance on police officers' credibility judgments.* Manuscript submitted for publication.

Masip, J., Garrido, E., & Herrero, C. (2004). Facial appearance and impressions of credibility: The effects of facial babyishness and age on person perception. *International Journal of Psychology, 39,* 276–289.

*Masip, J., Garrido, E., & Herrero, C. (2006a). *Heuristic versus systematic processing of information in detecting deception.* Unpublished manuscript, University of Salamanca, Madrid, Spain.

*Masip, J., Garrido, E., & Herrero, C. (2006b). Observers' decision moment in deception detection experiments: Its impact on judgment, accuracy, and confidence. *International Journal of Psychology, 41,* 304–319.

*Meissner, C. A., & Kassin, S. M. (2002). "He's guilty": Investigator bias and judgments of truth and deception. *Law & Human Behavior, 26,* 469–480.

*Millar, M. G., & Millar, K. U. (1997a). The effects of cognitive capacity and suspicion on truth bias. *Communication Research, 24,* 556–570.

*Millar, M. G., & Millar, K. (1997b). Effects of situational variables on judgments about deception and detection accuracy. *Basic and Applied Social Psychology, 19,* 401–410.

*Miller, G. R., deTurk, M. A., & Kalbfleisch, P. J. (1983). Self-monitoring, rehearsal, and deceptive communication. *Human Communication Research, 10,* 97–117.

*Morris, K. A. (2003). Teaching students about classic findings on the detection of deception. *Teaching of Psychology, 30,* 111–113.

*Murray, J. (1983). *The detection of interviewees' verbal deceptions from their accompanying overt nonverbal behavior.* Unpublished doctoral dissertation, Florida State University, Tallahassee.

Nunnally, J. C., & Bernstein, I. H. (1994). *Psychometric theory* (3rd ed.). New York: McGraw-Hill.

*Oberleitner, D., McLarney-Vesotski, A., Bernieri, F., & Okdie, B. (2004). *Musical mood induction and its effects on lie detection accuracy.* Paper presented at the annual meeting of the Society for Personality and Social Psychology, Austin, TX.

*Oldfield, S. E. (1999). *The influence of self-monitoring on the detection of deception.* Unpublished master's thesis, Radford University, VA.

*O'Sullivan, M. (2003). The fundamental attribution error in detecting deception: The boy-who-cried-wolf effect. *Personality and Social Psychology Bulletin, 29,* 1316–1327.

O'Sullivan, M. (2007). Unicorns or Tiger Woods: Are lie detection wizards myths or rarities? A response to On Lie Detection "Wizards" by Bond and Uysal. *Law & Human Behavior, 31,* 117–123.

*O'Sullivan, M., Ekman, P., & Friesen, W. V. (1988). The effect of comparisons on detecting deceit. *Journal of Nonverbal Behavior, 12,* 203–215.

*Park, E. S., Levine, T. R., Harms, C. M., & Ferrara, M. H. (2002). Group and individual accuracy in deception detection. *Communication Research Reports, 19,* 99–106.

Park, H. S., Levine, T. R., McCornack, S. A., Morrison, K., & Ferrara, S. (2002). How people really detect lies. *Communication Monographs, 69,* 144–157.

*Parker, R. J. (1978). *Age, sex, and the detection of deception through nonverbal cues.* Unpublished doctoral dissertation, California School of Professional Psychology.

Paulhus, D. L. (1991). Measurement and control of response bias. In J. P.Robinson, P. R.Shaver, & L. S.Wrightsman (Eds.), *Measures of personality and social psychological attitudes* (pp.17–59). New York: Academic Press.

*Pietras, K. R., & Bond, C. F., Jr. (1985). *The reliability of lie detection judgments.* Paper presented at the annual meeting of the Eastern Psychological Association, Boston.

*Porter, S., Campbell, M. A., Stapleton, J., & Birt, A. R. (2002). The influence of judge, target, and stimulus characteristics on the accuracy of detecting deceit. *Canadian Journal of Behavioural Science, 34,* 172–185.

*Porter, S., McCabe, S., Woodworth, M., & Peace, K. A. (2006). "Genius is 1% inspiration and 99% perspiration," or is it? An investigation of the impact of motivation and feedback on deception detection. *Legal and Criminological Psychology, 12,* 297–309.

*Porter, S., Woodworth, M., & Birt, A. R. (2000). Truth, lies, and videotape: An investigation of the ability of federal parole officers to detect deception. *Law & Human Behavior*, *24*, 643–658.

*Raichle, W. (1990). *The roles of verbal and nonverbal behavior in impression formation during an employment interview*. Unpublished doctoral dissertation, New York University.

*Rockwell, P. (1996). Hemispheric differences in detection of deception with content-filtered speech. *Perceptual and Motor Skills*, *82*, 1241–1242.

*Rudin, J. P. (1999). *Effect of reward size in performance of a deception detection task*. Proceedings of the annual meeting of the Southwest Academy of Management, Houston, TX.

*Sahlman, J. M., & Koper, R. J. (1992, May). *Do you hear what I hear? Deception detection by the blind*. Paper presented at the annual meeting of the International Communication Association, Miami, FL.

*Sakai, D. J. (1981). *Nonverbal communication in the detection of deception among women and men*. Unpublished doctoral dissertation, University of California, Davis.

*Schoephoerster, B. T. (1996). *Deception detection accuracy: The effects of suspicion and antisocial personality traits*. Unpublished master's thesis, University of Nevada at Las Vegas.

*Seager, P. B. (2001). *Improving the ability of people to detect lies*. Unpublished doctoral dissertation, University of Hertfordshire, United Kingdom.

*Steinberg, J. R., & Bernieri, F. (2001). *How locus of control affects accuracy of detecting deception*. Paper presented at the annual meeting of the American Psychological Society, Toronto, Ontario, Canada.

*Stiff, J. B., & Miller, G. R. (1986). "Come to think of it": Interrogative probes, deceptive communication, and deception detection. *Human Communication Research*, *12*, 339–357.

*Swann, W. B., Jr., Silvera, D. H., & Proske, C. U. (1995). On "knowing your partner": Dangerous illusions in the age of AIDS? *Personal Relationships*, *2*, 173–186.

*Swinkels, A. H. (1989). *The effects of cognitive busyness on human lie detection ability*. Unpublished doctoral dissertation, University of Texas at Austin.

*Taylor, R. (1999). *Relationships between accuracy of detecting deception and beliefs about the cues involved*. Paper presented at the Division of Forensic Psychology annual conference, Cambridge, England.

*Tetterton, V. S., & Warren, A. R. (2005). Using witness confidence can impair the ability to detect deception. *Criminal Justice and Behavior*, *32*, 433–451.

*Tornqvist, J. S. (2002). *The detectability and believability of lies and truths in the e-mail medium*. Unpublished doctoral dissertation, University of Virginia, Charlottesville.

*Vrij, A. (1993). Credibility judgments of detectives: The impact of nonverbal behavior, social skills, and physical characteristics on impression formation. *Journal of Social Psychology*, *133*, 601–610.

*Vrij, A. (1994). The impact of information and setting on detection of deception by police detectives. *Journal of Nonverbal Behavior*, *18*, 117–136.

Vrij, A. (2000). *Detecting lies and deceit: The psychology of lying and the implications for professional practice*. New York: Wiley.

*Vrij, A., & Baxter, M. (1999). Accuracy and confidence in detecting truths and lies in elaborations and denials: Truth bias, lie bias, and individual differences. *Expert Evidence*, *7*, 25–36.

*Vrij, A., & Graham, S. (1997). Individual differences between liars and the ability to detect lies. *Expert Evidence*, *5*, 144–148.

*Vrij, A., Harden, F., Terry, J., Edward, K., & Bull, R. (2001). The influence of personal characteristics, stakes, and lie complexity on the accuracy and confidence to detect deceit. In R.Roesch, R. R.Corrado, & R.Dempster (Eds.), *Psychology in the courts* (pp. 289–302). London: Routledge.

*Vrij, A., & Mann, S. (2001). Telling and detecting lies in a high-stake situation: The case of a convicted murderer. *Applied Cognitive Psychology*, *15*, 187–203.

*Vrij, A., Mann, S., Kristen, S., & Fisher, R. P. (2007). Cues to deception and ability to detect lies as a function of police interview styles. *Law & Human Behavior*, *31*, 499–518.

*Vrij, A., Mann, S., Robbins, E., & Robinson, M. (2006). Police officers ability to detect deception in high stakes situations and in repeated lie detection tests. *Applied Cognitive Psychology*, *20*, 741–755.

*Wilson, S. J. (1975). *Channel differences in the detection of deception*. Unpublished doctoral dissertation, Florida State University, Tallahassee.

*Yang, C. C. (1996). *The effects of training, rehearsal, and consequences for lying on deception detection accuracy*. Unpublished master's thesis, State University of New York, Buffalo.

Zebrowitz, L. A., Voinescu, L., & Collins, M. A. (1996). "Wide-eyed" and "crooked-face": Determinants of perceived and real honesty over the life span. *Personality and Social Psychology Bulletin*, *22*, 1258–1269.

*Zuckerman, M., DeFrank, R. S., Hall, J. A., Larrance, D. T., & Rosenthal, R. (1979). Facial and vocal cues of deception and honesty. *Journal of Experimental Social Psychology*, *15*, 378–396.

Zuckerman, M., DePaulo, B. M., & Rosenthal, R. (1981). Verbal and nonverbal communication of deception. In L.Berkowitz (Ed.), *Advances in experimental social psychology* (*Vol. 14*, pp. 1–60). New York: Academic Press.

*Zuckerman, M., Koestner, R., & Alton, A. O. (1984). Learning to detect deception. *Journal of Personality and Social Psychology*, *46*, 519–528.

*Zuckerman, M., Koestner, R., & Colella, M. J. (1985). Learning to detect deception from three communication channels. *Journal of Nonverbal Behavior*, *9*, 188–194.

*Zuckerman, M., Koestner, R., Colella, M. J., & Alton, A. O. (1984). Anchoring in the detection of deception and leakage. *Journal of Personality and Social Psychology*, *47*, 301–311.

About the Authors

Charles Bond is a research psychologist (Duke PhD, 1980). He has held appointments at several Universities and published widely in psychology and statistics. To study international deception, he moved to India for a year. The resulting research has drawn interest from the FBI, CIA, Department of Defense, and National Academy of Sciences. In 2004, Bond gave a US Congressional briefing on cross-cultural deceit.

Bella DePaulo (PhD, Harvard) is one of the leading scholars of the psychology of deceiving and detecting deceit. She has authored more than 100 scholarly publications. Her expertise on topics such as the psychology of deception, single life, and friendship has been recognized in the *New York Times*, the *Washington Post*, *USA Today*, the *Wall Street Journal*, and many other major national and international newspapers. Her work has also been reported in magazines such as *Time*, *Newsweek*, *Business Week*, the *New York Times Magazine*, and the *New Yorker*. Her op-ed essays have appeared in publications such as the *New York Times*, the *Chronicle of Higher Education*, and *Forbes*. Dr. DePaulo has discussed her work on ABC, NBC, CBS, CNN, CNBC, PBS, the BBC, and the Discovery Channel. She has lectured nationally and internationally, addressing such diverse groups as medical professionals, forensic scientists, school teachers, criminal attorneys, physicists, judges, women's centers, and mental health practitioners.

Dr. DePaulo writes the "Living Single" blog for *Psychology Today*, and is also a contributor to the Huffington Post. She has been a Visiting Professor of Psychology at the University of California, Santa Barbara since the summer of 2000. Much more information about her background, her books, and her contact information, together with her *All Things Single (and More)* blog, can be found at her website, www.BellaDePaulo.com. Her previous books are listed below.

The Hows and Whys of Lies

Behind the Door of Deceit:
Understanding the Biggest Liars in Our Lives

The Lies We Tell and the Clues We Miss:
Professional Papers

Singled Out:
How Singles Are Stereotyped, Stigmatized, and Ignored, and Still Live Happily Ever After

Single with Attitude:
Not Your Typical Take on Health and Happiness, Love and Money, Marriage and Friendship

Friendsight:
What Friends Know that Others Don't

The Psychology of Dexter